BIG QUESTIONS, WORTHY DREAMS

BIG QUESTIONS, WORTHY DREAMS

Mentoring Young Adults in Their Search for Meaning, Purpose, and Faith

Sharon Daloz Parks

JOSSEY-BASS
A Wiley Company
www.josseybass.com

Published by Jossey-Bass
A Wiley Imprint
989 Market Street, San Francisco, CA 94103-1741   www.josseybass.com

Jossey-Bass books and products are available through most bookstores. To contact Jossey-Bass directly call our Customer Care Department within the U.S. at 800-956-7739, outside the U.S. at 317-572-3986, or fax 317-572-4002.

Jossey-Bass also publishes its books in a variety of electronic formats. Some content that appears in print may not be available in electronic books.

Credits are on page 262.

Library of Congress Cataloging-in-Publication Data

Parks, Sharon.
Big questions, worthy dreams : mentoring young adults in their search for meaning, purpose, and faith / Sharon Daloz Parks.
    p. cm.
    Includes index.
    ISBN 0-7879-4171-9 (alk. paper)
    1. Religious education of young people. 2. Young adults—
Religious life. 3. Faith development. 4. Mentoring. I. Title.
    BL42 .P37 2000
    261.8'34242—dc21   00-09170

Printed in the United States of America
FIRST EDITION
HB Printing   10 9 8

CONTENTS

Preface   xi

1. Young Adulthood in a Changing World:
   Promise and Vulnerability   1

2. Meaning and Faith   14

3. Becoming at Home in the Universe   34

4. It Matters How We Think   53

5. It All Depends . . .   71

6. . . . On Belonging   88

7. Imagination: The Power of Adult Faith   104

8. The Gifts of a Mentoring Environment   127

9. Mentoring Communities   158

   ○ Higher Education ○ Professional Education and the
   Professions ○ The Workplace ○ Travel ○ The Natural
   Environment ○ Families ○ Religious Faith Communities

10. Culture as Mentor   206

Notes   223
The Author   243
Name Index   245
Subject Index   251

PREFACE

THERE IS SOMETHING particularly powerful and poignant about the "twenty-something" years, harboring, as they do, both promise and vulnerability. Young adults embody critical strengths and yet remain dependent in distinctive ways, upon recognition, support, challenge, and inspiration. Not only the quality of individual young adult lives but also our future as a culture depends in no small measure upon our capacity to recognize the emerging competence of young adults, to initiate them into big questions, and to give them access to worthy dreams. This book is intended to inform and inspire renewed commitment to the practice of mentorship, to invite reconsideration of some of the institutional and societal patterns that affect young adult lives, and to bridge the deepening divides between generations, increasingly evident as a consequence of dramatic shifts within a rapidly changing society.

In 1986, I published *The Critical Years: Young Adults and the Search for Meaning, Faith, and Commitment*. It revealed a new era emerging in the human life span, and a vital set of tasks in the development of meaning and faith. After it had gone out of print yet was still being used, I was invited by Jossey-Bass to "rewrite" the work. As an act of faithfulness to the original insight, I set about the task. But by the time the dust settled, I found I had written a new book. I trust that it retains the essence of the former, while conveying my ongoing learning about the significance of the young adult years and the importance of mentors and mentoring environments in today's world.

Since the earlier publication, a number of critical shifts have taken place that call forth deepening understanding of the anxieties and aspirations of young adults. For example, our economy continues to undergo dramatic changes that have profound implications for young adult lives, the extension of the life span now more obviously stresses the twenties decade, and we are yet more conscious of the religious pluralism that is a fact of our common life. It has become all the more essential to honor these realities by understanding *faith* in its broadest, most inclusive form as *the activity of making meaning* that all human beings share. Looking through a developmental lens, this book describes primary features of the development of meaning and faith in the young adult years, during which ways of thinking, forms of authority, and patterns of belonging may be recast. But it also recognizes that the "content" of faith—images, symbols, stories, concepts, beliefs—matters, whether expressed in religious or secular terms. In relatively few years, new media technologies have become a dominant feature of the young adult landscape; if we are to mentor the next generations well, it has become a matter of considerable urgency that we more adequately understand the formation of the young adult imagination and its implications for forming meaning, purpose, and faith.

Moreover, although there has been for some time growing appreciation of the critical role that individual mentors can play in the formation of young adult aspirations, this book argues for the even larger significance of mentoring environments in the formation of all commitments, especially commitment to the common good and the building of a more vibrant and just culture.

Although the earlier book was addressed primarily to higher education, *Big Questions, Worthy Dreams* is intended for all who find common cause in responding to young adults, whatever the context may be. It gives special attention to seven particular environments where young adults seek place and participation, as you will see in Chapter Nine. At an earlier time, a primary concern that fueled my research and writing was that young people would discover a critical perspective that would call into question their inherited, conventional faith, and then, though able to enlarge their respect for the faith of others, they would be unable to recompose a worthy faith of their own. This concern remains. But another and growing concern is that too many of our young adults are not being encouraged to ask the big questions that awaken critical thought in the first place. Swept up in religious assumptions that remain unexamined (and economic assumptions that function religiously), they easily become vulnerable to the conventional cynicism of our time or to the economic and political agendas of a consumption-driven yet ambivalent age.

This book draws on thirty years of teaching, counseling, and research with young adults in college, university, and professional school contexts, as well as in workplace, religious, and other settings both formal and informal. Unless otherwise cited, quotations from young adults themselves are drawn from my research at Whitworth College (in collaboration with Gonzaga University), Harvard Divinity School, Harvard Business School (in collaboration with the Tuck School of Business and the Darden School of Business), and the Kennedy School of Government; from the study reported in the book *Common Fire: Leading Lives of Commitment in a Complex World*; and from current study along with

occasional informal conversations. In most instances names and identifying elements have been changed because anonymity was a condition of
the research interviews; thus any similarity to actual people or organizations is accidental. To each of the interviewees who so graciously and continually confounded and informed my understanding, I want to express
my great gratitude.

There are, however, some in their young adult years (past or present)
who have made essential contributions to my understanding, who are not
otherwise acknowledged in the text, and whom I do want to recognize.
They are Peter Bloomquist, Peter Dykstra, Wendy Evans, Julie Neraas,
Scott Shaw, Cindy Smith, Greg Spenser, and Drew Tupper. I owe a special
debt of gratitude to Kate Daloz, who provided research assistance for this
book, bringing her considerable interviewing and writing skills along with
her thoughtful analytical talent to the enrichment of this work.

From the beginning and for always, I am grateful to Margaret Sharp,
David Erb, Timothy Tiemans, Robert Rankin, Beverly Harrison, James
Fowler, and George Rupp—apart from whom my study of young adult
faith might never have been launched, or, once launched, might never have
found a voice and a home. I am also deeply indebted to many colleagues
from a wide range of institutions and traditions—particularly faculty,
administrators, and campus ministers—who have generously shared their
insight, competence, and the inspiration of their commitment to the next
generation, informing my own understanding in a host of ways. These
include my colleagues at the Clinical Developmental Institute—Michael
Bassaches, Bob Goodman, Ann Fleck Henderson, Gina O'Connell Higgins,
Bob Kegan, Gil Noam, and Laura Rogers—in whose good company my
understanding of constructive-developmental psychology has been nurtured across fourteen years of sustained conversation.

This book would probably never have been written if it had not been
for the vision and elegant competence of Sarah Polster, my editor at
Jossey-Bass. To her and her very fine colleagues, I am especially grateful.
The work has also been graciously supported by a grant from the W. K.
Kellogg Foundation and the colleagueship of Betty J. Overton.

I am grateful to those who read and gave critical response in developing
this manuscript. These include Gary Brower, Donna DiSchullo, Thomas
Finnegan, Keith Morton, Michael Waggoner, and Elaine Wetterauer. There
have been other colleagues, friends, and family who in particular and
meaningful ways informed and supported this work. They include Jill
Carlino, Mary Romer Cline, Ron Frase, Rick Jackson, Kathie Koopmans,
Kay Millhon, Charlie Murphy, Eloys Parks, Suzanne Repetto, Joyce
Veatch, Cathy Whitmire, and my colleagues at the Whidbey Institute.

Twenty years ago, an exceptional young woman, Karen Thorkilsen, appeared in one of the first courses I taught at Harvard Divinity School, "Faith and Its Transformations Across the Life Span." She did not speak a great deal during the course, but on the last day she gave all of us a brief, powerful, and eloquently written reflection on the meaning of the course and the conversation we had shared. As her vocation continued to evolve, she became, in part, an extraordinary editor. Thus it has been my privilege to continue that conversation as she has worked with me as a research associate, editor, and colleague on five projects. Now, as before, she has been steadfast in bringing her uncommon thoughtfulness, intelligence, and sharp pencil, along with her gentle and fierce spirit, to the support and completion of this work. My gratitude is deep and boundless.

Finally, I am grateful to Larry Parks Daloz, my husband. In our life and work together, he is both spouse and colleague *par excellence*. He has not forgotten how to ask the big questions, and the strength of his love and commitment helps me believe that working on behalf of the next generations to reweave the bonds of civil society within a new global commons is indeed a worthy dream.

Whidbey Institute   Sharon Daloz Parks
Whidbey Island
Spring 2000

BIG QUESTIONS, WORTHY DREAMS

YOUNG ADULTHOOD
IN A CHANGING WORLD

PROMISE AND VULNERABILITY

A TALENTED YOUNG MAN, recently graduated from an outstanding college, still trying to heal from his parents' divorce, and somewhat at a loss for next steps in his search for a meaningful place in the world of adult work, is asked by his dad and stepmom, "When you think from your deepest self, what do you most desire?" To their surprise he quietly responds: "To laugh without cynicism."

A twenty-six-year-old law student also maintains a full-time position with a venture capital firm. Daily she makes thumbs-up or thumbs-down decisions on new technology companies. Her eyes sparkle as she reflects on how exciting it is to be alive at this time in history. Over lunch, an older adult asks, "What do you think about the environmental challenges we are facing?" Instantly, her face falls. She responds, "There's no hope." When asked why she feels that way, she makes reference to global warming, species depletion, toxic buildup.

A freshman in her spring term at a state university remarks that she wishes she could find a "church home," longing for what she had in her hometown three hundred miles away. She says she is coping in the meantime by attending an off-campus evangelical college youth group, where there is a lot of warmth, singing, and community. She also participates in a small, intellectually satisfying study series offered by the campus ministry. What's missing is a kind of wholeness or integration she can't quite grasp.

A young man from Guyana, twenty-six years old, is the proud owner of a small flooring company and a part-time student at the community college. One of his teachers observes that though last term he only occasionally slouched into class, he seems to have made some kind of decision and now attends regularly, alert and ready. "His papers have improved by about two hundred percent, and he contributes to the friendly, thoughtful tone of the class. He is obviously working *very* hard both for class and in his business. He has dyslexia, and writing is very labored for him, but he has shown a tremendous amount of thought, effort, creativity and truly beautiful insight—especially in a paper he wrote about being a young father. He is someone I really, *really*, respect and am generally rooting for."

In the bowels of the university physics lab, a sophomore, raised in middle America and steeped in a mainline conventional faith, is fascinated by the conversations he is having with some of his fellow students. He has discovered that the lab is a good place to learn how people from the Middle East and Asia make sense of today's world. It is his perception that the faculty is not aware of this conversation.

A young woman graduating from college with a major in religion and studio art and ambitions for further study in Islamic religious art bought herself a beautiful suit, wore it to one interview with a major computer company, and was invited to fly across the country for a second interview. Images of $40K straight out of college and a hip working environment got her on the plane. Once there, she received a couple of job offers (including stock options) from two good companies.

Then she happened to meet a guy starting a new Internet company that seemed like her kind of place—it was in a basement, she could wear what she wanted, there was a dog, and "it wasn't corporate at all." Having very little background experience, she offered to work for free for a short time to show what she could do as a web designer. Three years later, the company is now six hundred people located in six cities, and she is a reasonably wealthy art director. She supervises a team of six people she hired, most of whom are older than herself and have master's degrees.

Recently, she says, "I hired a vice president in charge of design; basically I hired my own boss. I'm learning so much from him. He's thirty-six, super smart, amazing, funny, down-to-earth. I watch him win a lot of battles that I'd been fighting for years as a twenty-three-year-old female—not listened to by the higher-ups, even though they are only twenty-eight."

Thinking about the future, she says, "I got here because I've worked hard, I'm a leader, and it was inside me. On the other hand, it is bizarre to be in a position of enormous responsibility over someone who is forty years old. But like others my age, I know the whole scene better, I'm quick, I'm on it, I grew up with it. It's not like it takes that much to learn. With a combination of luck and grace and talking to the right people, I fell into it. As my astrologer says, I can move on if I want with a certain amount of material *whatever*—but not necessarily have it define me for the rest of my life."

For each of these young adults—and, as a consequence, for all of us—there is much at stake in how they are heard, understood, and met by the adult world in which they are seeking participation, purpose, meaning, and a faith to live by.

In varying roles (residence director, chaplain, researcher, professor, and friend), I have taught, counseled, studied, and learned with young adults in college, university, and other professional workplace settings. In the late 1960s and early '70s, I witnessed the power of young adult energy to sway a society. I wondered at the apparent disappearance of that energy once the Vietnam War ended and the television cameras had departed from campus.

Then, over subsequent decades, I watched the same energy reconfigure and, in multiple strands, weave itself into the fiber of our cultural life. In the eighties and nineties, I watched young adults seeking a place in a new global commons that ambivalently welcomed, encouraged, exploited, and discouraged their participation.

Now, at the dawning of the twenty-first century, I continue to watch young adults reach for a place of belonging, integrity, and contribution that can anchor meaningful hope in themselves and our shared future—while the tides of cynicism and the prevailing currents of consumerism play big roles in charting their course. I have observed, among some of the most talented, many who simply have been lured into elite careers before anyone has invited them to consider the deeper questions of purpose and vocation. Others are fiercely determined to find a distinctive path and to make a difference in a complex maze of competing claims and wide-ranging opportunities.

Across thirty years, my scholarship has been primarily in the fields of developmental psychology, theology, education, leadership, and ethics. Insights drawn from these domains have served as useful interpreters of young adults as I know them. At the same time, young adults themselves continuously prompt me to notice that even some of the "disciplined" interpretations of young adulthood are misleading. By young adulthood, I mean young people typically between seventeen and thirty—the "twenty-somethings."

When I began my initial studies, important theoretical perspectives defined young adulthood as "prolonged adolescence," a merely "transitional" time or a period of idealism soon to be outgrown. Cultural assumptions implied that young adulthood ends, or should end, with the granting of a college degree around the traditional age of twenty-two. Later, such popular descriptions of young adults as Generation X extended the time frame but attempted primarily to describe and normatively define young adults in media-manageable terms, casting them as a market—yet finding them resistant to categorization.

The Ambiguity of Young Adulthood

When does one cross the threshold into adulthood? The response of North American culture is ambiguous. Chronological age does not serve as a consistent indicator, and the rites of passage that might mark the threshold of adulthood are various: obtaining a driver's license, social security card, or credit card; experimenting with sexuality; parenting a child; graduating from high school or college; establishing one's own residence; marrying; becoming financially independent; reaching the legal drinking age; becoming eligible to vote; becoming subject to military registration. Each of these serves to some degree as a cultural indicator of adulthood, yet the legally established age for these passages ranges from sixteen to twenty-one and is not uniform from one jurisdiction to another. Further, as conventional wisdom often asserts, "You may be twenty-one, but. . . !"

In this maze of contradictory cultural signals, it is difficult to have a clear sense of what to expect of either oneself or of others as adults. Establishing an occupation, finding a mate, and starting a family all endure as primary indicators of adulthood.[1] But the human life span has been extended, and a postindustrial, technological culture has made it both easier and more difficult to make one's way into the world of adult work. Thus even an indicator such as "becoming established" no longer seems useful when some young people are "on their own" because they have left dysfunctional families in search of healthier ways of life; when professional education may extend into the early thirties (and beyond); when it is common to change careers several times in one's lifetime; when what it is important to learn and know becomes increasingly complex and controversial; when there are significant changes in the relationship between the genders, often resulting in the postponement of marriage and childbearing; and when personal life is sometimes neglected in favor of career development (or the reverse).

In this changing milieu, many parents find themselves surprised and dis-mayed when, for a variety of reasons, their children seem to need to move back home after college. Parents ponder whether and for how long it is appropriate for them to provide financial support. Corporate planners are challenged by the fluidity and short-term horizons of young adult ambi-tions. Financial magazines feature young entrepreneurs earning "adult" salaries at the age of eighteen—appearing to bypass higher education alto-gether.[2] Young mothers, with partners who do not yet seem ready to be fathers, have few guidelines for determining what they may ask, claim, demand. Many young adults themselves, even those who achieve a bac-calaureate degree, wonder when and if they really are "grown up." All are bewildered if the sort of self-confidence, commitment, and stability that are associated with adulthood are not as evident as they expected.

Two Important Questions

Thus, embedded in this question of when one becomes an adult are two other important questions. The first is, What is the key marker that defines the task of the young adult era?

Young adults do many things. They seek work, find work, change their work. They party and play. They earn undergraduate, master's, doctoral, and professional degrees. They have a yen for travel—from one country to another, and from one company to another. Sometimes they protest and make demands, for themselves and on behalf of others. They create art, claim adventure, explore and establish long-term relationships, form house-holds, volunteer in their communities, become parents, initiate important projects, and serve internships. They try to become financially indepen-dent. They also go to prison. Some deal with major health and other phys-ical and emotional challenges. And some young adults die too young.

It is my conviction that the central work of the young adult era in the cycle of human life is not located in any of these tasks or circumstances per se. Rather, the promise and vulnerability of young adulthood lie in the experience of the birth of critical awareness and the dissolution and recomposition of the meaning of self, other, world, and "God." This work has enormous consequences for the years of adulthood to follow. Young adulthood is rightfully a time of asking big questions and discovering worthy dreams.

The second question is, When is it time to give a younger person the respect and trust due another adult? Older adults may become weary (if not irritated or angry) upon hearing that one more university somewhere on the globe has been shut down because of student protests against a policy or a government. Managers, whatever the institutional context, tend to resist inconvenient insights coming from their juniors. Some parents tend to want to see their adult offspring as children—or at least as still dependent upon parental authority, competence, and approval. Correspondingly, however, established adult culture feels at least mild uneasiness if its younger adults seem passive, dependent, oriented to absolute security, and bereft of idealism.

I suggest that, informed by insights from developmental psychology, we can strengthen our response to both of these questions if we recognize that every major era or stage in the life span is marked by its own way of making meaning. Typically, in the years from seventeen to thirty a distinctive mode of meaning-making can emerge, one that has certain adult characteristics but understandably lacks others. This mode of making meaning includes (1) becoming critically aware of one's own composing of reality, (2) self-consciously participating in an ongoing dialogue toward truth, and (3) cultivating a capacity to respond—to act—in ways that are satisfying and just.

Halfway though her sophomore year of college, a young woman recently reflected: "I have been thinking lately a lot about thresholds. When does one become an adult? When we graduate from high school? Or college? Can a piece of paper signify that we are adult? It seems at times that it is easier to meet new adults who recognize me as I am now, than to be with adults who see me as I used to be." Later, when I expressed appreciation for her comments, she added, "It seems to me that one becomes an adult when *you know that you have a life.* Do you know what I mean?"[3]

When we shift from just "being a life" to "knowing we have a life," we achieve an undeniably different form of consciousness. New possibilities and responsibilities appear for both self and world. How a young adult is met and invited to test and invest this new consciousness with its emerging new capacities will make a great difference in the adulthood that lies ahead. The dreams that are made available, embraced, and nurtured, and the promises that are made, broken, and kept, will shape our common future.

For these reasons, the questions surrounding young adults and the formation of mature adulthood are a matter of consequence for educators and policymakers in every sector. Invariably, issues pertaining to the development of character and conscience—competence, courage, integrity, freedom, compassion, responsibility, wisdom, generosity, and fidelity, all qualities associated with exemplary citizenship and the best of the intellectual life—are embedded in our assumptions about the formation of adulthood. How these qualities are formed and reformed in the twenty-something years appropriately shapes educational goals and the conditions of accountability for students, faculty, and all who interact with young adult lives. They are concerns that appropriately belong at the center of life in the academy and every other institution with a stake in the future. Thus, society finds its orientation, in part, in a commitment to the formation and flourishing of young adulthood.

To understand how this may be so, we examine the dynamics of adult meaning-making in its most comprehensive dimensions—that is, the formation, loss, and recovery of faith itself—as a primary perspective from which to reconsider the significance of the young adult years. Understanding the formation and reformation of meaning and faith may encourage us to reexamine our assumptions about the formation of adulthood, our participation in the lives of young adults, and our own capacity to live meaningful adult lives.

Meaning and Faith

We human beings seem unable to survive, and certainly cannot thrive, unless we can make meaning.[4] We need to be able to make some sort of sense out of things; we seek pattern, order, coherence, and relation in the disparate elements of our experience. If life is perceived as only fragmented and chaotic, we suffer confusion, distress, stagnation, and finally despair.

This capacity and demand for meaning is what I invite the reader to associate with the word *faith*. For most of us, this represents a shift from the usual connotations. Faith is often linked exclusively to belief, particularly religious belief. But faith goes far beyond religious belief, parochially understood. Faith is more adequately recognized as *the activity of seeking and discovering meaning in the most comprehensive dimensions of our experience*. Faith is a broad, generic human phenomenon. To be human is to dwell in faith, to dwell in the sense one makes out of life—what seems ultimately true and dependable about self, world, and cosmos (whether that meaning be strong or fragile, expressed in religious or secular terms). This way of understanding the nature of faith has value for secular and religious folk alike. It addresses our culture's current hunger for a shared language about things "spiritual."

To become a young adult in faith is to discover in a critically aware, self-conscious manner the limits of inherited or otherwise socially received assumptions about how life works—what is ultimately true and trustworthy, and what counts—and to recompose meaning and faith on the other side of that discovery. The quality of this recomposition and its adequacy to ground a worthy adulthood depends in significant measure on the hospitality, commitment, and courage of adult culture, as mediated through both individuals and institutions.

How faith is formed and reformed in the young adult years is clearly a matter of importance for young adults. It is also of enormous importance for our society as a whole. The day inevitably arrives, for example, when we find ourselves in the care of a physician younger than we are, or we elect an official half our age. Thus, how we meet young adults as they begin to know they have a life to live and invest has consequences for all of us. Moreover (as we shall see), young adulthood is the birthplace of adult vision, and within a positive mentoring environment it can galvanize the power of ongoing cultural renewal. Within a distracted, indifferent, or exploiting culture, however, young adulthood may be squandered on dreams too small to match the potential of the young adult soul, or it simply may be cast adrift in the unexamined currents of mere circumstance.

An Underrecognized Era

Young adults embody a postadolescent quality of emerging strength yet are at the same time appropriately dependent upon the presence and quality of mentors and mentoring environments—educational, economic, political, religious, and familial. But because we live in a time of cultural transition, this critical need is often eclipsed by the distortions of flawed psychologies, hidden in the press of presumably more important agendas, or masked by assumptions that tragically widen the gap between generations. When the promise and vulnerability of the critical decade that we call young adulthood is either ignored or wrongly seen as only an amorphous, transitional time, the opportunity to cultivate, protect, and later harvest its fruits for the renewal of culture is lost.

It has been three decades since Kenneth Keniston, a researcher at MIT, argued for recognition of this postadolescent era in human development and began to describe its significance in a new social reality calling for an increasingly skilled and educated citizenry. Though a few theorists in human and faith development have further articulated this perception,[5] young adulthood per se remains underrecognized in prevailing theories of human development and in the conventional mind. There is, however, a growing awareness that the process of human growth and maturity is being extended and is not tied exclusively to chronological age or traditional societal expectations. Becoming an adult is increasingly recognized as a complex process that includes changes in biological, cognitive, emotional, social, spiritual, and moral dimensions. Kotre and Hall have observed that if a new stage of life is emerging it is "confined primarily to the middle class, but that is where childhood and adolescence first took root. Wider recognition . . . will depend on the prosperity and educational demands of society at large. If young adulthood becomes accepted as a season of life in the twenty-first century the way adolescence did in the twentieth, it would be the second stage to fill the widening no-man's-land between the biological and social markers of adulthood. Twenty-five extra years of life . . . have stretched the lifeline. . . . Much of the resulting tension is being felt between childhood and adulthood."[6]

Becoming Adult in a Changing World

Wade Clark Roof has drawn attention to the power of a generation and recognized that "in times of social upheaval and cultural discontinuity especially, generations tend to become more sharply set off from one another."[7] We live in such a time. Valerie Russell, a veteran of the civil rights movement who for forty years has worked on behalf of a more just and humane society, commented that "in all the meetings I now attend, the greatest divides are between the generations."[8] Recognition of the importance of young adulthood and reappraisal of the relationship between generations and the work we need to do together are critical elements of the challenge of our time.

We live in "cusp time." The young adult task of composing and recomposing meaning and faith now takes place in a culture making its way through a similar set of rapids—a turning point in the flow of history, shaped by new technologies that have spawned accelerated, permanent change and unprecedented conditions prompting reconsideration of every feature of life. As we become aware of the power of our participation in an interdependent planetary reality, we increasingly recognize that we are birthing—and must birth—a new cultural imagination on a global scale. The nature and quality of this consciousness shapes our opportunities and options. Thus the tasks of human development in young adulthood are a microcosm of the transition we are now making as a culture.

The New Commons

A powerful image buried deep in the civil imagination of American society is that of the commons. In ancient societies, it was and remains the crossroads at the center of the village. It has also taken the form of the great plazas in Europe and elsewhere. In New England, it was the classic patch of green where everyone could pasture a cow; it was framed by an ecology of institutions—the general store, town meeting hall, school, church, bank, post office, the doctor's house, the dentist, and a flock of households with the farmlands beyond. People gathered on the commons for play and protest, memorial and celebration, and worked out how they would live together.

The commons is not a pristine romantic image. Whether in the form of Main Street or the wharf; the church, synagogue, or mosque; the *bodega* or the stoops of the brownstones; the city square or the ball field, the practice of the commons is always a mix of sins and graces. But wherever there is consciousness of participation in a commons, there is an anchored sense of a shared life within a manageable frame.

Today the commons is global in scope and personal in impact. Travel, communications, and entertainment technologies, along with the emergence of a global market and growing awareness of our interdependence within the natural environment, have cast all of us into a new global commons. On this new commons, society has become yet more complex, diverse, and morally ambiguous. As addressed in our book *Common Fire: Leading Lives of Commitment in a Complex World,*[9] there is an enormous need for an understanding and practice of human development that prepares people to become citizen-leaders in this new commons, able to engage the great questions of our time and to participate in discovering and creating responses to challenges both new and ancient. Democratic societies are dependent upon a complex moral conscience—a citizenry who can recognize and assess the claims of multiple perspectives and are steeped in critical, systemic, and compassionate habits of mind. Initiating young adults into viable forms of meaning and faith that can undergird these tasks is a critical feature of our vocation as a species on the edge of a new cultural landscape.

The Distinctive Role of Higher Education

In its best practice, higher education is one important expression of that vocation, playing a primary role in the formation of critical thought and a viable faith. It is not the only context within which critical awareness can be cultivated and informed. But higher and professional education is distinctively vested with the responsibility of teaching critical and systemic thought and initiating young lives into a responsible apprehension first of the realities and questions of a vast and mysterious universe and second of our participation within it. Higher education is intended to serve as a primary site of inquiry, reflection, and cultivation of knowledge and understanding on behalf of the wider culture. As such, institutions of higher education hold a special place in the story of human development, particularly in the process of becoming a young adult in faith.

This is a complex challenge. It is hard enough to make meaning, to compose a faith, within the intensified complexity of today's commons, but it is especially difficult to do so in the institution charged with teaching the value of critical reflection upon life in that world. Some would argue that meaning-making is not the business of higher education, that its proper task is discovering and teaching empirical truth, and that issues of purpose and meaning are more appropriately dealt with elsewhere in society. Yet society itself has not always made this assumption. At the beginning of the story of American higher education (the founding of Harvard College), we find this statement of purpose: "After God had carried us safe to *New England* and wee had our houses, provided necessaries for our livelihood, rear'd convenient places for God's worship and settled the government: One of the next things we longed for, and looked after was to advance *Learning* and perpetuate it to Posterity: dreading to leave an illiterate Ministry to the Churches, when our present Ministers shall lie in the Dust."[10]

For these forebears, learning and faith were integral to each other. Moreover, both were at stake in the establishment of higher education. The little college, which was at once a divinity school and the seed of one of the world's finest universities, was charged with preparing people who could responsibly nurture human faith for future generations.

Today, as our social reality has become dramatically complex, higher education is a multi-institutional configuration made up of colleges, programs, institutes, centers, laboratories, and graduate schools formally and informally invested in related professional sectors. Further, every college and university is linked to a vast network of trustees, alums, parents, funding agencies, and other members of the wider commons who have a stake in what we know and how we learn to become citizens in the twenty-first century. Within this dynamic complexity, the questions of the relationship between the extraordinary knowledge development of our time and questions of purpose, meaning, faith, and ethics have become both more difficult and more urgent.[11]

Mentors in Many Roles

This book, therefore, is addressed in a particular way to those who directly affect the lives of young adults within higher and professional education: professors, administrators, trustees, counselors, campus ministers, residence hall staff, and others. But higher education no longer dwells in any kind of reality separated from the fabric of our society as a whole. Young adults, whether or not they are engaged in higher and professional education, are affected by work supervisors, parents, older adult friends and relatives, and a wide range of professionals, including business executives and religious leaders, attorneys and social workers, and all who shape modern media—musicians and other artists, directors, producers, book publishers, and webmasters. Thus, while giving particular attention to the experience of young adults in the context of higher education, I examine the re-formation of meaning and faith in young adulthood in a way that recognizes the mentoring role of all who affect young adult lives.

For many reasons, the practice and wisdom of mentoring has been weakened in our society. We compensate for this loss with a professionalism that is too often delivered without the "life-giving, caring field once provided by elders."[12] But this has contributed to fragmentation and loss of transcendent meaning, for which no amount of professional expertise can compensate. Restoring mentoring as a cultural force could significantly revitalize our institutions and provide the intergenerational glue to address some of our deepest and most pervasive concerns. Thus this book is for all adults who are investing themselves in the promise of young adult lives, and it is for those who yet may be persuaded to do so. It is also for relatively older young adults themselves who, having traveled some of the terrain described here, may find confirmation of their own struggling and aspiring integrity and affirmation of their finest and boldest dreams.

Revealing the Elusive Young Adult Era

The perspective described here emerges in dialogue with perspectives from developmental psychology (Piaget, Erikson, Perry, Levinson, Kegan, Gilligan, Belenky and her colleagues, and others), linking this discipline with insights from the study of religion and theology, leadership and ethics. This work both stands within and critically elaborates the interdisciplinary study of faith development pioneered by James Fowler.

But the primary dialogue that shapes my thinking is with young adults themselves. My ongoing work with them continually challenges my assumptions about human development, the formation of faith, and educational-professional practice. Listening carefully to young adults grappling with the particular stresses of making meaning in these complex times has prodded me to significantly amend those theories (including my own) by which they have been interpreted.

Current developmental theories (represented by Kegan and Fowler) continue to describe the movement to mature adult faith as a three-step process whereby conventional (or adolescent) meaning-making develops into a critical-systemic faith (or order of consciousness), which then evolves into a mature adult faith that can hold both conviction and paradox. My own view is that this developmental journey is more adequately grasped as a four-step process. That is, I believe a distinctively young adult way of making meaning may be discerned in the often murky and overlooked territory between conventional faith and critical-systemic faith. Seeing young adults clearly through this lens can awaken our attention to a crucial era in human becoming. Since the future of our planet may depend upon us all becoming more conscious, mature adults, this book is dedicated to shedding light on that era and the critical transformation it harbors.

I draw attention also to the relationship between *how* we know and *what* we know, that is, to the difference between the form and content of knowing. Though developmental theorists to date have concentrated primarily on describing the formal structures of each stage or "order of mind" (Kegan), careful consideration must also be given to the formative power of the images (content) our structures of mind hold and to the role of imagination in human intelligence. As the contents of thought are the stuff of the young adult "Dream,"[13] they inevitably play a vital role in the formation of adulthood and in turn potentially shape (or misshape) the promise of a culture's future.

When seen from this perspective, every subject, discourse, and methodology in the curriculum of higher and professional education (as well as their analogues in the related contexts of adult work and the wider society) potentially contributes to the formation of young adult meaning-making and faith. Creating mentoring environments—formal and informal—is a primary means by which faculty and the many others who are directly and indirectly related to young adults inevitably, by intention or default, have a mentoring role in young adult lives. I suggest that by extension, not only the ecology of higher education and related institutions but also the wider culture as a whole play mentoring roles in the formation of each new generation of young adults, thus shaping the future of the culture itself.

Today's young adults must make meaning in the midst of an intensifying personal and global complexity and an expanding universe. Both younger and older adults stand on a new frontier in the history of human meaning-making. In reconsidering the formation of young adult faith, and particularly the power that mentoring adults have to determine its quality, we may recognize with new strength how young adults and their mentors serve to fuel the power and promise of cultural renewal, seeding the imagination of a worthy adulthood and the promise of our common future.

2

MEANING AND FAITH

WHEN I WAS INVITED to work with the faculty of a prestigious business school as they began to readdress ethics in the M.B.A. curriculum, a long-time colleague from another field said, with a cynical glint in his eye, "Oh, you get to ask those students what their ethics are!" I responded, "Well, yes, but what I really want to understand is how they make meaning."

Most of us recognize that we human beings may or may not act in a manner that corresponds with what we say our ethics are. But human beings do act in ways that are congruent with what they ultimately trust as dependable and real—what makes sense at the end of the day, what they think they can really count on. We humans act in ways that are congruent with how we make meaning.

As human beings, we all make meaning. We search for a sense of connection, pattern, order, and significance. In our ongoing interaction with all of life, we puzzle about the fitting, truthful relationships among things. We search for ways of understanding our experience that make sense of both the expected and the unexpected in everyday life.

Over time, we can grow in our capacity to make meaning in ways that are trustworthy and dependable because they increasingly align with the currents of life itself. A child may make meaning of his parents' divorce by telling himself, and us, that his parents are divorced because they caught it (like a disease) from another family in the neighborhood that suffered divorce just a few months earlier. We find this bit of heroic meaning-making poignantly charming, fitting for his age—and perhaps not without truth—but we know that in time he will tell the story differently.

But how does this change happen? How do our ways of making meaning become more adequate, dependable, and satisfying? How do we learn to make meaning in ways that orient and sustain a worthy adult life?

These are important questions that invite us to reflect on how adult faith is formed. Most people, however, do not immediately recognize that meaning-making is a central feature of the experience of faith and the ground of our ethics. When I told my cynical colleague that I was interested in the *meaning-making* of M.B.A. students as a way of understanding their ethics, he was intrigued. If I had said I was interested in their *faith,* he might have found it odd or inappropriate in a culturally plural, professional setting, or he might have simply concluded that ethics and faith or religion go together—all important, but somewhat marginal in the "real world."

Points of Departure: What Faith Is and Isn't

Faith is a multifaceted phenomenon, and we perceive it best when we consider it from several angles of vision.

Faith and Religion

Indeed, for many, faith is simply equated with religion. Thus the word *faith* has become problematic in a religiously plural world. This is particularly true within any setting—governmental, educational, or commercial— where the multiple perspectives characteristic of our new global commons are especially evident.

Among some people, personal and cultural ambivalence about matters of religion makes *faith* a charged, negative word, best avoided in any case. For others, it is a strong and positive word with a venerable history that dwells at the core of human life. For yet others, faith has simply become a matter of indifference. If recognized as a part of human life—even an important part—it is nevertheless seen as *only* a part and considered separable from other important elements of life, such as career, relationships, political commitments, economic life, and so on. Those who view faith this way assume it is something one may choose or not choose to incorporate into one's particular lifestyle. From this perspective, faith becomes merely a single element in the complex calculus that is required to negotiate contemporary adult life. Thus many in today's society assume faith to be at most a personal matter, preferably confined to the private sphere.

In contrast, there are those (particularly some who have a strongly defined and intensely held set of religious beliefs) who assert that a particular form of faith (theirs) fully interprets and may be arbitrarily imposed upon all experience (theirs and others'). Common to many understandings of the word *faith* is the assumption that it is something essentially static. You have it or you don't. When faith is linked with religious dogma, the word is not generally used to connote something dynamic that undergoes change, transformation, and development over time.

Faith and Spirituality

There is, though, some shift when faith is associated with spirituality. Growing numbers of people in professional and other walks of life are apt to say, "I'm not religious, but I am spiritual." In the corporate and educational spheres there is, at least in some quarters, growing comfort with speaking of spirit, spirituality, and soul. In large measure, these words seem to connote a personal rather than a public sensibility, although book titles addressing these dimensions of experience are highly visible in the public square.

This turn to a recognition of spirituality and an acknowledgment of soul is rooted in a longing for ways of speaking of the human experience of depth, meaning, mystery, moral purpose, transcendence, wholeness, intuition, vulnerability, tenderness, courage, the capacity to love, and the apprehension of spirit (or Spirit) as the animating essence at the core of life. As Parker Palmer has articulated so helpfully, it arises from the hunger for authenticity, for correspondence between one's inner and outer lives.[1] In a society and an academy grown weary and restless with hardening definitions of who and what counts in determining what matters—what we will invest our lives in and how we will name that investment—there is a desire to break through into a more spacious and nourishing conception of the common life we all share. In this context, the words *faith* and *faithfulness,* connoting trust, loyalty, and connection, find place and resonance.

Faith: A Human Universal

A reconsideration of the word *faith* assists us in reclaiming an enlarged sense of meaning and purpose and yields ways of understanding the contemporary resistance and attraction to things religious and spiritual. A central conviction of the perspective offered here is that faith is integral to all of human life. It is a human universal; it shapes both personal and corporate behavior. It is related to meaning, trust, and hope. Its expressions in language and ritual, ideology and practice are always particular and finite. Faith is a dynamic phenomenon that undergoes transformation across the whole life span, with the potential for a particularly powerful transformation in the young adult years.

A careful exploration of the word *faith* is more than an exercise in etymology. If we are to recognize the significance of the dynamics of faith in the experience of young adults and the implications for the role of mentors and the institutions that influence the formation of adulthood, faith must be emancipated from its too-easy equation with belief and religion and reconnected with meaning, trust, and truth.

Faith and Belief

In contemporary English usage, *faith* is used primarily as a noun, strongly associated with religion, and frequently used synonymously with *belief*. This has not always been so. The eminent historian of religion Wilfred Cantwell Smith elegantly traced the relationship between the words *faith* and *belief*. He has shown that since in English *faith* was used only as a noun, "to believe" was chosen as the verb. This was appropriate, for in earlier centuries "the Anglo-Saxon–derived word 'believe' meant pretty much what its exact counterpart in German, *belieben,* still means today: namely, 'to hold dear, to prize.' It signified to love, . . . to give allegiance, to be loyal to; to value highly." The Latin *credo,* meaning literally "I set my heart," was translated "I believe," and thus was not a mistranslation.[2] "To believe" connoted an essential human activity involving the whole person.

In recent times, however, the word *belief* has shifted. Smith traces three important migrations in the use of *believe* that have altered its meaning: first, from the personal to the impersonal—from a relationship with Being to dogma; second, a shift in the subject of the verb, from "I believe" or "believe me" to "he, she, or they believe"; and third, from conveying the linking of the heart with truth to increasingly connoting lack of trust and confidence—"Do you really think that is so?" "Well, I believe so."[3]

As a result, belief has come to suggest primarily a cognitive enterprise. Further, it connotes mere opinion—or even the dubious or false—rather than matters of truth, reality, and ultimate importance. To wit, when the word *faith* is used synonymously with belief, it takes on these same connotations. Consequently, these impersonal, propositional, and narrowly cognitive connotations separate faith from the personal, affective, visceral, and passional dimensions of being and knowing. In addition, the association of faith with what is dubious links it with "irrational knowledge" and consigns it to the private, emotional sphere, divorced from both public life and the life of the mind.

These shifts in the meaning of the words *faith* and *belief* have critical significance in contemporary culture. They are a part of the postmodern reorientation of our relationship to knowledge, affecting our most cherished institutions and assumptions—specifically our assumptions about faith, religion, belief—and what we can trust, imagine, and hope for. Religion itself has had a role in these currents of change. For example, Christianity, the prevailing religion in the Western world, in Smith's view has fallen into the "heresy" of requiring belief as the primary evidence of faith.[4] Faith, a more fundamental dynamic than belief, has been obscured.

Wherever belief has become mere intellectual assent to abstract propositions, and whenever specific religious propositions have become meaningless, impersonal, or at least dubious to a large number of Western, postmodern people, then by synonymous usage faith has come to be equally meaningless—particularly to the critically aware mind. If faith is discounted, the human landscape becomes arid, and hope and commitment wither; the human spirit grows parched, and not much more than a prickly cynicism can be sustained. Therefore, if we are to recover an adequate understanding of human faith, we must be clear that when we use the word *faith* we are speaking of something quite other than *belief* understood in these ways. Faith is not simply a set of beliefs that religious people have; it is something that all human beings do.

Faith and Truth

This distinction between faith and belief is particularly important when we are concerned with the relationship of faith to truth. Every person, profession, and sector of society has a stake in the adequacy of truth claims. Commitment to truth requires a questioning curiosity and ongoing and rigorous examination of one's most elemental assumptions. In the face of new understanding, one may come to perceive an earlier experience of faith or religious belief—an earlier way of making meaning—as now outgrown or otherwise irrelevant. Indeed, if faith is understood as static, fixed, and inextricably bound to a particular language or worldview, it must be discarded as obsolete if the integrity of intellect and soul is to be maintained in a dynamic world. A richer perception of faith, however, enables us to recognize that fidelity to truth may indeed require changing a particular set of beliefs—and yet be important to the ongoing tasks of finding a more adequate faith.

Faith and Skepticism

Any attempt to recover a generic understanding of the word *faith* in a way that may illuminate essential human capacities and commitments—including the commitment to truth—is bound to encounter skepticism.

Yet skepticism itself may be closely related to faith. For faith to become mature, it must be able to doubt itself. Cynicism functions as a kind of armor against disappointment and despair. Skepticism combines the power to question with an openness to being convinced. Skepticism can be a healthy form of doubt, or it may reflect the loss of a once-shared trust in a universe of meaning, however that was defined. It may also function as a thin veneer of public sophistication, glossing over a private, lonely void that neither the rational mind nor economic success can fill. In our time, we have become at once scientifically informed, philosophically relativistic, and disappointed and disillusioned in many quarters. Yet ironically faith can come alive in an engagement with radical uncertainty.

Faith: A Matter of Meaning

Though faith has become problematic, the importance of meaning has not. William G. Perry Jr., who has contributed so much to our understanding of meaning-making in young adulthood, often remarked that the purpose of an organism is to organize, and what human beings organize is meaning. Meaning-making is the activity of composing a sense of the connections among things: a sense of pattern, order, form, and significance. To be human is to seek coherence and correspondence. To be human is to want to be oriented to one's surroundings. To be human is to desire relationship among the disparate elements of existence.

Patterning, testing, and recomposing activity occurs in every aspect of human life and manifests itself in meaning. The mind does not passively receive the world but rather acts upon every object and every experience to compose it. This composing activity occurs even at the level of basic perception. For example, when we perceive a tree, we compose it, organizing its various parts into a whole—branches, leaves, trunk, roots, textures, colors, height, breadth, and whatever we may know of the intricate systems by which it is nourished or threatened through the seasons of its existence. Though we may all encounter the same tree, each of us composes a different one. Moreover, in interaction with the tree we compose, we each make different meaning of it. Some of us see the subject of a poem; others see a lucrative number of board feet; and still others see a source of shade, shelter, or a threat in a strong wind.

It is much the same with our experience of a handshake. We compose a sense of warmth or sincerity, strength, aloofness, ambivalence, or mere social custom according to how another grips (or fails to grip) our hand. This perception is ordered by our cultural history, our mood in the moment, our knowledge of the person, and a whole host of other elements in our environment. Though we may shake hands with the same person, each of us composes a different perception.

We compose the discrete elements of our every day, such as trees and handshakes, into an overall pattern that orients us and grounds us. Even to get out of bed in the morning we depend upon some familiar pattern of relationships between coffeepot, shower, and breakfast—whatever constitutes our ritual of initiation into a new day. There is, however, an important distinction to be made. Though there may be times when getting up in the morning is indeed a heroic act, nevertheless the primary concern here is not with meaning-making at the level of only the discrete and mundane. Rather, when we speak of faith, we direct our attention to the desire of human beings to live at more than a mundane level, and to make meaning of the whole of life.

We reserve the word *faith* for meaning-making in its most comprehensive dimensions. In other words, whenever we organize our sense of a particular object, series of activities, or institution, we are also compelled to compose our sense of its place in the whole of existence. We speak of this activity as composing a world. All human beings compose and dwell in some conviction of what is *ultimately* true, real, dependable within the largest frame imaginable. Human beings, either unself-consciously or self-consciously, individually and together, compose a sense of the ultimate character of reality and then stake our lives on that sense of things. It is this act of composing and being composed by meaning that I invite the reader to associate with the word *faith*.

Forms of Faith

Faith has many facets and is manifest in our experience in several forms.

Faith as Primal Force of Promise

The will to find meaning is a primal force that courses through human life as a demand for order, pattern, and relation. William F. Lynch, a Jesuit who reflected deeply on the nature of faith and hope, described faith as "the most elemental force in human nature."[5] He invites us to imagine faith as coming into force "as soon as promises begin to be made to it"[6]— that is, at the very dawn of human existence, in the womb. (Although he used this image only as a metaphor, prenatal psychology suggests that it may indeed be more than metaphor.)[7] We cannot remember, but we can imagine that we first come to consciousness in a rudimentary sense of trustworthy pattern, wholeness, and relation—a sense of an ultimate environment that intends our good.

Then, in the experience we call birth, we undergo what must seem like utter chaos: sound louder than ever before, light, touch, breathing for the first time. The task of the infant is to recompose that which was promised at the dawn of existence, a felt sense of trustworthy pattern and relation. Erik Erikson described an infant's first task as the establishment of "basic trust."[8] As I am describing the process, however, the first task of human being is to *re*establish basic trust.

In most religious traditions, a ritual occasion marks our entry into a social world of meaning and purpose. In Jewish and Christian tradition, the community gathers around the infant and does an extraordinary thing. The child is addressed as "child of the covenant"—child of the promise. What is most significant about this declaration is that the adult community knows that though the infant may with good care be able to reestablish a trustworthy sense of connection, relation, and wholeness, this task is not accomplished alone, nor is it then accomplished once and for all. Over and over again, life will require the encounter with the unexpected. Again and again, we undergo the loss of our most cherished patterns of meaning and anchors of trust as we discover their insufficiency. In the ups and downs of daily life, human beings experience an ongoing dialogue between fear and trust, hope and hopelessness, power and powerlessness, alienation and belonging. Yet mature faith has learned that though the forms of faith are finite, the promise is kept. It is from this struggled knowing that the adult community addresses the new infant as child of the promise.

Thus, to speak of faith is to point toward the meaning-making that frames, colors, provides tone and texture, and relativizes the activity of the everyday. All human action is conditioned by a felt sense of how life really is (or ought to be), or what has ultimate value.

A Center of Power, Value, and Affection

Fowler has described the activity of faith as "intuiting life as a whole"— a wholeness that is felt as a sense of relatedness among self, other, and "a center of power and value" that some would name God.[9]

Up to this point, we have spoken of faith without speaking of God per se. In the dynamic activity of composing meaning, whatever pattern of meaning we ultimately depend upon functions as "God" for us. In other words, whatever serves as the centering, unifying linchpin of our pattern of meaning and holds it all together—that center functions as "God." As the theologian H. Richard Niebuhr recognized, "To deny the reality of a supernatural being called God is one thing; to live without confidence in some center of value without loyalty to a cause is another."[10] In this sense, virtually all human beings may be understood as "theists." From this perspective, a "true atheist" would be one "who loves no one and whom no one loves; who does not care for truth, sees no beauty, strives for no justice; who knows no courage and no joys, finds no meaning, and has lost all hope."[11]

Many and Lesser Gods

In the times in which we live, many people might best be understood as "polytheists," juggling as it were many gods. They find themselves living fragmented lives, piecing together various scraps of discrete meaning, each with its own center of value, power, and affection, each with its own god. Polytheistic faith is composed by those who may have "intuited life as a whole" but have only been able to compose an assortment of "isolated wholes." For example, many people yearn for a sense of deep integration in their lives but experience even the worlds of home and work as separate, each sphere oriented to differing values, expectations, and loyalties.[12]

On the other hand, there are those who construe a single pattern of meaning and thus dwell in a faith with a single cause or center, such as the success of their career or other ambition. Yet they are unable to relate the center to any larger frame of trustworthy meaning. Niebuhr described this form of faith as "henotheism." Their sense of self, world, and God is cohesive because the boundaries are tightly drawn. The center they rely on to anchor ultimate meaning is, however, inadequate in the face of the variety, complexity, and tragic elements of human experience. Their henotheistic faith is vulnerable to competing centers and to any significant shift in the conditions of personal, professional, or cultural life. This form of faith can also be the "cramping faith of blind and fanatical particularism" or "narrow faith."[13]

Henotheistic faith also may take the forms of devotion to a child or of commitment to artistic achievement, scientific inquiry, a political dream, or a business venture. The question is not whether these are worthy and valuable forms of engagement with life. The question is, Do self, world, and "God" collapse when the child dies, or a permanently injured hand can no longer play a musical instrument, or the funding for the laboratory dries up, or one is defeated in an election, or the business enterprise ends in failure? The challenge that drives the motion toward mature adult faith is grounded in the question, Is there a pattern of meaning, a faith, that can survive the defeat of finite centers of power, value, and affection?

The One Embracing the Many

H. Richard Niebuhr directs our attention beyond polytheism (which depends for its meaning on many centers and gives its partial loyalties to many interests) and henotheism (which centers in a god who is "one among many possible gods"), to "radical monotheism." This is a pattern of meaning, a faith, centered in the "One beyond the many"—a center of power and value adequate to all of the ongoing conditions of the experiences of persons and their communities.[14] This could, however, be expressed as the "One embracing the many."

In a Buddhist sensibility, this ultimacy might be described as *Sunyata*, usually translated as "emptiness." This use of the word is intended to convey a consciousness of the very foundation of the universe, the vast "mystery underlying even darkness—from which the earth itself with its mountains, oceans, buildings, animals, people, and clouds is born."[15]

When we speak of faith as the composing of meaning in these most comprehensive dimensions, we mean a sensibility of life that not only transcends (is *beyond* us) but also permeates and undergirds our very existence (is *within, among,* and *beneath* us). To speak of God as the gift of faith is to seek to name an orienting consciousness that is both transcendent and immanent, both ultimate and intimate.

Faith as Truth and Trust

When the activity of meaning-making is recognized in these comprehensive dimensions, we begin to perceive how both truth and trust are at stake in the composing of faith. A worthy faith must bear the test of lived experience in the real world—our discoveries and disappointments, expectations and betrayals, assumptions and surprises. It is in the ongoing dialogue between self and world, between community and lived reality, that meaning—a faith—takes form.

Yet the meanings human beings compose range from "murky shadows to shimmering points of illumination."[16] If a person composes self and world in a manner that constellates an ultimate sense of mistrust, a conviction of a universe of, say, indifferent or malicious randomness, for her such randomness is what is true and trusted. This is her faith. But interestingly, the word *faith* is most typically used to convey the affirmation of a trustworthy ultimacy, having dependable characteristics in a more conventional sense.

Faith is generally understood as a form of meaning-making that is a quality of human living that at its best grounds capacities for confidence, courage, loyalty, and generosity—and even in the face of catastrophe and confusion enables one to feel at home in the universe (though one's apprehensions of it may be complex, dynamic, shrouded in mystery, and variously described). But the tension remains. If we understand faith as a human universal, two questions necessarily haunt us: If one composes a faith that is trustworthy, is it true? If one composes an ultimacy that is not trustworthy, is it faith?

This way of perceiving faith may trouble those who take for granted that faith always has to do with God as defined by their religious tradition. For them, to speak of faith in generic terms without necessarily referring to God as previously conceived seems confusing, if not beside the point. It is helpful, therefore, to explore further the intimate relationships among faith, trust, and truth.

To Set One's Heart

The relation of faith to trust and truth is illuminated by Smith's study of the notion of faith across cultures, specifically in his discussion of the Hindu word *sraddha*. The word *sraddha* permeates Hindu literature and is assumed in all religious sensibility. As such it functions as an Indian concept of faith. *Sraddha* "is a compound of two words, *srad* (or *srat*), heart, and *dha*, to put." *Sraddha* "means placing one's heart on." This tradition has said that "the religious life, whatever its form, begins . . . with faith; and faith, in its turn, is one's finding within that life (one's being found by) something to which one gives one's heart."[17]

Sraddha in itself leaves unspecified the object of faith. It can be recognized, however, that one gives one's heart only to that which one "sees" as adequate, trustworthy, and promising. Indeed, Smith notes the Hindu insight that "in fact, the universe and human beings were created in such a way that faith is the intrinsically appropriate human orientation towards what is true and right and real, its absence or opposite (*asraddha,* unfaith, disinterest) being recognized similarly as the proper human attitude to what is false and awry.[18]

"Faithing," then, is putting one's heart upon that which one trusts as true. It is a bedrock trust that the pattern one sees is real. Faithing, in other words, is the ongoing composing of the heart's true resting place. Thus, learning to see in increasingly adequate ways is critical to faith.

The Canopy of Faith

We may think of faith, therefore, as the deep ground, the warp upon which the rest of the particular threads of life's tapestry find their place. Or the activity of faith might be imagined as the weaving of an overarching "canopy of significance" that embraces, orders, and relativizes all of our knowing and being. Both metaphors convey faith as both infinitely *transcendent* in character and simultaneously profoundly *immanent*. Faith is an activity that at once reaches infinitely beyond and intimately within the particulars of existence.

The metaphor of the canopy of faith has been made accessible to many cultures through the classic play *Fiddler on the Roof*. When the second daughter chooses to follow her revolutionary lover into Siberia, her father waits with her for the train that will carry her far away from her family home. He acknowledges that they do not know when they will see each other again. Then his daughter gives him a special gift. She responds, "I promise you I will be married under the canopy." This is a gift to her father, for in the Jewish wedding, the canopy represents not only the home that is formed by that union but also the whole household of Israel. She is promising her father that the fabric of meaning into which he has woven his life will be sustained and will transcend both miles and ideology. Later, we watch his canopy of faith stretched to its limits—and perhaps beyond its limits—when his youngest daughter chooses not to be married under the canopy.

Particularly because many in contemporary life find their meaning in forms that are not articulated in religious terms, we are often unaware that we have nevertheless woven a canopy of significance—a faith that we hold and are held by—until people we value do not choose to affirm that upon which we discover our sense of life has ultimately depended. For some, awareness of the patterns that have been deeply woven into our personal and collective life emerges only in the suffering of the unraveling or rending of those weavings that held a personal or public trust.

If our daily living is dependent upon a comprehensive fabric of meaning, the questions of faith are at once both large and intimate, as all those who grieve or otherwise suffer meaninglessness know. "Why should I get out of bed in the morning?" "What is the purpose of my existence and the existence of others?" "Does anything really matter?" "What can I depend upon?" "Are we ultimately alone?" "What and whom can be trusted as real?" "What is the ultimate character of the cosmos in which I dwell?" "What is right and just?" "How, then, shall we live?" Whenever we allow such questions to permeate the fiber of our lives, we discover new depths, and enlarged vistas often catch us by surprise. Our sense of the possible and the impossible is vulnerable to being reordered.

Faith as Act

Faith—one's sense of the ultimate character of existence—not only centers the mind and provides a resting place for the heart. It is also the orienting guide of the hand. Faith determines action. Faith is manifest in act (and, as we shall see, is paradoxically birthed in action). Faith is intimately related to doing. We human beings act in accordance with what we really trust—in contrast to what we may merely acclaim. We act in alignment with what we finally perceive as real, oriented by our most powerful centers of trust (or mistrust). Thus our acts, powered by a deeper faith, often belie what we say (or even think) we believe. Our faith is revealed in our behavior.

Our actions are consistent with our verbal declarations only if these declarations reflect our actual convictions about ultimate meaning and are not superseded by unspoken commitments, loyalties, and fears oriented to other, more compelling centers of power, value, and affection. Faith makes itself public in everyday acts of decision, obedience, and courage.[19] Faith is the ground of ethics and the moral life. Faith is intimately linked with a sense of vocation—awareness of living one's life aligned with a larger frame of purpose and significance. It is from this perspective that I might have responded to my cynical colleague regarding the ethics of M.B.A. students by saying, "I want to understand their meaning-making at the level of faith—what they ultimately trust will work and count as they act to sort out the fitting relationships between themselves and others—as they make decisions and deals in their crafting of life."

Thus we may recognize faith in many manifestations: as the primal force of promise; as our everyday activity of meaning-making, both ultimate and intimate; and as act. As such, faith is powerful; this is well revealed in faith betrayed.

Through the Valley of the Shadow

Betrayal, loss, fear, and death pose fundamental challenges to faith, yet they may be integral to the life of faith most profoundly understood.

Faith Betrayed

Faith as a primal, elemental force of promise permeating the whole of life is manifest most inescapably and often treacherously in faith betrayed. Lynch refers us to the mythical Medea for an appreciation of the primal, elemental power of faith. Medea has been "terrible" in her fidelity to Jason the Argonaut. She has followed him everywhere and given up everything. When he abandons her for Creusa, the princess of Corinth, Medea says she made a mistake when she "trusted the words of a Greek." She then murders her own children and Creusa, demonstrating the limitless fury that floods the vacuum created by faith's disappearance, thereby revealing the power of this primal force transformed into one of its fierce forms. Lynch continues:

> The furies insert themselves in a terrible way into human affairs precisely where the greatest faith has been violated, where a mighty word has been given but is now betrayed. In every case the Fury attacks the violator of a *word* written out in the most primitive and earthly forms of nature, the form of mother, who is word to her child, the form of wife, the form of friend, the form of father. All these forms are words carved out in the deepest realities of nature itself, making promises without opening the lips and demanding belief for very survival's sake. . . . The energy and power of human faith become visible in the size of this fury. We tend to reduce faith to a sweet pious dimension, weak rival and challenger of knowledge. We know it best through its embodiment in fury. And through its incarvement, without words, in the very deepest structures of human life. Aristotle knew this well in *The Poetics* when he chose these violations of kinship and fidelity as the most tragic forms of tragedy. They are.[20]

In most societies, there is a legal distinction between crimes of passion and other crimes. Such tragic moments arise when the very fabric and center of one's meaning—one's sense of wholeness, connection, and belonging—is violated, broken, shattered. The promise is broken. Faith erupts into fury. These are the Furies who rage in witness to the world as it "ought to be."

Faith as a Suffering

Any attempt to rethink the category of faith in relation to contemporary life is insufficient without recognizing faith as a "suffering" as well as a virtue of reasoning and willing.[21] Suffering in its broadest sense means undergoing, and to be totally affected; thus suffering may include not only physical and emotional pain as we may typically think of it but also the kind of betrayal just described, as well as the suffering of doubt, of being overwhelmed, of drifting without moorage or goal, of prolonged struggle, of yearning, and of despair.

Shipwreck, Gladness, and Amazement

During my own graduate study, it happened that the professor I most frequently heard applauded was Richard R. Niebuhr. The reasons were not immediately obvious, since he did not seek to capture the student imagination either with entertaining anecdotes or with a lecture style designed to dazzle by the aesthetic of its systematic outline. Rather, when he lectured it was as though he was generously allowing others to be present to his own contemplation. As he reflected on the material for the day, he would sometimes, for example, pause and look out the window, waiting for the word to come that would fittingly name what he was learning to see and understand. When the word did come, it did seem to be the right, fitting word. And when applause broke out at the end of class, it was perhaps because we are especially grateful for the naming of intuitions that dwell in the deepest currents of our being.

When Niebuhr reflects on human faith, he does so, in part, with the metaphors of "shipwreck, gladness, and amazement."[22] These metaphors connote the subjective, affective, dynamic, often bewildering, and transformative nature of the experience of faith.

Metaphorical shipwreck may occur with the loss of a relationship, violence to one's property, collapse of a career venture, physical illness or injury, defeat of a cause, a fateful choice that irrevocably reorders one's life, betrayal by a community or government, or the discovery that an intellectual construct is inadequate. Sometimes we simply encounter someone, or some new experience or idea, that calls into question things as we have perceived them, or as they were taught to us, or as we had read, heard, or assumed. This kind of experience can suddenly rip into the fabric of life, or it may slowly yet just as surely unravel the meanings that have served as the home of the soul.

To suffer, I have said, means to undergo and be totally affected. If people undergo the break up or unraveling of what has held their world together, inevitably there is some degree of suffering. When we suffer the collapse of our sense of self, world, and "God," we are disoriented—drained of those rich connections that create significance, delight, and purpose.

When I first began to reflect on the experience of young adult faith, a colleague recalled that as a freshman in college his dream was to become a basketball star. He was not very tall, and he had come from a small-town high school. The second week of the season, he was cut from the team. He remembers going to the showers and sobbing for two hours. He suffered the collapse of meaning—his sense of self, world, and "God." To undergo shipwreck is to be threatened in a total and primary way. In shipwreck, what has dependably served as shelter and protection and held and carried one where one wanted to go comes apart. What once promised trustworthiness vanishes.[23]

Early in my experience of undergraduate teaching, I was a part of the teaching team for a freshman course in the Jewish and Christian traditions. I became aware that one of the young men in my section seemed less than satisfied with the course, so I invited him to linger for a moment after class for some conversation. I assumed that in general he was adjusting well to college. He was on the football team; his older brother (also an athlete on campus) had paved the way for him. But in our conversation, I began to realize that there were other dissatisfactions beneath the surface. He wasn't entirely sure that he was comfortable with being "just a football player"— feeling that perhaps this identity was forged more by his high school newspaper than by his own sense of self. Then, after telling me briefly about his parents' divorce, he looked directly at me and quietly said, "Do you know what it is like to have lost everything you ever really loved?"

We didn't get around to discussing the course very much that day. But in that moment, I felt some gladness that I could tell him that I did know something about it. My parents were not divorced, but I had undergone other experiences in my mid-twenties that, in retrospect, I realized had quietly devastated assumptions about my self, how the world worked, and even my sense of God.

On the other side of these experiences, if we do survive shipwreck—if we wash up on a new shore, perceiving more adequately how life really is—there is, eventually, gladness. It is gladness that pervades one's whole being; there is a new sense of vitality, be it quiet or exuberant. Usually, however, there is more than relief in this gladness. There is transformation. We discover a new reality beyond the loss. Rarely are we able to replace, to completely recompose, what was before. The loss of earlier meaning is irretrievable and must be grieved and mourned. But gladness arises from the discovery that life continues to unfold with meaning, with connections of significance and delight. We rarely experience this as a matter simply of our own making. As the primal, elemental force of promise stirs again within us, we often experience it as a force acting upon us, beneath us, carrying us—sometimes in spite of our resistance—into new meaning, new consciousness, new faith.

This gladness is experienced, in part, as a new knowing. Though this knowing sometimes comes at the price of real tragedy (which even the new knowing does not necessarily justify), we typically would not wish to return to the ignorance that preceded coming to the new shore. We do not want to live in a less-adequate truth, a less viable sense of reality, an insufficient wisdom. There is deeply felt gladness in an enlarged knowing and being, and in a new capacity to act.

But here we must resist any temptation toward glib piety. To repeat, when we wash up on a new shore of knowing, there may be diminishment as well as enlargement. Something is always lost. This diminishment may potentially lead, however, to a more adequate understanding of how it is that human beings are continuously both enlarged and diminished in the course of ongoing lived experience. Yet surely some tragic outcomes challenge a notion of faith as a dynamic of shipwreck, gladness, and amazement.

My own reflections on this matter in relation to young adulthood continue to be tugged into discipline and mystery by the suicide of a close friend, the husband of one of my college roommates, when we were all twenty-seven years old. When Dan died, another of his friends said of us, "Before Dan died, we were all 'star-spangled.' After he died, we knew that tragedy could strike any of us." In the face of a promising life seemingly unfulfilled, and another (his wife's) forever set upon a path quite different from her choosing, we suffered a kind of shared shipwreck. We were initiated into yet larger dimensions of consciousness and deepened questions of meaning, purpose, and significance. Three decades later, life and faith have been recomposed, but there remains a shared ache, a shared knowing, and a sweetness among us that from time to time render us reverent again before the Mystery we all share.

The questions that suffering and death pose to us are questions of faith: Is there any form of meaning, any faith, that can without delusion embrace both our small and great sufferings? In today's world, not only our own suffering but that of millions of others is made known to us through modern media. The threats to meaning that confront us on the scale of collective experience surely challenge any cursory affirmation of the dynamic described here as faith. Specifically, the task of making meaning on the scale of vast shared suffering has been almost overwhelmingly confounded by the suffering of Jews and others in the Holocaust in Europe, compounded further by the recognition that this Holocaust represents other holocausts in other places and times, including our own. Yet it is Holocaust sufferers themselves who give us some of the most compelling examples of the capacity of the human spirit to reconstitute meaning and faith of the most profound integrity. Victor Frankl, a Holocaust survivor, has written, "But not only creativeness and enjoyment are meaningful. If there is a meaning in life at all, then there must be a meaning in suffering."[24]

Thus the gladness on the other side of shipwreck arises from an embracing, complex kind of knowing that is experienced as a more trustworthy understanding of reality in both its beauty and terror. It is in this sense that Richard Niebuhr describes such gladness as an "intellectual affection."[25]

Such gladness is accompanied by amazement. The power of the experience of shipwreck is located precisely in one's inability to immediately sense the promise of anything beyond the breakup of what has been secure and trustworthy. Until our meaning-making becomes very mature, in the midst of shipwreck there is little or no confidence of meaningful survival. The first time we are self-consciously aware that faith itself has been shattered is, after all, the first time; how could we know that even this might be survived? Even if we accept the dissolution of our self, world, and God with steely and sophisticated courage, we may expect nothing more; the possibility of surviving and going on to more has hitherto not been a part of our experience. Then, when we are met by the surprise of new meaning, we are amazed. Passover is the celebration of amazement. Easter is what happens to us when we look back and say, "I survived that?!"[26] Faith is recomposed by joy as well as by pain.

The Power and Motion of Faith

As we become more conscious of living in a dynamic reality, our notions of faith necessarily undergo change.

Faith as the Motion of Life

The metaphors of shipwreck, gladness, and amazement point toward the dynamic, transformative nature of faith. They help us recover *faith* as a verb, a powerful activity provisionally distinguished from static notions of religion and belief. Faith is a dynamic, multifaceted activity, an active dialogue with promise.[27] The motion of shipwreck, gladness, and amazement describes not only major crises of meaning that punctuate the story of our lives but also the tumbling, rocking, flowing motion of our every day, as we dwell in a continuous dialectic between fear and trust, hope and hopelessness, power and powerlessness, doubt and confidence, alienation and belonging.

This ongoing, meaning-making motion of faith is named in many traditions as the activity of spirit and Spirit. Across traditions, the word *spirit* is typically rooted in words such as *air, breath, wind*—the experience of power moving unseen. Faith is formed and transformed through many forms of spirituality. As we are beginning to see, it is the strategy of Spirit to "release our tight hold on the foreground of life and turn toward the vast background"[28] over and over again. The ongoing process of shipwreck, gladness, and amazement shakes us loose from our focus on little loves and puts us in touch with the mystery of the wider force field of our lives. Each time, our souls are stretched and reordered, at least in some small measure. We find that all we love and wrestle with is recast as something closer to a sense of right proportion. We are perpetually invited to participate more consciously in the vast tissue of life, and if we are attuned to the motion of faith, we learn to wonder in a larger frame and are awakened to bigger questions and larger dreams.

Faith as Rational and Passional

The power and motion of faith includes, but is more than, cognitive activity and a reordering of mind narrowly understood. Yes, faith is intimately related to knowledge; yet it is also prior to knowledge in any formal sense. The faith of the infant, for example, is composed by a rudimentary cognition that relies on, discovers, and composes meaning through sensory, affective modes of knowing. Trust (or mistrust) is grounded in an affection that informs cognition. So it is with adults. As Fowler has put it, "in faith the 'rational' and the 'passional' are fused."[29] A trustworthy ultimacy is composed by feelings as well as thoughts, by being touched as well as by intellectual persuasion. This is not to say that faith is irrational. It is to say that faith has both affective and cognitive dimensions. As in all knowing and being, affect has an ordering power.

Verb and Noun

To suffer shipwreck, gladness, and amazement on the journey of faith is to relinquish the pattern of ultimacy one has seen, known, felt, and acted upon; it is also to discover a new faith. Therefore, even as the word *faith* is recovered as a verb, it remains also a noun. Faith is a composing and a composition. We journey from faith to faith. Faith is not only the act of setting one's heart; it is also what one sets the heart upon. When we say people have a strong faith, we mean first that they confidently engage in the activity of faith in their ongoing meaning-making, testing, trusting, and acting; and second that they have found the pattern of shipwreck, gladness, and amazement to be true and trustworthy. They hold it dear and believe. They dwell in a consciousness of an intricate, intimate pattern of life that is continuously in motion and yet holds at the level of ultimacy. Their faith is manifest as trust, knowledge, emotion, value, and action, permeating every facet of their existence. Their faith changes—it develops—over time, undergoing transformation and growth toward greater adequacy.

Mature adult faith composes meaning in self-conscious engagement with the repeated dissolution and repatterning of one's perceptions of the fabric of life, in the dynamic reconceiving of the assumed connections among persons, things, ideas, events, symbols, the natural and social order, space, and time. The suffering of adult faith is located in learning how to hold on to, and when to let go of, the perceptions, patterns, and relationships that one experiences as partaking in ultimate value and truth.[30] The journey through shipwreck, gladness, and amazement can have particular power in young adult lives, and it can be recognized as one way of describing the deep process by which we become at home in the universe.

3

BECOMING AT HOME
IN THE UNIVERSE

REFLECTING ON THE political cynicism of American society and the ironic detachment that characterizes many in his generation, twenty-four-year-old Jedediah Purdy writes: "We doubt the possibility of being at home in the world, yet we desire that home above all else."[1]

It has been said that *home* is the most powerful word in the English language. It is where we start from. It is what we aspire to. To be at home is to have a place in the scheme of life—a place where we are comfortable; know that we belong; can be who we are; and can honor, protect, and create what we truly love.

To be at home within one's self, place, community, and the cosmos is to feel whole and centered in a way that yields a sense of power and participation. Parker Palmer has described his experience in midlife of contending with the ill-fitting dreams of his future and toxic expectations of self he had carried for many years. This journey took him though the slough of depression. When asked how it felt to emerge from depression with, as he put it, "a firmer and fuller sense of self," he responded, "I felt at home in my own skin, and at home on the face of the earth for the first time."[2] Wilfred Cantwell Smith wrote: "Faith, then, is a quality of human living. At its best, it has taken the form of . . . a quiet confidence and joy which enable one *to feel at home in the universe*. . . ."[3] To be at home is to be able to make meaning of one's own life and of one's surroundings in a manner that holds, regardless of what may happen at the level of immediate events. To be deeply at home in this world is to dwell in a worthy faith.

Young adulthood has much to do with big questions about home: Where do I live? Whom do I live with? Where and with whom do I belong? What can I honor? What is worthy of shelter and protection?

Where can I be creative? If Robert Frost was right that "home is the place where they have to take you in," young adults do indeed also ask: "Does my society have a place for me? Am I invited in?"

These are questions of meaning, purpose, and faith; they are asked not just on the immediate horizon of where to spend the night. In young adulthood, as we step beyond the home that has sheltered us and look into the night sky, we can begin in a more conscious way to ask the ancient questions: Who am I under these stars? Does my life have place and purpose? Are we—am I—alone?

In our time, however, I believe that these ancient questions are being slightly recast. We continue to speak of composing a world, yet we are sensing that *world* is too small a frame. Consciousness of the circuitry of life—ecological and technological—increasingly expands world into universe. Today's young adults grew up within the imagination of *Star Trek* and *Star Wars*. For many, such planetary odysseys have held spiritual significance, shaping a sense of orienting myth. At the same time, a new story of the universe is coming to us from science and creating a new dialogue with religion. Either directly or indirectly, through the shifting forms of culture, these myths have cast the psyche into an enlarged field of awareness. That we as individuals, a species, and a planet inhabit a vast universe has been confirmed and further informed in the conventional mind by scientific space exploration. These are the first generations who have seen the earth rise (the earth as seen from space) and taken account of black holes as features of their geography.

I remember a conversation with Timothy Hull, a friend of mine who is now thirty and an accomplished and committed composer and musician. We were talking one afternoon when he was about eight years old, and I noticed that he was playing with a globe. I assumed that it was a map of the earth, "our world." When I actually focused my attention on it, I was a bit surprised that it was, in fact, the moon, with the craters and valleys mapped and named. Timothy was quite familiar with them. I learned from his mom that he often flew his toy spaceships around that globe and that he asked her one day if she ever thought about how we could be standing upside down as well as right side up, depending on how we thought about our planet moving through space. Yet when, shortly thereafter, I speculatively asked him if he would like to live in space someday, he responded with a bit of distress on his face: "No." When I asked why, he said that he would miss his mom and dad.

Distant realities of many kinds are increasingly brought into our immediate experience. Our sense of place necessarily expands, our stance has become relative to more points of reference, and the field of awareness in which we search for meaning, purpose, and faith has become more vast. Particularly for young adults, up and down (along with top-down) has rapidly become a less meaningful way of speaking. It is thus that the ancient question shifts: "Who am I *under* these stars?" is becoming "Who am I *among* these stars? Can I be at home in the universe; among vast stellar spaces; among my own varied and conflicting yearnings; among diverse cultures; among multiple perspectives, theories, and ideologies; among a wide array of possible futures? And if I make this move rather than that one, who and what will I miss?"

Ironically, the same set of dynamics can conspire to cause people to draw smaller boundaries, or carve out some manageable frame so as not to be obliterated by the vastness. This is the temptation to fortify, especially acute when global awareness and the accompanying encounter with greater diversity prompt and require a refined definition of self. Awareness of an expanding universe can thus go hand in hand with greater differentiation of the participants within it. There can be a tendency to identify home as only a small distinct unit rather than the whole panoply of life within the larger frame.[4] This move toward greater differentiation can be life-enhancing, or it can become tribalistic and dangerous. To avoid the latter, it is vital that the capacity for trust, confidence, and humility be developed in ways that make it possible for the soul to wade into the diversity and complexity of today's world.

The Formation of Trust and Power

If it is a responsibility and privilege to participate in the process by which others become at home in the universe, what do we know as to how this may come about? One of the perspectives that informs my respect for another's becoming is the discipline of constructive-developmental psychology, careful study of the unfolding of competence and consciousness through time and space. This perspective, like other disciplines, has been composed over time through successive conversations among theorists and the populations we have studied over the years. Although there are a host of voices in this conversation, it is useful to recognize the particular contributions of certain key voices in composing the point of view we are using here to understand the potential and vulnerability of young adult lives. There are two well-known grandfathers of this discipline.

In his classic *Childhood and Society,* Erikson traced "eight ages" of human unfolding, linking biological development to a series of life tasks that we all recognize:

1. **Infancy:** trust vs. mistrust
2. **Toddlerhood:** autonomy vs. shame
3. **Early school age:** industry vs. inferiority
4. **Later school age:** initiative vs. guilt
5. **Adolescence:** identity vs. role confusion
6. **Young adulthood:** intimacy vs. isolation
7. **Adulthood:** generativity vs. stagnation
8. **Later adulthood:** ego integrity vs. despair

As each stage with its corresponding task is engaged, if the task is resolved in the positive direction then the person gains strength and more satisfying participation in his or her emotional and social world.

Erikson believed that there is a particularly ripe time for each life task to be taken up. But he also believed that once a task is taken up and worked initially in its own ripe time, it is also continuously reworked in relation to the tasks of the following eras. It is interesting that Erikson's first tasks (the ones planted at the core of our unfolding, to be reworked and strengthened throughout life) are *trust* and various aspects of *power*. These basic life tasks, successfully achieved, create the capacity to trust that one is held well and that one can affect one's world. In whatever measure they are not taken up well, they yield mistrust, shame, guilt, and feelings of inferiority. Although no life does (and perhaps should not) avoid these feelings altogether, resolving these tasks in a positive direction honors the potential of human life. Erikson's later stages can be seen as yet more complex elaborations of the dynamics of trust and power that are foundational to our lives. In our study of people committed to the common good in the face of the complexity, diversity, and moral ambiguity of the new commons, a good enough sense of trust, and confidence that one has power to make a difference, were, indeed, key elements in the formation of their lives and commitments.[5]

Erikson's original scheme (and its later refinements with his spouse and colleague, Joan Erikson) has significantly influenced both educators and clinicians and been widely critiqued and elaborated. Its broad application has long since confirmed its intuitive power and fundamentally shaped our maps of change and growth through the human life cycle. In the Eriksons' view, people move through these life stages and their tasks ready or not, as biological changes inevitably unfold across a lifetime.

The popular radio personality and cultural commentator Garrison Keillor has observed, however, that though we move through life and its tasks ready or not, we do not necessarily become adult. It is said that he has remarked, "You don't have to be very smart to be an adult; some people prove it to you. They get promoted every year at their birthday when they ought to be held back because they still have work to do." Being an adult in terms of chronological age is not necessarily the same as having the capacity to negotiate the rapids of life, in ways that can be trusted as competent and mature. If we focus only on the number of birthday candles— or, as we shall see, only on the tasks Erikson describes (vital as they are)—we may find we become adults without growing either knowledgeable or wise. We need additional perspectives to understand adequately the development of consciousness that is now needed. Understanding the gap between just getting promoted every year at our birthday and learning to see, know, and act in the complex ways that can lead to competence and wisdom is the passion that animates the discipline of constructive-developmental psychology.

Evolving Capacities of Mind

Jean Piaget is the second grandfather of constructive-developmental psychology. His understanding of human development was grounded in the intellectual tradition of Immanuel Kant, James Mark Baldwin, George Herbert Mead, and John Dewey. Originally a biologist (and at the age of sixteen a recognized expert on mollusks!), Piaget became a genetic epistemologist as a result of his fascination with the consistency of logic displayed by children regarding the "wrong" answers they gave in IQ tests. This fascination led to another set of powerful insights into human development.

We can begin to grasp what Piaget was after by reflecting on this now well-known passage from another popular author, Robert Fulghum:

> All of what I really need to know about how to live and what to do and how to be, I learned in kindergarten. Wisdom was not at the top of the graduate-school mountain, but there in the sandpile at Sunday School. These are the things I learned:
>
> Share everything.
>
> Play fair.
>
> Don't hit people.
>
> Put things back where you found them.
>
> Clean up your own mess.
>
> Don't take things that aren't yours.

Say you're sorry when you hurt somebody.

Wash your hands before you eat.

Flush.

Warm cookies and cold milk are good for you.

Live a balanced life—learn some and think some and draw and paint and sing and dance and play and work every day some.

Take a nap every afternoon.

When you go out into the world, watch out for traffic, hold hands, and stick together.

Be aware of wonder. Remember the little seed in the styrofoam cup. The roots go down and the plant goes up and nobody really knows how or why but we are all like that.[6]

What is delicious about this passage is that we hear it through two differing forms of consciousness. We are at once both our present age and also six years old. We know what Fulghum is writing about because of how we knew these things as children. We also know that the passage conveys more than what we knew as children because of our subsequent experience and the meanings we have made of it. Thus his words take on more meaning. Though they refer to concrete things that are supposedly simple, they simultaneously hold a subtle complexity—if, that is, we have learned to see, hear, and act in ways that are more complex than when we were six years old. Not everyone does.

Piaget deepens our understanding of why some people are able to compose a larger and more adequate sense of truth over time. He has helped us to see that not only do we human beings compose our world but we also develop in our capacity to do so.

Through careful and elegant observation, Piaget discerned that human beings, in interaction with their environment, develop increasingly complex structures (or capacities) to receive, compose, and know their world. He observed, for example, that infants know their world through performing certain sensorimotor operations by means of which they can begin to dependably relate to their environment: grasping, sucking, and the like. But infants cannot hold in the mind the rattle they learn to grasp and hold in their hand. For them, out of sight is literally out of mind. Toddlers, in contrast, can hold an image in mind but cannot coordinate images—cannot, for example, put items in sequence. Nor can they distinguish between dream and waking reality. School-age children, however, can become liberated from a world in which all images float free as they develop the capacity for "concrete operations," the capacity for ordering and categorizing the world of concrete reality. This is the age of beginning to organize things in a more fixed way, recognizing cause and effect, and creating "collections"—rocks, stamps, or a series of cards.

It is not until later—the cusp of the teenage years—that one can begin to practice abstract, symbolic thought, or what Piaget called "formal operations." This capacity makes it possible to think propositionally, hypothetically, inferentially, and symbolically. Possibility is no longer a subset of concrete reality. Reality becomes a subset of possibility. It becomes possible to "spin out an 'overall plan' of which any concrete event . . . is but an instance. Put most simply . . . 'what is' [becomes] just one instance of 'what might be.' "[7]

Thus Piaget has helped us understand that all knowing is shaped, in part, by an underlying structure of thought as well as its particular content. Even a bright child of nine who uses concrete operations to receive and compose his or her reality simply cannot know, cannot make meaning, in the same way that may be possible for a fifteen-year-old who has developed formal operational structures of thought. Consequently, such life events as achievement or defeat in school or athletics, or the death of a parent, or the potential consequences of drug abuse are grasped and known differently in each era of human development. Terror and comfort, understanding and wonder, may take quite different forms for an infant, a child, an adolescent, and an adult.

Moreover, we do not move through this kind of development ready or not. Piaget would have agreed with Erikson that biological maturation plays a significant role in human development, but not all of the potential of our becoming is tied to biological maturation. Rather, aging is a necessary but insufficient condition for developing some aspects of cognition and affect. The nature and quality of our interactions with our environment are also critical. A fourteen-year-old, for example, may be ready biologically to develop the abstract thought required for basic algebra but will have difficulty developing this capacity if her environment does not encourage the development of abstract and symbolic thought. We develop the capacity—the structures—to think and feel in increasingly complex ways only if the situations we encounter present us with both the challenge and the resources to do so. Thus, this school of psychology is best understood as a social psychology, because it pays attention not only to the unfolding of an individual's life but also to the power of the context—the quality of relationships and institutions—within which individuals live and do or do not become at home in the universe.

We are still discovering the implications of Piaget's insight. Though not easy, it is intriguing to consider what it means that how a person perceives reality, makes meaning of it, and consequently acts is dependent in part upon his underlying pattern or structure of thought, and that this underlying structure can grow and develop in identifiable ways. (Using a computer metaphor, we might say that a person's grasp of reality is dependent upon the capability of the inner software program as well as the nature and quality of the information available.) When we explore the implications of this insight, not just for child development but also for adult growth and development, the implications for learning; teaching; parenting; advertising; management practice; and social, political, and religious life are enormous.[8] Above all, this perspective reminds us yet again that what is said is not necessarily what is heard. What is intended is not necessarily what is received. And each of us plays a part in the becoming of others.

A Powerful Conversation

Theories of human growth and development have become powerful at this time in our cultural life primarily as a consequence of two new conditions in our society: (1) People are living longer and thus undergoing more change across the life span, and (2) our society is becoming more complex and requires people to develop the complex strengths required of workers, spouses, parents, and citizens.

It is not surprising, therefore, that one of the places where this perspective has been seriously explored is in graduate schools of education. In the 1970s and early 1980s at Harvard's Graduate School of Education, a notably generative conversation convened around the work of Lawrence Kohlberg, who pioneered the implications of Piaget's work for moral development. Among the many who participated in those seminars were Robert Kegan, Carol Gilligan, and James Fowler.[9]

Kegan: Shifting the Focus

Piaget focused his attention on the development of cognition in the individual child. As a consequence, Piagetians and neo-Piagetians were often perceived as concerned only about childhood, cognition, knowing, the individual, stages, and the discontinuities in human development (what is new and changed in the person). As important as these dimensions are, however, they neglect other dimensions that are also integral to becoming at home in the universe: adulthood, emotion, being, the social process, and continuities in development (what in the person persists through time).

Robert Kegan has contended that these "neglects" are actually unitary. He has effectively argued that all of the neglects in the Piagetian story of development are embraced if we return to Piaget's central insight: human becoming takes place in the interaction between the person and his or her environment, between self and other, self and world. These neglects become unitary when they are gathered up in a larger conception: the transforming motion of the self-other relation, which is the daily motion of life itself.

In his two primary books, *The Evolving Self: Method and Process in Human Development* (1981) and *In Over Our Heads* (1994), Kegan observes that ongoing self-other differentiation and relation is one of the most significant, robust, and universal phenomena to be found in nature. In the relationship of self and other, we are constantly sorting out what is what, who is who, and how we are all distinctive yet related. But, he says, the full significance of the self-other relation is obscured if we fail to recognize the motion that gives rise to it. He calls this motion "meaning-constitutive evolutionary activity," by which he refers to "something that is more than biology, philosophy, psychology, sociology, or theology, but is that which all of these, in their different ways, have studied . . . the restless creative motion of life itself."[10]

Individual persons are not their stages of development but are a motion, within which what has been called stages of development are merely moments of dynamic stability—a temporary balance. In his most current work, Kegan has shed the language of stages altogether and prefers to speak of "orders of consciousness": distinct patterns of making meaning that, evolving over time, can hold complexity with increasing adequacy.[11] The more adequate our pattern of meaning-making, the more developed, conscious, and (in this sense) mature we may become.

Kegan has pushed Piaget's theory of cognition in childhood to a broader theory of the formation of persons across time and space—a theory of the self in motion. The activity of cognition is but one actor in a larger drama: the composing of meaning. This drama has everything to do with adulthood as well as with childhood.

Kegan is moved by the dignity and the "astonishingly intimate activity" of a person—at any age—laboring, struggling, and delighting in making sense. If we look through a developmental lens, we see that the heart and art of life is not a static structure—a stage or a series of stages. It is a motion in which what one is "subject to" evolves so as to become "object." Growth involves a process of emergence, from embeddedness in the assumed truth of one's perceptions to the dawn of a new consciousness in which those same assumptions become available for more conscious assessment. Thus Kegan has suggested that it is useful to recognize that a person is always both an individual and an "embeddual," meaning that we are embedded in our perceptions until we can distinguish between our perceptions of the other and the other itself.

An important step toward mature adulthood, for instance, is the evolution from "I *am* my relationships" to "I *have* relationships." Whether I cherish, wrestle with, or despair over my relationships, if I *have* them instead of *being* them, I participate in them differently. Though I continue to depend upon them in profound ways, I am less fused with them. I can respond as a self to the other from a more self-aware "ordering of consciousness"—a more complex way of making meaning.

This perspective is grounded in the conviction that truth is a relational phenomenon. It modifies the sharp divisions between subject and object that have dominated Western ways of knowing, without dismissing the importance of these distinctions. A person remains "in relation to" that which one may also "take as object." Thus, how we compose knowledge and make meaning is shaped by the context in which we love and work, think and feel.

Gilligan: A Different Voice

It is, however, Carol Gilligan, seeking to understand moral decision making in real time and using the lens of gender, who retold the story of human development in a manner that most directly reveals the power of connection as well as differentiation. Listening to the voices of women as they made moral judgments, she and her associates described an evolving understanding of moral choice in a world in which "all things being equal never are." The journey of development, as she tells it, unfolds in a language—a voice—that seeks to express more adequately the reality of ongoing relation and responsibility. This voice (expressive of both male and female experience, but tending to be more evident in the voices of women) contrasts with the juridical voice of differentiation and rights identified in Kohlberg's account of the development of moral reasoning in males.[12] The voice Gilligan identified focuses not upon the differentiation of subject from object but upon the *relation* that orients subject to object, self to other, self to truth, self to possibility.

Gilligan has portrayed the distinctions between these two voices with the example of two young children playing together and wanting to play different games. The girl says, "Let's play next-door neighbors." The boy replies, "I want to play pirates." The girl responds, "OK, you can be the pirate that lives next door." The children might have resolved the conflict by the fair solution (Kohlberg). They could have taken turns playing each game for an equal period. This solution would honor the rights of each child and keep the identity and truth of each child intact, while providing opportunity for each child to experience the other's imaginative world. But, observes Gilligan, "the inclusive solution, in contrast, transforms both games: the neighbor game is changed by the presence of a pirate living next door; the pirate game is changed by bringing the pirate into a neighborhood." The inclusive, relational solution creates not just a new game but a new image of self, a new relationship, and a new truth.[13]

The importance of this relational perspective is heightened in a society and world in which growing numbers of neighborhoods feel threatened in some measure by intensified social diversity and the specter of random or organized violence. Because together we must create new, life-bearing realities, the potential contribution of this perspective cannot be overestimated.

Fowler: Development as the Motion of Faith

The developmental perspectives of Erikson, Piaget, Kegan, and Gilligan are deeply resonant with the dynamics of the formation and reformation of faith, as described in the previous chapter. In them we hear a process of composing meaning, making sense, and ordering the relationships among things, in ways that transform being, feeling, knowing, and doing. Indeed, James Fowler, a theologian and ethicist, and already familiar with Erikson's perspective, joined the Kohlberg seminar and became the most significant pioneer in bringing a constructive-developmental perspective to our understanding of the formation of faith. In response to Fowler's work, early on Kegan affirmed that to incorporate a dynamic notion of faith into the constructive-developmental insight is not to add something at the periphery of the developmental perspective but to speak from its heart.[14] For when constructive-developmental theory moves beyond focusing on stages to focusing on the deep motion of life that gives rise to consciousness, it moves into the experiences and phenomena that have been a feature of people and their communities of faith for as long as people have given expression to the reality of being alive: "The constructive-developmental perspective has not yet found a way to do justice to what Whitehead called the ultimate reality of the universe—its motion. Much less has it recognized the religious dimension of our relation to this reality, what Buber spoke of both as an inevitable lifelong tension between the I-Thou and the I-It, . . . the sacredness of the everyday."[15]

Incorporating the methodology used by other constructive-developmental theorists, Fowler and his associates mapped the relationship between developmental psychologies and transformations of faith across the life span.[16] Informed by theological and psychological perspectives and by the patterns that began to emerge from analyzing hundreds of interviews, he enunciated a framework by which to interpret the development of faith in a series of six stages.

Beginning with his now-classic *Stages of Faith: The Psychology of Human Development and the Quest for Meaning,* across two decades and in a wide variety of publications and forums, Fowler has shown how evolving forms of logic, perspective taking, moral judgment, world coherence, the boundaries of social awareness, symbolic function, and the locus of authority all affect the life of faith.[17] Like the work of other Piagetians, Fowler's has had a cognitive and stage-structure bias. He has, however, not only forged linkages between psychological development and human faith but has contributed significantly to the extension of constructive-developmental insights into adulthood.

Fowler's attention to shifts in the locus of authority in the maturing of faith provided a key girder for building a bridge in my own thought between the formation of faith and human development in the young adult years. It was Perry, however, who drew the essential outlines of an architecture that spans the chasm between unexamined trust and a critically aware form of making meaning in the young adult years.

Perry: The Art of Listening to Young Adult Meaning-Making

William G. Perry Jr., or "Bill" as we knew him, was a master educator, therapist, and theoretician who, with his colleagues, forged the most groundbreaking and widely applied study of human development in the context of higher education. Founder of Harvard's Bureau of Study Counsel, Perry and his colleagues accompanied scores of students as they made their way through the rapids of young adult life. As described in his *Forms of Ethical and Intellectual Development in the College Years: A Scheme,* Perry identified nine ways in which students composed truth as they pitched and bucked from assumed ways of knowing to taking responsibility for their concepts and commitments. His work is characterized by an extraordinary quality of careful and compassionate listening and by a sensitivity of interpretation that serves as a model for researchers who are willing to value the integrity of human experience more than theoretical tidiness. One of his favorite axioms was, "The person is always larger than the theory."

Perry embodied practiced reverence for the courage and costs of growth. He paid deep respect to how difficult it is to compose and recompose reality and truth on the other side of discovering the finitude of every form of "Authority." He described with careful nuance the journey of intellect and soul that requires holding on while letting go—making one's way through the valley of the shadow of doubt, struggling to retain something enduring, while a new way of seeing and trusting is being configured. He understood how it feels from the inside when certainty must be relinquished for integrity. He believed that to be present to the growth of another is "to worship before great mysteries." The insights into the development of young adult faith elaborated in the chapters that follow are substantially informed by Perry's capacity to listen with rigorous respect to the underlying patterns of young adult meaning-making, or, as he put it, to the "music beneath the words."[18]

A New Place in the Life Span

In American society prior to the Civil War, the human journey was typically described as a movement from infancy and childhood to adulthood. Major transformations in society after the Civil War effected such real change that adolescence emerged as a "new" stage in human development. Keniston has observed that now the same magnitude of change has "created" yet another recognizable era in the human life span. Employing philosophical, sociological, and psychological perspectives, he has demonstrated a rich appreciation of the dynamic, shifting interaction between culture and person:

> . . . psychological development results from a complex interplay of constitutional givens (including the rates and phases of biological maturation) and the changing familial, social, educational, economic, and political conditions that constitute the matrix in which [people] develop. Human development can be obstructed by the absence of the necessary matrix, just as it can be stimulated by other kinds of environments. Some social and historical conditions . . . slow, retard or block development, while others stimulate, speed and encourage it. A prolongation and extension of development, then, including the emergence of "new" stages of life, can result from altered social, economic and historical conditions.[19]

Among the changes he has cited are a shift in the percentage of students who finish high school and begin college, and acceleration of social change: "a rate of social change so rapid that it threatens to make obsolete all institutions, values, methodologies and technologies within the lifetime of each generation; a technology that has created not only prosperity and longevity, but power to destroy the planet, whether through warfare or violation of nature's balance; a world of extraordinarily complex social organization, instantaneous communication and constant revolution."[20]

In this social milieu, Keniston has argued that we would do well to notice that many young people are not adequately described as either adolescent or adult. This is because "the twenty-four-year-old seeker, political activist, or graduate student often turns out to have been *through* a period of adolescent rebellion ten years before, to be all too formed in his or her views, to have a stable sense of self, and to be much further along in psychological development than his or her fourteen-year-old high school brother or sister."[21]

Long before the popular media created Gen Xers and a subsequent parade of other generational tags, Keniston's description of the characteristics of this new era in human development was an early signal, drawing attention to emergent, identifiable forms of postadolescent meaning-making. Keniston's observations illuminate the contemporary journey into adulthood as it is increasingly experienced by many; along with my research and that of others, it significantly informs our understanding of the development of adult faith.

Keniston provided compelling confirmation of my own perception that within Kegan's and Fowler's fourth stage there are actually two separate, identifiable stages. Between the assumed knowing of stage three and the critical, systemic knowing of stage four's "full adulthood," we can see the outlines of a critically aware, but yet young, adulthood. This era is recognized colloquially in the use of the term *twenty-somethings* as a way of identifying the distinctive experience of many young adults in today's world.

Discovering Another Neglect

After reflecting on my own experience with young adults and allowing my perceptions and thinking to steep in the strength of these developmental perspectives, I published an initial critique and elaboration of theory.[22] Though the insights that had emerged among those of us who were working to elaborate constructive-developmental theory were proving strong and useful, I noticed that I was vaguely but persistently uneasy. From the beginning, there was a healthy recognition within the field that every theoretical perspective has its limits. I knew, nevertheless, that there was some sense of a significant deficit in these powerful, useful perspectives, and it subtly haunted me.

I was already well aware that though the metaphor of development itself was a rich one, with an imposing pedigree, it was also problematic. *Development* connotes incremental but qualitative growth, an enhanced adequacy. As some critical social theorists have well argued, however, the language of development is aligned also with certain imperial economic and political impulses (requiring "them" to be like "us").[23] I was keenly attuned to how the force of this critique alerted us to conditions of exploitation in the service of development and had to be taken into account.

But it was not until I was reading the draft of a manuscript that would subsequently receive two national awards,[24] written by a then-distant colleague, Larry Daloz, that I discovered the still deeper source of my uneasiness. I was disturbed by a chapter in which Daloz described the relationship between a mentoring professor and three older adult students, a man and two women. All three had been affected by their encounter with higher education; each underwent a significant challenge to assumptions about self, world, and "God." In the author's analysis, however, only one of the students, the male, had "grown" or "developed." The two women seemed not to have "moved" because they were choosing to "stay" in their context, maintaining commitments to family and community in settings that appeared to place constraints on their opportunities for enhanced thought and being. Yet it was fully apparent to me that both of these women, having recomposed their ways of seeing, knowing, and being, were undoubtedly acting in new ways, though remaining within their same context.

I urged him to think some more about his analysis, and after some discussion sorting out the distinctions between movement and growth, he recast that portion of the manuscript. Meanwhile, I discovered a key to another feature of the story of human development: its prevailing metaphors.

Journey

As typically told, the story of human development is framed by the primary metaphor of journey. Developmental psychologies are attractive, in part, because they are so resonant with the many secular and religious myths that feature the journey motif. The journey metaphor is powerful; it grasps essential elements of our experience of moving through life. It has special power in relationship to spirituality and the life of faith. Our desire to soar is readily fused with a conviction of aliveness, a confidence of spirit. Journey language is a language of transcendence, crossing over, reaching and moving beyond. When we feel we are not yet *what* we ought to be, we are prone to feeling we are not *where* we ought to be. The journey metaphor can also convey a sense of movement down into, through, and beyond the swamps of confusion or despair.

The metaphor of journey evokes adventure, courage, and daring. In Western culture, it is linked strongly with the metaphor of battle, the slaying of dragons, and the triumph of conquest. Going out to conquer is a primary element in all of the heroic myths, from the ancient Gilgamesh down to Luke Skywalker: "The hero ventures forth from the world of common day into a region of supernatural wonder: fabulous forces are there encountered and a decisive victory is won: the hero comes back from his mysterious adventure with the power to bestow boons on his fellowman."[25]

The journey metaphor is strong within religious-spiritual imagery. At the heart of Jewish and Christian experience is a language of covenant, of promise; this promise is envisioned primarily as something not yet fulfilled: the Promised Land, the Kingdom or Commonwealth of God. The language of exodus along with the imagery of a journey toward greater enlightenment or sanctity are dominant motifs across many cultures.

The metaphor of journey is strong in American culture. Increasingly, however, journey has signified going forth without necessarily leading to a return. Upon discovering the New World, explorers went out and often did not go back. In a culture of emigrants, the dominant experience is departure and journey without return. Since the Enlightenment, we have become profoundly aware of the relativized nature and partiality of our knowledge, particularly our knowledge of "Truth, God, and Ultimate Reality." We feel, as it were, bound to an ongoing, uncompleted search, an infinite quest for more adequate approximations of reality.

Yet if we build on the work of Robert Kegan, Carol Gilligan, and Nancy Chodorow (a social psychologist), a larger imagination comes into view. The map of the psyche that portrays a journey is perhaps particularly salient in male experience, yet only half of a larger human reality. Chodorow has suggested that the emphasis upon heroic separation may be shaped significantly by the fact that for most children the primary caregiver is female. For males, therefore, a central task in becoming a self is separation or differentiation, going forth and heading out. In contrast, for females the task of becoming a self requires identification with, attachment, and connection.[26]

Thus the dance of self and other in the story of human becoming might best be understood as reflecting "two great yearnings"[27]: one for differentiation, autonomy, and agency, and the other for relation, belonging, and communion. There may well be a polar preference between the genders, but each gender has the capacity and the need to fulfill both yearnings. Men tend to tell their stories primarily in terms that celebrate moments of separation and differentiation. Women tend to tell their stories in terms of moments of attachment and relation. Thus if we listen to the voice that Gilligan identified in the development of moral decision making, and if we listen to the story of finding our voice that Mary Belenky, Blythe Clinchy, Nancy Goldberger, and Jill Tarule have described in their account of the development of women,[28] we hear additional metaphors. I began to realize that it was insufficient to work exclusively with the metaphors of journey, traveling, and adventuring. The story of human growth and development is more richly comprehended if we cast it also in the metaphors of home, homesteading, dwelling, and staying.[29]

Indeed, men and women alike know that a good life is composed of both venturing and abiding.[30] The ventures that matter most are the ones that enable us to become truly at home in the universe. If we embrace this larger conception of the story of human development, we recognize the power of home places as well as the power of travel. The image of journey in the story of optimal human development is transformed into pilgrimage. The word *journey* is rooted in the French *jour,* meaning simply a day's travel. A journey can be a profound and life-changing experience, or it can be endless and without purpose. The practice of pilgrimage is a going forth and a return home that enlarge the meaning of both self and home.

Home

From this perspective, we should be concerned that some of our most powerful contemporary myths presuppose the destruction of home, or even the home planet, as in *The Hitchhiker's Guide to the Galaxy* and the *Star Wars* epic. Simultaneously, a primary suffering of our time is homelessness, both domestically and in the growing number of refugees worldwide. Moreover, a fundamental question of our time is, "Can we all dwell together on the small planet home we share?" Martin Heidegger observed, "to be a human being means to be on the earth as a mortal. It means to dwell."[31] Thomas Ogletree has well argued that an ethical orientation for our time can be formulated in terms of hospitality to the stranger.[32] Yet with the industrial revolution, the household was separated from the means of production, bifurcating the relationship between the genders and shearing the home away from the workplace and the public place. As a consequence, the arts of dwelling have been associated with one gender alone. They have become a subjugated knowledge, removed from public discourse, and we are all the poorer for it.[33]

Thus at this pivotal, dangerous, and promising moment in history, the development of human life and adequate forms of meaning and faith may be dependent in part upon the liberation, reappropriation, and renewed companionship of the metaphors of detachment *and* connection, pilgrims *and* homemakers, journeying *and* homesteading, pilgrimage *and* home.

Psychotherapist and Zen trainer John Tarrant has reflected on the legend of Shakyamui, the historical Buddha, observing that in setting off to bend his life toward prayer and meditation, Shakyamui abandoned his family:

> It is said that on the night he left, he paused in the doorway in silent farewell to the woman and child sleeping there, and didn't dare to wake them. If we imagine their confusion when they woke the next morning, we see that if the man has found a sure path, he has asked his family to bear the desolation and loss that is the underside of his certainty. . . . By leaving the child and the woman, Shakyamui conformed to the familiar pattern that for the sake of developing the spirit, we must turn away from the world and our ties. The same gesture appears in Jesus' rejection of his mother. But this means to turn away also from the trees and the fate of the planet and the soul, which loves these things. If we are to have a marriage of soul and spirit, we will have to find a way to walk back eventually through the charged doorway and find the wisdom of the sages in that small, quiet room where the woman and her child are sleeping still.[34]

Again, it has become increasingly clear that there is value and healing in incorporating into our understanding of human development an imagination of becoming at home. A part of becoming at home in the universe is discovering our place within it, in the new global commons in which we now find ourselves. We are beginning to recognize that this becoming is not so much a matter of leaving home as it is undergoing a series of transformations in the meaning of home. We grow and become both by letting go and holding on, leaving and staying, journeying and abiding— whether we are speaking geographically, socially, intellectually, emotionally, or spiritually. A good life and the cultivation of wisdom require a balance of home and pilgrimage.

In this way of seeing, though we may move from one geographical location to another the growth of the self and the development of faith may be understood as transformation of the boundaries that have defined home. These boundaries may be continually revised outward to embrace the neighborhood, the community, the society, the world, and even the inexhaustible universe in which we dwell. While we make this journey of transformation in which our sense of inclusiveness and ultimacy is continuously expanded, we experience home as a familiar center surrounded by a permeable membrane that makes it possible both to sustain and enlarge our sense of self and other, self and world. Our imagination of development becomes not only a ladder but also a series of concentric circles, or perhaps a spiral that honors both.

As we explore critical features of young adult development, it is vital that we learn to do so with an eye to both venturing and dwelling. If we understand human development not simply as departures and arrivals but also as transformations in the meaning of home, then the young adults with whom we have the privilege of making meaning may become more viably at home in the universe. If we accompany them well, they may grace us all by becoming citizen-leaders, adults who can both belong and distinguish themselves, connect and separate, venture and dwell. To be good company, we need to understand the transformations in thinking, feeling, and belonging that are embedded in the promise of young adult lives.

4

IT MATTERS HOW WE THINK

AMONG LIFE'S biggest questions are: Who and what can I trust? Can I trust others? Can I trust myself? Where is the heart's resting place?

These questions dwell at the core of faith and are asked again and again across a lifetime. How we respond is in part a matter of how we think, and our patterns of thought may undergo significant transformation over time. Noticing whether and how we shift in our trust in authority is one way of observing these changes.

Who or what has authority in your life? In a society riddled with strong allegiances to the values of self-sufficiency, freedom, and infinite choice, questions of authority (intimately linked with trust) are often hidden from view. Yet every day we are not simply making choices. We are also swayed, moved, enticed, compelled, persuaded, and more or less swept along, in varying measures obedient to powers that are acting authoritatively upon us, influencing our perceptions and judgments.

There are many such powers in our lives. We sometimes trust the opinion of a friend, without actually checking the facts. We assume a published report in a reputable journal is accurate. We look to the boss or CEO for orientation and direction. We may respect traditional scriptures. We want to trust our physician. The opinion of a valued colleague carries weight with us. We may be cynically sophisticated about advertising, yet we know we are affected by it. We pass on to the next generation admonitions given to us in our youth. We believe in the scientific method. We entrust people we love to the care of professional people whom we do not know. We may pray—at least under certain circumstances. Placing our trust and vesting authority are an integral part of weaving the fabric of life.

Over time we may learn the appropriate limits of our trust. Recently, I heard a young child explaining a scrape on his face: "I hurt my nose, but not very badly because God is always with me and taking care of me."

He is being taught by authoritative voices in his world that he lives in a caring and dependable universe. By the time he is a young adult, however, he is likely to run up against experience that will cause him to wonder about God's care in ways he can't ignore.

In young adulthood there is a deepened readiness to become aware of our assumptions about whom we trust, what to believe, and how reliable the meanings we live by actually are. Learning to assess the strengths and limits of whom and what can be trusted as authoritative is important work in the process of becoming a mature, responsible, and wise adult. In part a cognitive process, this work is an essential element in the development of the intellectual life, a vital feature of preparing for citizenship in democratic societies, and integral to the formation of mature adult faith.

Forms of Knowing

The relationship of the self to authority can undergo considerable transformation during the young adult and subsequent years. Perry's study of nine shifts in students' relationship to knowledge in the context of higher education provides us an interpretive lens. Here, however, I modify and elaborate them into four primary positions, or "forms of knowing." Later, I add a fifth that is particularly useful in interpreting the potential and vulnerability of young adults.

Forms of Knowing	Authority-bound Dualistic	→	Unqualified relativism	→	Commitment in relativism	→	Convictional commitment

Authority-Bound

The first form of knowing Perry identified is oriented to Authority outside the self.[1] Within this form, what a person ultimately trusts, knows, and believes is finally based on some Authority "out there" who can, as it were, know truth by reading "tablets of Truth written in the sky."[2] In some way regarded as self-evident, Authority "knows." Belenky, Clinchy, Goldberger, and Tarule have described this as "received knowing."[3] In this mode of knowing it is assumed that you "get" knowledge from somewhere outside yourself. Authorities are trustworthy because they have done this—or because "we all think alike" (that is, we all see things simply as they are).

Authority may take the form of a particular person or group, for example a parent, teacher, or religious leader. Often, however, Authority functions in diffuse but subtly powerful forms that pervade a person's conventional ethos: media (films, the Web, television, newspapers, magazines, books, and journals, including the power of name brands); culturally affirmed roles and personalities (experts, government officials, religious figures, recognized artists, entertainers, other celebrities, and admired peers); and custom (expected conventions of thought, feeling, and behavior, whether broadly based throughout a society or within a small subgroup). These various authorities are confirmed by the stories, myths, and symbols (traditional or contemporary) that hold the meanings of a people, their institutions, and their communities.

This form of knowing may be characterized as "Authority-bound" (not Perry's term), and it functions in an all-powerful, determinative manner. When people compose their sense of truth in this form, they may assert deeply felt and strong opinion; but if they are asked the basis for their knowing, eventually they reveal their assumed, unexamined trust in sources of authority located outside the self. When this form of knowing prevails, people cannot stand outside of their own perspective, or reflect upon their own thought. Their knowing is inextricably bound up with the power of the trusted Authority.

This form of knowing also tends to be dualistic. People who compose self, world, and "God" in this form can make clear divisions between what is true and untrue, right and wrong, us and them. There is little or no tolerance for ambiguity. It is important to recognize, however, that *what* they hold absolute certainty about—the content of their sense of truth—varies from person to person, though they share the same cognitive structure. Thus, even though the structure of this form of knowing is quite rigid, the content that is known so absolutely may appear to be fluid. The language of relativism, for example, is now commonplace enough to be part of the conventional ethos. Thus one person may say "Toleration is a sin," and another may say "You must *always* be tolerant," yet both may be making meaning in this Authority-bound form of knowing.

In this form of knowing, even the inner self is primarily composed by others. For example, sometimes this form of knowing is heard in the young person who is working very hard to prepare for medicine, law, or another career. Listening carefully over time, we may discover that "I want to become a doctor" actually means "My family has always expected me to become a doctor."

Reflecting on how he felt after the first exam of his freshman year, a college senior reveals how easily the Authority-bound form of knowing may be composed by values, circumstances, and judgments outside of one's self:

> In terms of studying, I didn't know how I would stand in a class. Like
> I remember the first test I took was in History of Asia. I didn't know
> at all what I would get on the test . . . anything from a C to an A. I
> didn't think I had flunked because I had studied for it, but I didn't
> know quite how I stood. And I got the test back and I got an A. And
> that seemed to set a precedent, you know, what goals I set for myself.
> It's kind of strange. I look back, and if I'd gotten maybe a B or a C on
> that test I might have . . . set lower standards for myself.

A key point of awareness that emerges from a constructive-developmental perspective is the recognition that this uncritical, Authority-bound, and dualistic form of knowing is characteristic not just of children and adolescents but also of some people throughout the whole of their biological adulthood. Further development beyond this conformist way of knowing does not occur inevitably.

Thus, some who enter higher or professional education or the workforce, at whatever age, arrive with this mode of making meaning very much intact. For others, this form of knowing has already begun to dissolve. In either case, the transformation that can occur (and of which higher education at its best has been a primary sponsor) is a movement from this unexamined, uncritical form of certainty to another form of knowing.

This shift typically emerges in the uncomfortable discovery that established patterns of thinking do not fit lived experience. For example, while taking notes from several trusted professors, a student may begin to realize that one professor's point of view seriously conflicts with another's. The student may put them in separate compartments, thus ensuring that each point of view is sealed off from the other and conveniently obscuring the conflict. Or the student may place the two perspectives in some hierarchy of value, deciding, for example, that the sciences hold "truth" and the arts hold only "opinions," or that personal decisions can be simpler than professional decisions. As an illustration, here is a young woman's reflection on the pressures and choices in a business context:

> I'm very hard-line, straight and level when it comes to an ethical
> choice. . . . But here we are being challenged with, "OK, yes, there's
> clear right and wrong maybe when it comes to a personal choice. But
> when it comes to a public, professional choice in a business decision
> you have other stakeholders, other people are involved, and you have
> to think about every segment when you're making this decision and
> the effects that it will have on that." And so in my mind I see a lot
> more gray than I did before, and I find it very uncomfortable.

The discomfort reflected here is likely to persist. The validity of competing points of view is difficult to ignore and seriously undermines even heroic attempts to hold simplistic, either-or forms of true and untrue, good and evil, whether in personal or public life. For a time, it may be possible to trust that there is still a right answer that some Authority has or will surely discover, since the existence of such a right answer is still assumed. But a cataclysmic shift occurs in the revolutionary moment when the relative character of *all* knowledge becomes the only truth.

Unqualified Relativism

In the course of ongoing experience, as Authorities conflict or fail, awareness dawns that the human mind can compose many perceptions of reality and does not simply receive reality "as it is." The person becomes aware that if he or she had been born into a different family or society, or had attended other schools, or listened to some other music and watched different films, or worked in another lab, the same phenomena might be perceived and known quite differently. Thus knowledge becomes relative, meaning that all knowledge is shaped by, and thus relative to, the context and relationships within which it is composed.

It becomes slowly apparent that even the most trusted adults (or other Authorities) must compose reality within a relativized world. Now it appears that every perception leads to a different "truth," and every opinion and judgment may be as worthy as any other. This form of knowing falls at midpoint in Perry's scheme,[4] and in its most substantial form it might appropriately be described as "unqualified relativism."[5]

This shift may occur gradually or abruptly in the course of ongoing experience. It may be precipitated by a lead from the head, when, for example, a person in a stimulating seminar is introduced to a new idea that counters previous assumptions. Authority-bound and dualistic thinking may also come unraveled outside the classroom. Wherever one undergoes experience that does not fit the assumptions of one's conventional, assumed world, there is an invitation to develop critical thinking: the ability to stand outside one's own thought.

Sometimes this happens in relatively smooth, uncomplicated, and intriguing ways. A freshman in college described what a "great roommate" she had: "I'm an athlete, and she's not. She does arts. I don't. I'm learning that what time I get up, when I shower, could be different. I've always been conscientious about my schoolwork. She says, 'That paper is only worth five points, come play.' But sometimes I say to her, 'You'd better finish that paper.' We come from different backgrounds, and living with her I realize that I value what I've been given, but the patterns I've developed don't have to stay that way."

Sometimes, however, as we began to see in Chapter Two, learning to wonder about familiar assumptions may happen in more difficult ways. For example, a person may be involved in a romance or some other close and emotional relationship. It is assumed to be trustworthy because it fits the myths that the person holds about life, how life works, and how life will unfold. Yet when *the* romantic relationship (or perhaps *the* career opportunity) collapses, the person may suffer the obvious loss and then also the loss of an assumed life script: the shipwreck of self, world, and "God." The truth of life itself feels betrayed. One may begin rather ruefully to wonder, *Why did I ever think the way I did?*

In this moment, both subject and object are recomposed. The person is no longer subject to her earlier assumptions; these assumptions may now be held as possible points of view among others as objects of reflection. This new way of seeing and knowing may offer some new power and freedom, but it is achieved at the cost of an earlier certainty. Perry describes the experience as it may be felt from the inside:

> Soon I may begin to miss those tablets in the sky. If this [one possible interpretation among others] defines the truth for term papers, how about people? Principalities? Powers? How about the Deity? . . . And if this can be true of my image of the Deity, who then will cleanse my soul? And my enemies? Are they not *wholly* in the wrong?
>
> I apprehend all too poignantly now that in the most fateful decisions of my life I will be the only person with a first-hand view of the really relevant data, and only part of it at that. Who will save me then from that "wrong decision" I have been told not to make lest I "regret-it-all-my-life"? Will no one tell me if I am right? Can I never be sure? Am I alone?

Then Perry observes, "It is not for nothing that the undergraduate turns metaphysician."[6]

As this realization begins to form, a person may cope by saying, "I have my truth, you have your truth, and they have their truth. It doesn't matter what you think, as long as you are sincere." "The Truth" seems to become one truth among many (giving rise to the current vernacular "whatever"). But this stance discloses, on the one hand, the hope that absolute certainty still dwells somewhere (in this case in sincerity), while on the other hand it reveals a sort of bravado defending against the increasing awareness that conventional certainty just isn't holding up very well. Doubt is further deepened when someone points out that both Martin Luther King Jr. and Adolf Hitler were in a sense "sincere."

Thus a position of unqualified relativism is difficult to sustain over time. One discovers that there is a difference between just any opinion (even one's own) and an opinion that is grounded in careful and thoughtful observation and reflection and that takes more into account. One may move into a qualified relativism, increasingly aware that discriminations can be made between arguments based on such principles as internal coherence, the systematic relation of an argument to its own assumptions, external data, and so forth. But the dilemma remains: If thinking doesn't bring us to certainty, why think? The answer usually comes from the imperative of ongoing life.

Commitment in Relativism

Certainty may be impossible, but we still make choices that have consequences for ourselves and those we love. Particularly in relation to important life choices, a person may begin to look for a place to stand, a way of dwelling viably in an uncertain world. He or she may begin to value those ways of composing truth and making moral choices that are more adequate than other options. This is a search for a place of commitment within relativism.

The formation of commitment in a relativized world requires taking self-conscious responsibility for one's own thinking and knowing. Now one becomes conscious of joining other adults in discerning what is adequate, worthy, and valuable, while remaining aware of the finite nature of all judgments. Fowler describes this shift as a movement from a "tacit" form of world coherence to an "explicit system" formed in a desire to make explicit and coherent the meaning of life, as best one may. One young person expressed it this way: "I still feel my Big Picture is only so valid because so far I've only been able to look at it from a couple of angles. The more angles I have and have the opportunity to gain perspective from, the more valid my sense of meaning will be. But I have learned that a couple of angles is better than none and should not stop me from doing as much as I can with the limited picture I already have."

This awareness reflects the great shift that makes intellectual reflection possible and thus serves as the threshold into the life of the mind. This shift into critical reflective thought is a primary facet of becoming an adult in faith and, as we shall see, a central feature of the potential and vulnerability of the young adult years.

Convictional Commitment

Because Perry focused particularly on the young adult years, his elaboration of forms of knowing "ends" with commitment in relativism. Fowler, however, described the development of yet another form of knowing beyond it. Along with Fowler, I believe that this form typically does not emerge until well after the young adult years—indeed, not until midlife. I describe this place as *convictional commitment*. It seems to me that this form of knowing was expressed well by Carl Jung in a film made near the end of his life. As I recall it, when the interviewer asked, "Do you believe in God?" Jung immediately responded, "Now?" I happened to watch this film with a large university audience, mostly undergraduates, and many spontaneously laughed, assuming that of course, Jung was too sophisticated to believe in God. Jung, however, continued his response: "I don't need to believe; I *know*." This time, no one laughed.

Jung exemplified a quality of knowing that is quite other than the Authority-bound, dualistic knowing described earlier. Aware that all knowledge is relative, he knew that what he knew on any given day could be radically altered by something he might learn the next day. Yet he embodied a deep conviction of truth, a quality of knowing that we recognize as wisdom. This wisdom is also reflected in a statement of Oliver Wendell Holmes, who is reported to have said: "I do not give a fig for the simplicity on this side of complexity. But I would give my life for the simplicity on the other side of complexity."[7]

Mature wisdom is not escape from, but rather engagement with, complexity and mystery. Our response to this form of knowing is not necessarily agreement, but it does arrest our attention and compel our respect. Such knowing does not put us off the way Authority-bound and dualistic knowing may. Rather, we seek it out, or sense that we are sought by it. Without abandoning the centered authority of the self and a disciplined fidelity to truth, this way of thinking represents a deepened capacity to hear the truth of another, or even many others. This form of knowing can embrace paradox. This convictional knowing is a still more mature way of holding and being held in the ongoing motion of meaning-making and faith.

Reconsidering the Three-Step Model

Tracing forms of knowing in this way suggests that the movement toward mature adult faith (convictional commitment) leads from the assumed, received, tacit knowing of the adolescent (Authority-bound), through some sort of transition, wilderness, or at least "sophomore slump" (unqualified relativism), to a critically aware and responsible adult faith (commitment in relativism). This three-step process—authority-bound, unqualified relativism, commitment in relativism—has been the pattern generally assumed by faculty, administrators, supervisors, and others in the culture at large who in varying roles accompany the adolescent-becoming-adult. Many presume, for example, that as any young adult moves out into the world to take on increasing responsibility, he or she will bump up against naïve assumptions, flounder a bit perhaps, and then take up residence in the discovery of how things really are. It has been assumed, for instance, that in four years of college one can essentially complete the first leg of the journey from Authority-bound and dualistic faith to an informed yet committed stance on the other side of discovering the relative character of all knowledge—arriving at what we have called commitment in relativism as an intellectually and socially adult place.

Constructive-developmental theories have in large measure shared and reinforced these assumptions. Fowler's theory of faith development describes this first leg of the journey as a movement from "synthetic-conventional" faith (stage three) to "individuative-reflective" faith (stage four). This development is described, in part, as a shift in the locus of authority from outside the self to within, with the place in between regarded as simply "transitional." Likewise, Kegan's most recent description of the evolving self (1994) continues to describe evolution from a third order of consciousness to a fourth order, the place in between likewise described in transitional terms.

However, in my ongoing experience of teaching, counseling, and consulting, I have consistently encountered behavior that these models do not account for. It is indeed helpful to recognize the broad movement from conventional thought to a critically aware form of knowing. But I observe that the transition in between holds a kind of equilibrated integrity that itself constitutes a distinct form of faith—a developmental balance worthy of attention.

Teaching and counseling undergraduates first compelled me to notice how complex the dynamics of *emerging* adult faith were—that is, the faith that begins to form just beyond adolescence. Students who seemed confidently beyond Authority-bound knowing (and unqualified relativism) in their junior year often seemed fragile in their senior year, or reflected a subtle but surprisingly persistent dependence on authority outside the self in their early years as alums.

Not wanting to be a professor who cultivated a cadre of dependent followers, I delighted in offering the well-timed push from the nest that would enable students to discover their own wings and soar away. Why, then, did the long-distance phone calls come in every so many months, "just to touch base"? Though obviously distinctly different, they seemed faintly reminiscent of the way a two-year-old goes off exploring, returning periodically to touch in with the parent, only to go off again. For example, why were two former students, both of them bright, talented, and responsible, sitting at my breakfast table one morning, delaying their scheduled departure? Both had moved through the ups and downs of undergraduate years, developed critical thought, and demonstrated a confident sense of direction upon graduation. One was now enrolled in a prestigious graduate program, the other was going abroad for travel and study, and both were surely about to miss the bus that would take them to their train. It was my sense that each was less confident about his or her own knowing than I had presumed, and perhaps dependent in some way I didn't quite understand upon the security, affirmation, and haven I represented. Yet the possible description of regression did not quite apply. I took them to the train myself and returned, bewildered.

These puzzling dynamics continued to confront me when I began to teach at the graduate level and perceived rather sophisticated graduate students still engaged in recomposing a place to stand on the other side of the dissolution of their received, conventional faith. As they sat in my office and talked about the questions they struggled with, the strength, suffering, richness, and compelling integrity of their meaning-making simply could not be adequately described by the adjectives *adolescent, transitional, regressive,* or *arrested*—nor by the notion of *moratorium.* Yet these were the only images that prevailing developmental theories offered.

What were we all failing to see? As I kept listening to both students and theorists, I "found," embedded in the place called transition, a distinct form of composing meaning, a recognizable stage. I began to see the power, promise, and vulnerability of the young adult soul.

Some of the clues clustered around the formation of identity and the searching for a fitting role in society. To see them, we must return to adolescence and proceed slowly, paying particular attention to the shifts that occur at the thresholds first between adolescence and young adulthood and then between young adulthood and tested adult strength.

Identity at the Threshold of Young Adulthood

Adolescence begins with puberty. Erikson describes it as "the last stage of childhood."[8] Along with biological changes, puberty brings new cognitive possibilities: the capacity for formal operational thought and for thinking symbolically and abstractly. This new mental power also makes third-person perspective taking possible. This means that one can hold both one's own perceptions and those of another at the same time. Initially this leads to new (and often painful) self-consciousness, as the adolescent can for the first time see the self as perceived through the eyes of others. Thus the adolescent lives under the "tyranny of the *they*." The great task becomes the development of a self that has the strength to counter this tyranny and to mediate among the powerful images reflected in the adolescent's house of mirrors. This new strength is the power of identity. Cultivating this strength, and doing so in such a way as to achieve recognition in the social world, is, in Erikson's view, "the adolescent ego's most important accomplishment."[9]

Whether or not the achievement of both identity and social recognition can be fully accomplished at the end of adolescence is increasingly problematic, as we shall see shortly. But what may well be achieved in adolescence is what Erikson points to as the hallmark of identity: a self-aware self. This self has enough ego strength to recognize that one can make some choices about how one becomes. With this new power comes a corresponding new quality of responsibility for the development of self. This new awareness of responsibility for self, and thus also for one's world, corresponds to the diminishment of a received, conventional, Authority-bound form of knowing. This is an enormous achievement. It means that one can consciously choose to differ with conventional Authority, and not merely for the sake of "pushing away from the dock." One begins to choose differently out of a responsible loyalty to one's own perception and knowledge.

This is not to say that the critically aware postadolescent necessarily speaks of composing a self. Rather, there is a conscious sense of needing to make choices and take responsibility for their consequences for the future of self (and others). A young woman choosing a college other than the one her parents had hoped she would choose expressed this awareness: "If I went to that college it would fit the person I have been. I am choosing this college because it fits the person I am becoming."

This self-aware process often includes some struggle and acceptance of that struggle. In describing her sense of movement to a new place on the other side of the loss of an assumed world, another young woman said: "I guess . . . I'd give myself the freedom to struggle; then when I was done with a particular struggle and saw how I grew from it, . . . it was less threatening to me when other people would struggle with things—people that were really close. It wasn't like, 'Oh, no—what's gonna happen?' It was like 'Oh, yeah, this is part of growing so it's OK for them.'"

This newfound freedom to struggle for an identity and to take responsibility for it are signals that an adolescent has crossed the threshold into young adulthood.

Setting One's Own Heart

When we focus on the development of faith, it is significant to note that in Erikson's view the corresponding virtue developed in tandem with identity is fidelity. This suggests the development of a new capacity "to set one's heart." I propose, then, that the most profound marker of the threshold of young adulthood is the capacity to take self-aware responsibility for choosing the shape and path of one's own fidelity.

Thus, depending upon the scope of the questions life poses to the young adult soul, the young adult may realize, however partially at first, that one must take responsibility for the faith one lives by. This is sometimes a chilling recognition. Faith can now doubt itself; it is no longer possible to simply adopt the convictions of another, no matter how weighty and respected they may be. One becomes a young adult in faith (at whatever age) when one begins to take self-conscious responsibility for one's own knowing, becoming, and moral action, even at the level of ultimate meaning-making. This moment in the journey of faith does not typically occur until at least the age of seventeen.[10] For a few it may emerge as early as sixteen, and for many people it emerges much later—or never.

What claims the heart's trust at this important threshold? By what process will this newly emerging identity locate a worthy place for itself in society? It is here that Keniston's pioneering work on the young adult era helps to clarify what other theories missed.

Seeking a Place in Society

The people Keniston described have achieved a self-aware self and individuated from their family in significant measure. This new self, however, is as yet "over-against" society or the world as it is. It is not yet a full participant in what is perceived as the adult world. Newly equipped with the power of critical reflection, it is aware of its own emerging identity, values, and integrity as distinguished from societal (and conventional) norms. The self-aware self is able to "sense who he or she is and thus to recognize the possibility of conflict and disparity between his or her emerging selfhood and his or her social order."[11]

In other words, Erikson described the formation of self-identity as an adolescent task that included achievement of both self-awareness and an effective social role. Keniston recognized, however, that although in earlier historical eras these two tasks might have been achieved simultaneously, now the composing of a self that is also effective in society is more likely to occur in two steps. First, the critically aware self comes to birth.

But the task of integrating it into our increasingly complex society with integrity—that is, in a way that is both effective and satisfying—may well constitute an effort of its own.

What this postadolescent-not-yet-full-adult still needs to accomplish is finding a home where the integrity, promise, and power of the emerging self can dwell together with the perceived realities of the social world. This means that the big questions whose answers once defined adulthood remain to be settled: purpose, vocation, and belonging ("Where, why, and with whom will I dwell, love, and work?"). We might say that living with the questions has become a task unto itself and is often a primary characteristic of the young adult era.

A Pervasive Ambivalence

As noted earlier, the period of this life task has been described as "extended or prolonged adolescence"—certainly a pejorative description at best and, as we are beginning to see, inaccurate. As Keniston observed, "For, while some young men and women are indeed victims of the psychological malady of 'stretched adolescence,' many others are less impelled by juvenile grandiosity than by rather accurate analysis of the perils and injustices of the world in which they live."[12]

The young adult capacity for critical thought also makes possible a sense of the ideal. Young adults can dream of a better world than that which they find around them. What's more, they long to play a role in forming that world, rather than simply fitting into the real world as they presently find it. At the same time, they may question whether they have the requisite power to bring such a vision into being.

This new self-awareness and the emerging consciousness of an unresolved relationship between self and world was elegantly captured by Ernie Boyer Jr. When he was a young man of nineteen, he left the harbors of his good upbringing and literally went to sea. In the journal he kept as a sailor and later printed on an antique press, we can hear the postadolescent longing for a simpler world now lost, the consciousness of both a new power and a new vulnerability, the awareness of composing a balance between self and world, and a clear sense of living in relationship to transcendent forces more powerful than the self alone:

> I often imagine myself skippering a small sloop, out on the deck in the
> dark hours of morning while the small crew sleeps below. I would feel
> the ship beneath me slipping through the water, feel the sails above me
> tugging against the breeze, and dream until I fell asleep only to dream

more deeply. As the wind shifted I would awaken, check the compass, and readjust the sails to put us back on course. Then I would wait for the sun to rise.

Always when I watch the sea . . . I think of the times when I would have to fight it. I realize now, after seeing the height of these waves and feeling the power of this wind, that sailing is the living of a deadly balance. At times these forces would carry and caress me. But there would be other times when forces would rise and tilt the balance against me. Then I would be struggling for my life. I might win once or twice—I might—but if I did, it would be the sea's mercy more than my skill that had saved me. I have seen the sea; I have watched its moods, and I know: it has power as absolute as death itself, and no man rides above it as long as he would like.

But everything would be so simple, life in its bare energy or death, none of these squalid shades in between. I long for this life of the sailor.[13]

In "these squalid shades in between" is embedded a dynamic that strikingly illuminates our understanding of the young adult years: the dynamic Keniston observed as the "pervasive ambivalence" toward *both* self and society."[14] It became apparent why this place in the journey of faith was difficult for developmental theorists to recognize as other than merely transitional. The ambivalence characteristic of this era may easily be confused with the dynamics of transition. But ambivalence, wariness, exploration, and tentativeness are the warp and woof of the tapestry woven in the young adult era of faith. The dynamic of ambivalence, which might best be described as a quality of searching that is steeped in a new integrity, has confounded a theory looking for a stable equilibrium of the sort that Kegan and Fowler described in their formulations of postadolescent, adult meaning-making. Rooted in a healthy and fresh recognition of ambiguity, ambivalence is a hallmark of the equilibrium of young adulthood.

Probing Commitment

A return to Perry's nuanced description of intellectual development helps us recognize the integrity, stability, and structural power of this ambivalent young adult place. He identifies several positions within the discovery of relativism and the necessity of commitment: commitment foreseen, initial commitment, orientation in implications of commitment, and developing commitments.[15] Perry's observations suggest that commitment within a relativized world initially takes the form of a tentative, or what I choose to term *probing commitment.* One explores many possible forms of truth—as well as work roles, relationships, and lifestyles—and their fittingness to one's own experience of self and world.

Thus commitments formed on the other side of the encounter with the relativized character of self and world may initially last for two weeks, six months, or perhaps a few short years (a phenomenon that frustrates faculty hoping for commitment to a discipline, department, or program, and discourages managers seeking to recruit solid commitment to a long-term project). In this developmental moment, even deeply felt affirmations have a tenuous, exploratory, and divided quality. Listen again to the voice of the sailor, now in the midst of a second voyage:

> What can I do? All day I have flitted from one book to another, from one impulse, one dream to another, never mustering the resolution or sustaining the inclination to follow through my intentions. There is so much I want to do, must do, not just today, but with my life, with what time I have left. Not a second can be wasted. . . .
>
> I try for too much. I try for nothing less than a mastery of the world aesthetically, intellectually, and physically. To do this I need not only a momentous strength, but a divided self; for each of these three is incompatible with the other, and I must be a butcher, severing myself into three segments to be used only one at a time while the others are shelved and forgotten. What if I am too long with one? Will the other two die? After spending some extra time with philosophy my aesthetic impulse is harder to revive, and my physical impulse is all but dead. It worries me.
>
> It seems intolerable. And yet three is a very small number, and life has so many more aspects, those which many would say are its most valuable and rewarding, all of which I have renounced. I am a man very much alone. The scope of my choices is both infinite and far too narrow. What is the remedy? There must be a solution, but I thought and thought about it until that too has become frustrating. Too much to ever be accomplished, too little for an adequate life, this is my dilemma. What shall I do?[16]

In this account, we hear what Keniston described as the "divided self" and the "wary probe" of both self and world. This ambivalent and wary searching is qualitatively different from adolescent experimentation in search of self-definition. The probing commitment of the postadolescent is a serious, critically aware exploration of the adult world and the potential versions of a future that it offers (which the adolescent, in contrast, receives uncritically), through which society's vulnerability, strength, integrity, and possibilities are assessed. A corresponding self-probing tests the strength, vulnerability, and capacity of the self to withstand or use what society will make, ask, and allow.[17]

For example, a campus minister described a twenty-five-year-old alum who dropped by the campus ministry office just to muse out loud about his unfolding path. He had been an economics major, and in his junior year he worked for a term with Mother Teresa. "He is," she said, "now working as an administrative assistant for an educational nonprofit organization, and he is also working in a coffee bar. He is living with two roommates, one of whom is getting rich in a high-tech job. For himself, he is wondering whether he should go to work with a community that is exploring organic agriculture or seek more schooling. He isn't in a hurry, and in the meantime, he is also advising a freshman who got swept up in the heat of a political demonstration and may face a felony for destroying a sign."

This exploratory quality of young adulthood should in no way suggest that young adult commitments are always of the sort that can be redesigned at will. Many young adults are, for example, parents, a relationship that is not negotiable in any fundamental sense. Yet at the same time, the extension of the life span and the educational demands of a postindustrial culture have altered the assumptions by which such commitments are engaged. The phenomenon of probing commitment is affecting assumptions about marriage and partnership, the timing and meaning of becoming a parent, and patterns of work. These changes in the social contract with young adults are affecting young adult decision making and becoming features of faith. A young woman shares a section from her journal from a time when she was trying to choose between two very different forms of employment:

> The question is, what balance to strike between your life now, at 23, and your life as you hope it to be at 35. Do you predict what you want (now) for yourself at 35 and sacrifice things now for your goal for yourself at 35? Or do you ignore what you think (now) you want for yourself later and just live like you want to now? But if you do the first, will you have regrets at 35 of things you should have done at 23? Or when you get to 35 and aren't where you wanted (at 23) to be (at 35), do you regret not having set yourself up and made those sacrifices?

Then she reflects:

> These are the questions I was grappling with earlier this year, with a friend who has an even worse situation because his chosen career is really dependent on working your way up the ladder and suffering through stupid starter jobs. It's hard to figure out how faith fits in—

will it really all work out for the best? Is there really a master plan? Is what I'm doing now fitting into the master plan? Am I wasting time I'll regret later? Or will I regret, later, not wasting enough time when I had the luxury to? How come I can't *see* the master plan? It's a really frustrating feeling to have the impatient sense you should be working toward something, but not having any idea what it is, or even if you should know what it is now.

Another example of the changing cultural milieu and its effects on young adult meaning-making is reflected in the choices of a young man in his late twenties. After serving for a few years as an officer in the military, he married a recent law graduate. He then chose to go to a two-year business program rather than law school, calculating that it would require one less year of schooling. He speculated that he would then have the credentials to achieve the same level of income that his spouse would have to give up in order to pause in her career to have a child. This two-career family-in-the-making will probably negotiate their way through a great many tangles in the years ahead, sorting out what it means to be a parent, lover, and worker in the context of new and ancient biological-cultural patterns.

Forms of Knowing Revised

I propose that this period of probing commitment characterizes the first of the two eras within the single place earlier described as commitment within relativism. If we are to recognize and sponsor adult meaning-making, we need to make a distinction between the probing commitment of the young adult and what I term the *tested commitment* of the more fully adult. Tested commitment begins to take form when one can no longer be described as so divided, nor as simply exploring one's worldview, marriage, career commitment, lifestyle, or faith. One's form of knowing and being takes on a tested quality, a sense of fittingness, a recognition that one is willing to make one's peace and to affirm one's place in the scheme of things (though not uncritically). In the period of tested commitment, the self has a deepened quality of at-homeness and centeredness—in marked contrast to the ambivalence or dividedness of the earlier period.

We are now ready to recompose our understanding of the development of cognition as it is manifest in forms of knowing:

	Adolescent/ Conventional		Young Adult	Tested Adult	Mature Adult
Forms of Knowing	Authority-bound	→	Unqualified relativism	Probing commitment →	Tested commitment →	Convictional commitment

Since altered social conditions may merely reveal stages that are not new but have been present in earlier historical eras without being recognized, Brinton's analysis of Quaker journals from the seventeenth, eighteenth, and nineteenth centuries are particularly interesting when set alongside the ambivalent, probing character of the postadolescent period we are describing here. He has identified phases in the faith journey of Quakers that appear to corroborate the pattern described here. The first phase is "childhood piety," which is followed by "youthful frivolity" (adolescence, when Quaker youth of that era wanted to dance and have fancy clothes). Brinton then describes a postadolescent period that he terms the "divided self." During this period, the young person struggles between Quaker values and alternative values in the wider culture. This period of division is resolved in the choice to be at one, centered in the affirmation of the image of the "Inner Light" and the adoption of Quaker ways. (It is also interesting to note that the average age at which the Quakers he studied made the decision to be "at one" was twenty-six.)[18]

Young Adult

Keniston named this postadolescent period *youth*. However, since *youth* is a term that generally applies to most young people, and even children, I have chosen to name this early period of postadolescent, probing commitment *young adult*.[19] *Adult* connotes one's having achieved the composition of the critically aware self, with its attendant responsibility *for* the self. The qualifier *young* connotes the ambivalent exploratory, wary, tentative, and dependent quality that is manifest in early adulthood.

Henceforth, I shall distinguish four eras in the developmental spectrum spanning adolescence to mature adult faith: adolescence or conventional, young adult, tested adult, and mature adult. As we shall see, the appropriately dependent quality of young adult meaning-making has a particular cast and is the dimension of faith to which we now turn.

IT ALL DEPENDS . . .

OBSERVED FROM THE OUTSIDE, the transformation of an Authority-bound form of faith to a more reflective, critically aware faith may appear to be a merely cognitive development. Experienced from the inside, however, this is decidedly not the case. This shift in thinking affects not only cognition but also our feelings and relationships.

A person undergoing the transformation of his or her sense of truth, reordering "how things really are," may feel curiosity, awe, fascination, delight, relief, and joy. But it is likely that along the way there is also some measure of challenge, threat, bewilderment, frustration, anxiety, loss, emptiness, or other suffering. In other words, there may be some element of the shipwreck described in Chapter Two.

The presence of suffering in the process of cognitive-intellectual development is captured in a conversation between Bill Perry and a young woman recounting her experience in a physics class. There was, she said, a particular apparatus, the Ames window, that appeared to revolve in a circle. However, if the light cast upon it was changed, it then appeared instead only to be oscillating back and forth. This change in perception, which occurred with the flick of a light switch, catalyzed her recognition of the relative character of all perception. Might everything, seen in a different light, be recast into another perception of reality? She concluded her telling of the incident by remarking that in the midst of the experience her physics professor was very helpful to her. When Perry asked how, she said, "Well, now that I think about it, I realize that he didn't say anything. But the way he looked at me, I knew that he knew what I had lost."

To undergo the loss of assumed certainty, to have to reorder what was presumed to be dependably real, involves emotion as well as cognition. Cognition and affect, mind and heart, are intimately interwoven in the fabric of knowing and integral to the fabric of faith. To make this episte-mological journey is to be affected and moved. Kegan has stated it nicely: "A change in how we are composed may be experienced as a change in our own composure."[1]

In other words, as the discovery of knowledge and new meanings occurs in interactions between self and world, the whole self—body, mind, and heart—is affected.[2] Developments in intellectual awareness naturally set in motion a reordering of one's sense of person and place. Things that previously upset us are now seen in a new light; our response is conse-quently transformed, and we may become, for example, more tolerant. Or something that heretofore we would have accepted as "how things are and always will be" may in a new light be recognized as changeable, and we become less tolerant of things as they are. The evolution of meaning occurs in the dance of being affected in one's world coupled with evolv-ing cognitive power. Thus the motion of life is manifest as "e-motion" (even when constrained by conventions of supposed reasonableness within the academy, the corporation, or any other social context that may mute the expressions of surprise, disappointment, pleasure, or sorrow that reg-ularly accompany the discovery of new insight).

For example, development of new technological vistas, complex chemi-cal formulas including both medicines and biological weapons, and our abil-ity to manipulate DNA all reorder our relationship to the earth and to each other, enlarging both our power and our vulnerability, and fundamentally threatening the arrangements of those matters that ultimately concern us. We are affected. We watch the delicate relationships among peoples and nations unravel and reknit themselves in new patterns, alliances dissolve, borders are redrawn, slumbering forces awaken with renewed strength. We understand our vulnerability to political realities, and we hope that things won't get too out of balance. Yet we know that our inner sense of a depend-able universe can precariously shift upon hearing tomorrow's news.

We live with growing awareness that more depends upon us than previ-ous generations have supposed—even as we are continually defeated in our attempts to entirely grasp, much less control, the full measure of the chal-lenges and opportunities with which we now contend. Whether we cope by means of psychic numbing[3] or resolute engagement with the terrors that have become our daily reality, we are moved. Individually and collectively, we long for a trustworthy, dependable equilibrium in a dynamic, roiling world. (This longing is one way of understanding some of the tremendous attraction of fundamentalist religion at this time in history.)

Within this ongoing motion of life, we repeatedly reassess our felt understanding of what is ultimately dependable (our sense of "God"). We

are continuously moved to compose more dependable, trustworthy patterns of knowing and being. Whatever our age, we seek viable ways of
making meaning and search for a vital faith. At whatever level of sophistication, how we "depend" is a matter of ultimate importance.

Forms of Dependence

Since the discovery of knowledge and faith occurs in this interaction
between self and world, it follows that we learn in the context of relationships. We learn in relationship to the natural, more-than-human
world, in relationship to texts, people, and institutions. We learn because
we dwell in the dynamic interconnectedness of all life. We participate in
a shared tissue of being, which we experience as a physical, economic,
political, religious, and cultural reality. Fundamentally and inescapably,
we are social, interdependent beings.

Thus dependence is an integral dimension of life. We dwell in the power
of the relation of self and other. To depend means to be "held by" or "subject to," but it also means "to hold." The nature of our holding and being
held and how it may change over time affects the ongoing formation of
meaning and faith. Whereas focusing on cognition gave us access to how a
person *thinks* in her or his composing of meaning at the level of faith, focusing on dependence gives us access to what a person *feels*.[4]

Patricia Killen and John de Beer have observed that when "we enter our
experience . . . we find it saturated with feeling. . . . Feelings are our embodied affective and intelligent responses to reality as we encounter it. . . . Feeling joins body and mind. . . . Feelings . . . are clues to the meaning of our
experience. . . . They incarnate questions, values, and wisdom that we are
living but which we cannot yet articulate and of which we may be
unaware."[5] Killen and de Beer also observe that in the prevailing culture
feelings are often viewed primarily as problems because we cannot necessarily control them. But feelings are facts, and they cannot be ignored in the
life of faith. Thus dependence, which always challenges control, serves as a
particularly appropriate window into the affective dimensions of making
meaning. Holding, being held, depending and being depended upon within
the fabric of life (even in adulthood) all touch the core of the self so profoundly that elemental emotions such as trust, strength, power, and vulnerability are inevitably evoked.

Just as our forms of cognition can transform and develop, so too can
the forms of dependence. Tracing transformations in our ways of depending is one means of observing and describing the affective dimensions of
the development of faith.

	Adolescent/ Conventional		Young Adult	Tested Adult	Mature Adult
Forms of Knowing	Authority-bound, dualistic	Unqualified relativism $\rightarrow$	Probing commitment $\rightarrow$	Tested commitment $\rightarrow$	Convictional commitment
Forms of Dependence	Dependent/Counter-	dependent $\rightarrow$	Fragile inner-dependence $\rightarrow$	Confident inner-dependence $\rightarrow$	Inter-dependence

Dependent

At the time of Authority-bound knowing, it follows quite logically that a person's sense of world is dependent upon an uncritically assumed Authority. If a person is in his thirties or beyond and still making meaning in this way, the power of his social role may mask the profound dependence that is, in fact, in place. Dwelling in this form of knowing, he may be able to give a variety of logical reasons for holding a particular point of view but, if pressed, eventually reveals an unexamined trust in an authoritative other outside the self.

Feelings of assurance, rightness, confidence, hope, loyalty, fear, disdain, or alarm can be determined by Authority. One depends in a primary way upon the voice of a news commentator, the Pope, a political leader, a celebrity, one's parent ("always there and always right"), a favorite author, a spouse, or others who serve individually or collectively as trusted mediators of Truth.

Kegan quite fittingly has described this era in development as "interpersonal," for here a person's sense of self and truth depends upon his or her immediate relational and affectional ties in a primary way. With equal fittingness, Fowler described this era as "conventional," for here the person uncritically accepts the conventions of group and societal norms. The boundaries of the group may be rather narrowly drawn, as in the case of "my family" or "my soccer team," or broadly construed, as in the case of a "conventional" Democrat, Marine, or investment banker. In each instance, the person's sense of reality and what is fitting and true is dependent upon a sense of felt relationship to a shared ethos of assumed Authority and remains unaware of the prevailing ideology that shapes it. In this form of dependence, one can participate in the unreflective high of being swept up in the joy (or terror) of the crowd, whether in a sports arena, in a movie theater, in a worshipping community, or on the trading room floor.

Counterdependent

A person's feelings continue to be shaped by assumed Authority until the day there is a yearning (or the absolute necessity) to explore and test truth for oneself. This may occur in the midst of the utter shipwreck of the truth one has depended upon (which may be accompanied by feelings of devastation, bewilderment, or the like), or it may emerge as simply a restlessness, signaling readiness for more adequate and satisfying ways of knowing and being. In the latter instance, it is as though a new strength is taking form, one that can now push away from the dock of what has been sure moorage, to move out into the deep waters of exploring for oneself what is true and trustworthy. Initially, however, this move is essentially another form of dependence: counterdependence.

Counterdependence is the move in opposition to Authority; it provides momentum for the expansion of self into the still unknown horizon. It is a dimension of the earlier dependence, because the person can push against the pattern of meaning-making that is familiar, but she is not yet able to perceive or create a new one. Here, the *I* dwells in negative tension with whatever truth is now beginning to be tested. Yet a kind of absolute dependence remains in place. For example, after participating in a political demonstration for the first time, an eighteen-year-old woman who was arrested for trespassing said that before she had always trusted the police, but now she knew she could never trust them. Clearly, her experience was the beginning of a complex understanding of her relationship to the law and law enforcement. But she was as yet only pushing away from her earlier assumption and was caught up in the rhetoric of others as a defining, diametrically opposing interpretation, giving her a new, counterdependent, but still essentially Authority-bound, stance.

In the time of counterdependence, one is dependent upon moving apart and creating some distance. Yet the very need for distance obscures continuing participation in a relationship that is still (and in many instances will continue to be) quite powerful. Here, for example, are the words of a young woman from a tight ethnic community who, after an initial period of counterdependence in relation to her family, began to find a new, self-authoring pattern of relationship:

> I was so determined to break away from my family and the entire community that I drove to college with a vengeance. The more they told me not to go out, the more I'd go out. . . . I told them this: "If you told me to go left, I'd go right." Now I realize I can't keep making

decisions based on what my parents don't want me to do. I have to
think of what I really want. I've had my escape for four years and it's
time to return to reality. . . . In my freshman year, when I used to think
about a career it was kind of exotic: It was like I'd see something in a
movie. I would see a picture of myself out there. Now I know I don't
belong in that movie. I would feel ostracized from my community.[6]

Thus counterdependence is an important part of the motion of life in
preparing to venture out into the deep water of knowing for oneself what
is dependable and trustworthy, in ways that can finally embrace both the
past and a yet wider world of experience.

This move can occur in relatively nontraumatic forms if the person is
in an environment of wise parents, sponsoring teachers, effective supervisors, and public figures who consciously encourage or nurture it. Little
pushing-against is then necessary, because one is invited to explore and is
supported in doing so. However, if this motion is misunderstood, deval-
ued, and resisted, or if the bonds of relationship have been particularly
strong, good, and trustworthy, the person may have to push away from
the dock with greater force if a new relationship is to take form. (Also
note, people with little prior experience of positive trust may suffer
counterdependence over an extended period of time because, ironically,
negative relationships feel most familiar and safe.)

In any case, this may be a complicated time for parents and children,
teachers and students, managers and employees, or spouses trying to
repattern their marriage bond. For example, when a person wants to
move in the opposite direction from Authority, Authority may recognize
this and astutely suggest the opposite of what is really wanted. Clever
young people figure this out, however, and any real collaboration becomes
quite impossible for everyone. (This is most obviously the case when
Authority resists the now-necessary recomposing of the relationship and
becomes authoritarian.) Frustrations abound as earlier forms of communication seem to dissolve and alternative patterns of relationship have not
yet taken form (and cannot, so long as connection feels like a return to
earlier, now ill-fitting patterns of dependence).

Yet in time, a person may begin to recompose Authority and recognize
that, indeed, Authority doesn't hold ultimate truth or power. The counterdependent pilgrim then begins to look less toward resisting Authority
and more toward the self, taking responsibility for fuller participation in
the discernment of the truth. The person begins to move toward inner-
dependence.

Inner-Dependent Versus Independent

I use the term *inner-dependence* to signify something quite different from independence. Western culture places an extraordinary value on individuality and autonomy. In myriad ways, we signal that all should aspire to a kind of independence that implies not only a healthy strength of self but also the utter absence of an adult's practical dependence upon affectional (in contrast to merely utilitarian) relationships with others in the commonwealth of being. The presumed needs of industrial societies (for example, a mobile workforce and autonomous consumers) have spawned an almost pathological fear of dependence, reinforced by Freud's insights about infantilization.[7] Thus all psychological dependence has tended to be regarded as infantile, especially those forms of dependence that claim religious justification.

Reflecting the same industrial and Enlightenment influence, Protestant religious faith simultaneously has fostered a cultural ethos in which ethical reasoning focuses primarily on formation of the individual conscience and individual acts perceived as independent choices. Yet, as William Rogers observed, "while there is solid conviction as well as psychological wisdom in both religious and general cultural manifestations of independence, the excess of such claims easily leads us to the suspicion that they may betray more underlying anxiety about forms of dependence."[8] Not all forms of dependence are appropriately defined as weakness, immaturity, or regression to infantile relationships. Dependence simply affirms the relational dimension of all life. An absence of this recognition impoverishes our cultural myths and our overindividualized lives.

In contrast to the common associations we make with independence or autonomy, inner-dependence is not intended to connote standing all by oneself. Rather, the developmental movement into inner-dependence occurs when one is able self-consciously to include the self within the arena of authority. In other words, other sources of authority may still hold credible power, but now one can also recognize and value the authority of one's own voice.[9]

One young woman, reflecting on the differences between her experience of faith in high school and later in her senior year at a state university, wrote: "In high school my faith was more of a passive process—an assumed backdrop for my life. Now it is much more of an active process, something that I think about every day as a component of so many different aspects of my life." In her experience, this is not something that has occurred simply by her individual choosing. Rather, "a key factor in the growing sense of seeking faith/meaning and having it come more alive has been based on being surrounded by so many others that are also actively searching/challenging all the time." She continues:

> As a younger person, God was more of a higher up, all wise authority figure (father figure). Now I still sense in him this likeness, but there is an even greater sense of friendship quality. I think this may be because as I am becoming an adult, the parent role becomes less distinctive from the comrade role. I think I also have a gentler sense of him now and this may be because I have a gentler sense of myself as well. I think the two are inextricably related: my changing sense of God with my changing sense of self. . . . At this point, as I find the individual I am myself, I find that I feel much closer to God and my spiritual center, like we are getting more on the same wavelength. . . .

This shift in the construal of authority is interestingly linked with a gentler sense of self. Indeed, Gilligan's studies suggest a corresponding motion in the dimension of care. People (especially women) who have tended in the context of prevailing cultural assumptions to extend care almost exclusively to others while neglecting themselves (because only others had the authority to claim care) can now as a consequence of the capacity to include the self in the arena of authority extend care also to the self (who now also has the authority to claim care).[10]

Responsiveness to authority outside the self is thereby relativized but not necessarily demolished. With the term *inner-dependence,* then, I am signifying not a negation of the essential relatedness upon which all human life depends but rather new consciousness of the authority of the self in the composing of truth and choice. Here a person begins to listen within, with new respect and trust for the truth of his or her "own insides." That is, the person begins to listen and be responsive to the inner self as a source of authority and as an object of care. There is greater trust in one's own experience and in one's own "gut" or intuition. Again, this does not mean that sources of insight outside the self, or the claims of others for care, necessarily become irrelevant; it does mean, however, that the self can now take more conscious responsibility for adjudicating competing claims.

In this movement of the soul, there emerges the possibility of a new quality of correspondence between inner and outer realities, and the potential for new bonds of relation between self and world, faith and life. But the path is not always direct or smooth. Sometimes outer realities threaten to eclipse the nascent inner authority. One young adult said, "As I developed an awakening to the material inequalities in the world, I felt like there was no point in dealing with anything else . . . [that dealing with inner/personal struggles] would be an insane privilege—who am I to think about God when people can't eat? In my mind there was a line, an orderly way of dealing with things—material, and then inner. Now I realize you can't do social work without doing inner work. I burned out, not seeing the connection between myself and the world."

This awakening of the need to honor inner as well as outer demands while finding the right relationship to a wider and more complex world is manifest in today's parlance as a hunger for things "spiritual" in contrast to "religion." One young man, for whom church was "routine" when he was growing up, describes a transition he entered about age nineteen. He began to think more for himself and to formulate his own understanding of God, which transcended what he saw as hypocrisy in the religion he knew. He was reaching for a deeper congruence between his inner experience and a way of living in the world. Looking back a decade later, he said, "I had religion but *no* spiritual understanding. My family was *so* not spiritual but they are *so* religious." For him, being spiritual represented a postconventional form of faith in which his own inner authority began to play a stronger role.

The transition toward greater reliance on inner authority can be a time of significant vulnerability and uncertainty, as discrepancies between the claims of the self and the claims of the world come into sharp relief. One may question both self and world, wondering if either the social structures of one's world or one's own resources will prove sufficient for resolving the discrepancies. Before a new relation between self and world is created, the claims of each may threaten the other.

For example, young adults who become aware of the discrepancy between the haves and the have-nots find themselves buffeted by competing definitions of success. Those who have access to the "have" side may well find themselves asking the big question "Can I have what will make me happy and still make a difference?" and then spend a good deal of time exploring each pole.

A campus minister described a student who is majoring in humanities and business. When they spoke recently, the student happened to mention that he had that day invested $1,000 in day trading. He wondered about how to combine commitment to service with his need to be financially secure. He was trying also to be a success as a good son and grandson by taking care of his grandfather and helping to make significant family decisions, financial and otherwise. He was actively involved on campus in a program advocating changed economic conditions on behalf of the poor worldwide. As this young man begins to claim a sense of his own inner authority, he does so within a force field of competing claims and moral ambiguity. Again, young adult integrity can look like ambivalence.[11]

Once inner-dependence begins to take form, the young adult (being young) may long to return to a former kind of dependence, but the new knowing makes that difficult. One young woman, recently graduated from college, was keenly aware of the problematic character of turning back, even as she felt its allure. As she was making her way through a maze of challenges and disappointments, she recognized that she harbored a wish that at the same time she knew would not be satisfying. She said, "It's no accident that I've been reaching for something new. . . . After what this past year dealt me, I found myself wishing I were Catholic or a devotee of Santeria so I could have someone in authority just tell me which god/saint I needed to burn a candle for to change my luck."

Another said: "In high school I trusted others, the universe, to take care of me. . . . I trusted that my soul would be taken care of. Now I'm coming back to that point and it's an uphill battle. *I'm teaching myself* to trust. But when you start to learn about injustice, it's clear we aren't being taken care of—it can never be as easy again as it was in high school. Then I lived much more by instinct, versus now, I think through decision." That is, she now has a sense of responsibility for reflecting on what she can and cannot believe.

A New Kind of Authority

Many developmental accounts have assumed essentially a single movement in the shift of the locus of authority from an uncritical trust in assumed Authority "out there" to a critically aware sense of authority within. Yet it seems to be more the case that this shift occurs through a two-step process. When the locus of authority shifts from assumed authority outside the self to a sense of inner authority, it does so most solidly by moving from dependence upon an *assumed* Authority to dependence upon authority that is still external—still out there—but that *I* now choose, because this authority makes sense to me in terms of *my* observations and lived experience. Having some awareness that there are other authorities, other points of view, I nevertheless self-consciously choose *this* authority that has the power to beckon and draw forth *my own* sense of truth and emerging critical awareness.

That is, the transition into young adulthood occurs most gracefully and with optimum potential when the emerging self is recognized and invited into a wider arena of participation by wise and trusted adults. Thus, this is the fitting time for the presence of mentors—whether guru, guide, coach, sponsor, aunt or uncle, supervisor, professor, author, or important friend. Those who serve this mentoring function, however, can be distinguished from the heroes and heroines of adolescent devotion. The mentor holds a significant degree of power, but the "fusion" usually characteristic of the adolescent hero/heroine relationship is absent. When interviewing college seniors, for example, I found that if I posed the question, "Is there someone whom you wish to be like?" the students resisted it. They typically rephrased the question in their response: "No, there is no one who is a model for me, whom I would want to be *exactly* like, but there are people who exemplify certain qualities that I would like to have." Then they were able to name one or several people who served as an image of aspects of their emerging self.

The power of mentoring relationships is that they help anchor the vision of the potential self. They beckon the self into being and, in so doing, help to ground a place of commitment within relativism. As such, mentors exercise both cognitive and affective appeal, offering both insight and emotional support. But the young adult exercises a rudimentary sense of critical choice, at least on the level of requiring correspondence with his or her own experience. Indeed, the young adult will make do without a mentor rather than betray the integrity of the emerging self.

For instance, a young woman we will call Shelly, torn between traditional and potential images of womanhood, reflected upon the significance of a woman who served her as a mentor. Recounting how a course in the psychology of women taught from a feminist perspective helped her do some important integrating of conflicting tensions, she said:

> Probably this course was extremely significant. . . . See, one thing I have not found at the college until this year with [name of woman professor] was a person with as strong a career interest as I have who is also very interested in men. And that has been very lacking. I've done without it, but it's been lacking. All my close friendships at home are with women for whom career is secondary, and they're mostly interested in getting married. . . . My women friends here have been career oriented but not all that interested in men. . . . So what I finally did during the course was that I resolved that feeling . . . really feeling comfortable with being a woman [interested in men] and being very career oriented and being very independent. And that eased . . . conflict there.

Note that Shelly reveals the integrity of the emerging self along with the still appropriate dependence of young adulthood upon another who can authoritatively anchor her own emerging aspirations. The dependence we can detect here differs from the dependence of either the adolescent or the full adult. Though the adolescent is profoundly subject to the power of the conventional milieu, the young adult has a larger capacity to hear those voices that draw out the still vulnerable but increasingly inner-dependent self. In a healthy mentoring relationship, the young adult neither worships the mentor as a hero nor needs to push off counter-dependently. Rather, he or she is appropriately dependent upon a chosen (self-selected) "authority out there" to beckon and confirm the integrity emerging from within.

As Belenky, Clinchy, Goldberger, and Tarule have reported, there appear to be some who move to this more inner-dependent place without much outside support. Such people may say something like, "One day, I just knew that what I had been told I had to be, do, and believe, wasn't true."[12] Yet when we look closely at their life context, we can see precursors of this moment: influences that helped prepare the soul (whether in large or small ways) for this courageous, developmental moment. If the experience is to be sustained, the person needs to be met in ways that enable the new voice to flourish. Without such support, it is vulnerable to being crushed.

Fragile Inner-Dependence

One might, therefore, describe the emerging inner-dependence of the young adult as initially a *fragile inner-dependence*. *Fragile* here is not intended to connote weak, feeble, or puny. Rather, it is more like the fragility of a young plant as it emerges from the soil: healthy, vital, full of promise, yet vulnerable. The young adult may in her or his own personal style express this new inner-dependence and palpable strength with a kind of brazen pride, or a tentative, almost shy sense of new power to declare one's own sense of things and to take important initiatives. Either way, the new inner strength represents a horizon of promise, hope, deepened capacity for responsible action, and glimmering possibility. In some this new strength and voice may take the form of subjective knowing, described by Belenky, Clinchy, Goldberger, and Tarule.[13] The young adult, steeped in newly gained inner-dependence, may frustrate professors and others who want the young person to recognize the value of carrying on discourse with additional voices who have worthy points of view. The young adult may be bewildered when her or his own opinion is not enough for a term paper. To cite "experts" may feel like going back to always just trusting Authority, when now one can see in whole new ways for oneself: "Isn't that what you wanted me to do? Think for myself?"

The feelings to which the inner-dependent young adult is therefore correspondingly vulnerable are special forms of bewilderment, loss, and being at sca. One young woman, discovering a whole new horizon of opportunity and promise for her life, spoke poignantly of a sense of loss: knowing that she "would never be at home again in the same way—with my extended family, or in the place where I worked during high school." These would remain part of her life and landscape, but she knew she was choosing to step into a wider world—cognitively, emotionally, and geographically—and that these familiar people and places would be recast within a larger frame of belonging and choice. Her ecology of depending would be reordercd as she began to make meaning in new ways.

This fragile inner-dependence is evident also in the young adult's own experience of ambiguity regarding being a grown-up. Blake, for example, is a twenty-four-year-old college graduate living in a major city several hundred miles from her parents. She is an outstanding teacher in a community college, where the students in her classroom are one, two, or three decades older than herself, seeking their high school diplomas. It is Blake who decides when her students are ready to take the standardized exams that for many of them determine access to adequate employment.

Blake carries a faculty ID card, but she is not paid benefits. She pays for her own household and general expenses, but her parents are paying her health insurance because they feel she should not yet have to be responsible for her full support. These mixed messages about how adult she is echo a dialogue within her where "switching between adulthood and childhood minute to minute, happens in little ways." It still feels kind of "weird" to buy groceries *by herself,* but "buying mundane, day-to-day things with money you earned one hundred per cent by yourself, is a small moment of realizing you can make it on your own." Blake heard another twenty-something friend remark: "Every once in a while, like I'm standing on a subway platform dressed for my work, and I get this paralyzing feeling that I'm about to be found out. Like everyone is going to discover that I am a kid masquerading as an adult."

But there are yet deeper streams of vulnerability in young adult lives. When a senior at a large university was asked, "What do your friends 'count on'?" his answer revealed a complex set of vulnerabilities. Some of his friends were students who, despite their university education, seemed to be remaining in Authority-bound and dependent ways of making meaning. As he put it, "For some, God has all the answers—they will just rely on God to get them through it. Others count on whoever they can around them, which leads to their sometimes being crushed even further because no one can be completely dependable for everything." These students were vulnerable to an unexamined faith and the inevitable failures of present or future Authorities.

But then the student went on: "Others just don't count on much—some of these friends have a constant struggle with depression—just passively hope that some day will be different. And a few count a lot on themselves: 'If I just do something more, it will get better somehow.'" These friends seemed to have stepped beyond counting on Authority out there but encountered new challenges for which they are not fully prepared; steeped as these young adults are in cultural messages of "you are and should be on your own" (that is, independent), they are vulnerable to a special kind of disappointment, failure, isolation, abandonment, and depression. They cannot go back, but their emerging adulthood needs to be met and welcomed by a mentoring milieu that offers stepping stones into the promise of their future.

Confident Inner-Dependence

In contrast to the experience of those just described, if the fragile inner-dependence of the young adult is met with encouragement and confirmation, over time a confident inner-dependence can take form. The more tested adult has a deepened capacity to order his or her own sense of value and promise and has become strong enough to let the mentor be other— even to have feet of clay. The tested adult, however, does not cease to need others; rather, others are depended upon in a different way. For instance, as the young adult becomes more fully adult, mentors become peers. The nature of this transition was captured by a man in his forties who recalled that his mentor once said to him: "My job is to accompany you until you see yourself as I see you." When this occurs, authority previously located outside the self, though ratified within, becomes more fully equilibrated within (yet does not cease to require appropriate confirmation from one's community in the ongoing process of making meaning). The tested adult manifests a *confident inner-dependence*.

Interiority and the Ethical Life

In today's world, it is increasingly important to recognize that this movement to inner-dependence is critical to the formation of interiority, the capacity for what may be described as an inner dialogue. Inner dialogue is vital to the formation of conscience and the ethical life. The ethical life as it is lived out in a complex and morally ambiguous world is dependent less on the ability to do everything right the first time and more on the ability to reflect on past and potential action and make good choices.

How this works is described by Robert Quinn in his book *Deep Change: Discovering the Leader Within*.[14] There he recounts the story of Steve Thompson, newly working with Ron Cedrick, a man known for his command of deep-sea engineering and construction. Cedrick had a reputation for executing huge projects and completing them ahead of schedule. Steve was responsible for lowering the diving bell into the sea and bringing the divers back up on deck. The most dangerous time in this operation occurs when the diving bell is between the surface of the water and the deck. If cables snap then, divers can rarely be recovered.

As Quinn tells the story, the sea was growing rough as Thompson's first project with Cedrick neared completion. Cedrick passed by Thompson and said, "I know that the weather's gettin' up a bit, but those boys respect you and will do what you ask—I've seen it. We need to keep that bell in the water just as long as we can before we let a little 'ole weather shut us down." Thompson continued the operation in twenty-four-foot seas, and they beat the deadline without mishap.

Later, however, Thompson gave himself "the mirror test." He stood back and reflected on himself, what he had done and why. He recognized that in his overwhelming desire to succeed, he had accomplished the task, but at significant cost. He had tolerated unacceptable risk and had set a poor precedent for permissible operating parameters.

This ability to reflect on past action and compose future action is dependent upon the development of interiority: a dialogue within the self. The Society of Friends (Quakers) speak of listening to the "Inner-Light" or Spirit within. Jesuits speak of discernment and cultivate exercises for discovering the presence of God within. Others speak of listening for that "still, small voice." Perry was fond of saying that part of learning the art of life is to discover that there is not just a still, small voice but a whole committee of voices inside—parents, family, teachers, advertising, threats from competitors, expectations of friends and coworkers—and the challenge is to become a good chairperson! Among the gifts of the great spiritual traditions are the practices that have been honed across generations for becoming conscious of the power and processes of the inner life.

This capacity for an inner life is a way of holding the competing claims of various authorities together with the perceptions and judgments of the inner-dependent self. Thus the power of conscience can be substantially deepened by this particular movement in the journey into adult faith. If it does not occur or is limited to discrete domains, the conscience is blunted. If interiority is well cultivated, the capacity for responsible adulthood and faithful citizenship is enlarged.

Interdependence

After inner-dependence is established and the trustworthiness of the inner self is confirmed, there is the potential for yet another movement toward further awareness of trust and responsibility. This movement again expands the arena of authority and care. It does not typically occur in its fullest measure until post-midlife.

Midlife occurs at different times for different people, because it is determined primarily by an inner sense that one has probably lived half of one's life, and that the future is no longer infinitely revisable. One's sense of lifetime becomes more focused. This is a transition in consciousness, usually marked in part by both physical and social changes.

In the midlife period, a person may simply move through a transition from the first half of his or her life to the second half. But every transition can be an occasion for transformation. The transformative potential of the midlife transition lies in the strength achieved in the formation of the inner-dependent self, for only when one has become strong enough can the deep self be allowed to reemerge in the service of a further repatterning of truth and faith.[15]

The deep self is composed of those buried dimensions of oneself, particularly the sufferings and joys of childhood, the unresolved issues of adolescence, and (as we shall see) the most luminous dreams and hopes of young adulthood. This deep self may now come to the surface to be healed and fulfilled, or at least to be known and lived with nondefensively. If it is not resisted, it may thus lead to deeper trust of the self and also to profound awareness of one's relatedness to others.

This transformation constitutes another qualitative shift in the balance of vulnerability, trust, and faith. Now more at home with both the limitations and the strengths of the self, one can be at home with the truth embedded in the strengths and limitations of others. A person's center of primary trust now resides neither in the assumed authority of another, nor in the courageously claimed authority of the inner self. Rather, trust is now centered in the meeting of self and other, in the recognition of the strength and finitude of each, and in the promise of the truth that emerges in relation. This trust takes the form of a profound, self-aware conviction of interdependence.

When meaning-making moves into an interdependent form, it is not the fact of interdependence that is new. As we are beginning to recognize more fully, from infancy through adulthood a person is always interdependent. What is new, however, is one's awareness of the depth and pervasiveness of the interrelatedness of all of life and the important yet limited strength of one's own perceptions. One now becomes increasingly angered and saddened by assertions of truth that exclude the authority of the experience of others. For example, a manager may have been tolerant of shared inquiry and decision making, and even affirmed the notion ideologically—all the while silently harboring a sense that her own inner experience, knowledge, and intuition would lead to the best decision. When she dwells in this more interdependent conviction, however, she perceives dialogue to be not merely politically expedient but essential. Yet she can still bring to that dialogue the strength of her own capacity to author truth—a strength that is now joined with a capacity to listen to others with deepened attention and responsiveness.

Dwelling in this conviction of interdependence makes it possible to depend upon others without fear of losing the power of the self. For example, when this transformation into a deeper consciousness of interdependence occurs within a marriage, a yet more profound intimacy becomes possible, for the person is a self but can also hold that self as a gift to be given to the other. The person now participates in a new freedom that can hold the paradoxes of weakness and strength, needing and giving, tenderness and assertiveness—without anxiety that in the recognition of the other the self will be diminished.

A person who has composed, and is composed by, this form of dependence—interdependence—comfortably dwells in the truth that the needs of nurturance, affection, and belonging extend throughout life and into every domain of being, both public and private. Interdependence can now be profoundly owned at the affective level. The person now most trusts the truth that emerges in the dialectic, or, better, in the communion between self and other, self and world, self and "God." The person can recognize and know with the whole self the truth of the interdependence that we are. This knowing may involve feelings of delight, wonder, freedom, responsiveness, responsibility, and often a deep sense of the tragic dimensions of life as a consequence of the capacity to see what others cannot or will not.

Attention to the development of dependence gives us some access to the ebb and flow of feelings of trust, constraint, threat, fear, confidence, and communion. These feelings are rooted in inner experience. But the motion of affective life and its development emerges neither in a merely private inner world nor in abstract reflections upon relationship, but only in the pleasures, frustrations, and transformations of relationships lived out in the every day. The character and quality of our ways of depending and their transformations have everything to do with the forms of community within and through which we make meaning and seek a worthy faith.

6

. . . ON BELONGING

YEARS AGO, I was teaching in a liberal arts college in the Northwest that encouraged off-campus study, particularly during its January term. Therefore, with another colleague, I traveled with a group of students to San Francisco, where we studied the city for a month. I noted with interest that some students who had little or nothing to do with religion on campus were choosing to explore the cathedrals in San Francisco, as well as other notable and diverse religious communities. Some were also asking questions about religion, again in contrast to their behavior on campus. At first, I assumed that this was simply because of a change in environment; San Francisco, after all, did offer more cathedrals and more religious diversity. Only later did I recognize another dynamic at play with us in the city: a change in the students' network of belonging.

On campus, students tended to choose patterns of affiliation partly on the basis of their religious orientation. Once these were established, any significant departure was a threat to belonging. This meant that for some, religious practice or inquiry was out of bounds, though for others it was required. But when they were in another social constellation, new questions and new behavior became possible.

We expected that when students returned to campus those who had not traveled would benefit from association with those who had. We discovered, however, that the travelers tended to form new patterns of affiliation. They formed community—a network of belonging—with those who had also traveled and with whom they could confirm their new ways of seeing and knowing.[1]

Our location, social context, and general surroundings play a central role in the formation of meaning and faith. One of the distortions of many psychological, developmental, economic, and religious models is a focus on the individual that obscures the power of the social context in shaping personal reality. Reified distinctions between the disciplines of psychology and sociology, for example, reflect the split in much of Western thought between private and public, subject and object, the human and the rest of the natural environment. These overdrawn distinctions mask the growing importance of recognizing the interdependent realities of self and social context.[2] A young woman who had been listening carefully to her friends (male and female, some who went to college and some who did not) remarked that their faith experience was "fully based on what they were going through, who they were around, and where they were living. Everyone, across the board, identified their different moments of spiritual awakening and new understanding based on location and their experience at that location."

Networks of Belonging

An underrecognized strength of the Piagetian paradigm is its psychosocial conviction that human becoming absolutely depends upon the quality of interaction between the person and his or her social world. The individual is not the sole actor in the drama of human development. No single relationship can satisfy the casting needs for the drama of our becoming. We "interlive" with many others.[3] Just as the infant is dependent upon a network of others for confirmation of a universe of care and promise, even so everyone throughout life is dependent upon a tangible "network of belonging." Everyone needs a psychological home, crafted in the intricate patterns of connection and interaction between the person and his or her community. Networks of belonging provide the trustworthy holding upon which all humans depend for their flourishing within the wider world and the universe it spins though. The ultimate meaning we compose is determined partly by our relationships with the many in our lives who are "those who count"[4] and partly by a host of others, of whom we may be only dimly aware. Faith is a patterning, connective, relational activity embodied and shaped not within the individual alone but in the comfort and challenges of the company we keep.

The Power of Tribe

We all need "tribe." The power of tribe is a strong feature of how we as human beings have made meaning throughout the ages and continue to do so throughout our lives. For most of human history, we have lived in relatively small tribal groups. We need a place or places of dependable connection, where we have a keen sense of the familiar: ways of knowing and being that anchor us in a secure sense of belonging and social cohesion.[5]

Networks of belonging take various forms. Some are manifest as an obviously present and easy-to-identify circle of face-to-face relationships confirming identity and security: families, neighborhoods, workplaces, athletic teams, religious communities, or the regulars at the local cafe. But they may also be scattered geographically or otherwise dispersed. One might, for example, live and work far away from colleagues who share one's vision and commitments, and yet be able to sustain committed action (even when criticized in the immediate situation) because of the felt linkage with others who confirm one's very being.[6]

Increasingly, many find their tribe linked by phone, fax, and e-mail—with only the occasional direct encounter—a network of belonging stretched thin. Even those who choose a life of total solitude still carry with them a self formed by a history of relationships with those who count, both living and dead. One could, for instance, have a strong sense of identification with an historical figure one has never met but who serves nevertheless as a touchstone for one's life and values. A growing ecological consciousness has reawakened many to meaningful kinship that includes animals, trees, birds, and the creatures of the sea.

Freedom and Boundaries

The power of any network of belonging is twofold. First, the sense of connection and the security it offers affords the freedom to grow and become. Second, every network of belonging has norms and boundaries that one cannot cross and still belong. Thus every network of belonging simultaneously represents freedom and constraint.[7] Social norms, for example, may manifest collective wisdom that protects and nourishes the individual, but they can also distort reality, or in time unnecessarily limit the promise of human life. Transformations in the meaning of the self, therefore, may also require transformation of the social world—a mutual recomposing.

If we recognize the power of "the surround" in the story of human becoming, we begin to see that learning to recognize a particular form of meaning-making or a stage is not a matter of diagnosis and treatment. Rather, it prompts questions: What do we now mean to each other?[8] How does the community respond to the life of a developing person? What does a person's growth mean for the life of the community? Is the relationship mutually nourishing and sustainable?

Thus, embedded in the story of human development is a story about transformation in forms of community.

Balancing Two Great Yearnings

The importance and the power of the social milieu has been reasonably well acknowledged in psychological descriptions of children and adolescents. We know that children are profoundly affected by parents, families, teachers, playmates, and schoolmates. Peer groups are well factored into the story of adolescent development. But as people move into adulthood, their relationship to community may become confused. Because the notion of independence is so powerful in Western society and in the canons of adult psychology, if the need for family and community is strong, it may appear to contradict the achievement of adulthood. If the mark of psychological adulthood is autonomy, and maturity is measured in terms only of degrees of individuation, the ongoing and essential role of community in adult life can become almost invisible.

The communion features of the psyche at the threshold of adulthood remain in focus, however, if we remember that the motion of meaning-making is located in the oscillation between "two great yearnings": the yearning for exercise of one's own distinct agency (one's own power to make a difference) and the yearning for belonging, connection, inclusion, relationship, and intimacy. Human becoming can be partially understood as a series of temporary resolutions of the desires for differentiation and connection; every developmental era is a new solution to this universal tension.[9]

Forms of Community

Earlier, we explored the development of forms of knowing (cognition) and forms of dependence (feeling and affect). Now we are prepared to recognize the corresponding forms of community that nourish the development of human life.

	Adolescent/Conventional		Young Adult	Tested Adult	Mature Adult
Forms of Knowing	Authority-bound, Dualistic (tacit) →	Unqualified relativism →	Probing commitment (ideological) →	Tested commitment (systemic) →	Convictional commitment (paradoxical)
Forms of Dependence	Dependent/Counter-dependent →		Fragile inner-dependence →	Confident inner-dependence →	Inter-dependence
Forms of Community	Conventional	Diffuse →	Mentoring community →	Self-selected class/group →	Open to other

Conventional Community

If meaning and faith are composed in Authority-bound, dependent forms, composing self and world takes place within the assumed value of membership in a group or groups characterized primarily by some form of face-to-face relationships.[10] These groupings (which may also occur in some measure in virtual forums) are conventional because they are marked by conformity to cultural norms and interests (including the interests of subcultures). They may be defined by loyalty to any one, or a combination, of ethnic-familial ties, social-class expectations, regional perspectives, a religious system, a technoscientific ethos, peer values, gender roles, or media-crafted attractions. Conventional community includes simply "those like us." This form of community corresponds to the Authority-bound and dualistic form of cognition, in which Authority defines *us* and *them*.

Diffuse Community

As one begins to want to know for oneself, however, and moves into a relativized world, often it is precisely the conventional social ordering that one begins to question. Experiencing an other (someone who was previously "them") who contradicts assumptions about who we are and who they are may be a first step in questioning familiar social arrangements.

As the social horizon thus expands, the form of community may shift from a well-defined set of assumed associations to a considerably more diffuse form of belonging. An exploratory, experimental, and tentative quality of relationship may prevail as one ventures into a wider horizon of belonging. One young woman recalled how, when she began to discover that she was "clueless" about what the world was really about, she actively put herself in as many different social contexts as possible to challenge her assumptions. This was part of questioning her stability and security in the universe—"a major upheaval and a period of searching."

If any one truth or perspective is as good as another, there can be a corresponding sense that perhaps any sort of relationship may be as good as any other. If unqualified relativism prevails, it becomes problematic to sustain any particular relationship. This is not to say that relationships become a matter of indifference. Quite the contrary may be the case as the person, now feeling a bit at sea, has both a new freedom to explore the widening horizon of life and a new vulnerability to the potential power of every possible relationship. Thus (and somewhat ironically) the person awash in the sea of unqualified relativism may be sustained by the subjective experience of the importance of human connectedness of some sort—a spar we cling to when the shipwreck of certainty dumps us into a seemingly meaningless world.

Since, as we have recognized earlier, unqualified relativism is difficult to sustain in the real world of choices and consequences, a person begins to seek an adequate pattern of meaning, a place of commitment within a relativized world. It is here that a new network of belonging plays a key role, as it serves to confirm the self in composing a new (and sometimes hard-won) faith. Fowler described this form of social awareness as a "self-selected class or group," but here again, we can discern two forms: one that is characteristic of the young adult era, and another that signals full adulthood.

Mentoring Community

For the young adult, community finds its most powerful form in a *mentoring community*. As we have seen, the emergence of a critically aware and inner-dependent self should in no way suggest that the need for a network of belonging disappears. Quite the opposite is the case. But there is a readiness for a new kind of belonging. Young adulthood is nurtured into being, and its promise is most powerfully realized through participation in a community that poses a trustworthy alternative to earlier assumed knowing. A mentoring community offers hospitality to the potential of the emerging self, and it offers access to worthy dreams of self and world.

A critical, cognitive perspective on one's familiar ethos alone is not enough to precipitate a transformation in faith. Critical awareness combined with a single mentoring figure, though influential, may still be insufficient to reorder faith itself. Rather, it is the combination of the emerging developmental stance of the young adult with the challenge and encouragement of the mentor, grounded in the experience of a compatible social group, that ignites the transforming power of the young adult era. A mentoring community can confirm the faith that there will be a new home.

This sense of having a viable network of belonging is key. If a person becomes critically aware and begins to take responsibility for his understanding of faith, then recomposing truth includes recomposing his own sense of trust and power. In such moments, the recognition, presence, care, and faith of others can make all the difference. Boundaries of awareness can expand, and the person begins to move in new ways in the adult world of responsibility for discerning the nature of life itself, making judgments, and choosing actions—in the intellectual life; in the world of work; and within one's family, community, and the wider commons.

Thus it is particularly useful here to think less in terms of developmental journeys and more in terms of transformations in one's sense of home. Imagine a series of concentric circles. The innermost is the family of origin; the next, the neighborhood; the next, the larger community; then the world of first adult work; and so on. The person, remaining at the center yet transcending each new threshold, experiences a growing sphere of belonging and participation. To become a young adult is to make one's way across another threshold into a wider sphere of consciousness and participation. Upon crossing this threshold, the young adult finds her antennae out and highly tuned to assess what will be asked and allowed in this newly enlarged sphere of becoming.

Developing the kind of inner-dependence that grounds responsible participation within this expansion of reality does not happen easily or all at once. The emerging, still fragile inner-dependence of a young adult self remains significantly vulnerable to the prevailing sociality, on both sides of the new threshold. The young adult is both strong and vulnerable in new ways.

One young adult, age twenty-six, reflecting upon the first year in a prestigious graduate school, recalled:

> Everyone who gets here is such a strong individual, and then you really give up a lot of that individuality, I think, and sort of succumb to all these group pressures and learn in the way that the school wants you to learn, and the whole group thing is very powerful. It's incredibly strong, and you find yourself succumbing to these norms that you might not necessarily believe in.
>
> I think in the beginning I felt like, "Oh, that's the way it is, and I have to fit into this in order to be here," because I don't think I have the confidence to say, "Well, I feel differently than all of the seventy other people in this classroom." I think it's hard to get out of the mind frame that there's *an* answer, there's *a* way of analyzing, there's *a* way of thinking. . . .
>
> You have to . . . realize that there are many more people out there like you, and you just have to find them . . . but when you are only in the second month, you don't have that kind of perspective.

Notice that this young adult does not search for a way to transcend the need for a compatible community; rather, she seeks one in which the emerging self can flourish with integrity.

Thus the character of the social context to which the young adult has access may be the most crucial element in transforming or maintaining what a young adult "knows." Indeed, John Henry Newman was so convinced of the power of the social environment to train, mold, and enlarge the mind that he proposed that if he had to choose between a school without residence hall life and one with only the life of the residence hall, he would choose the latter, where "the conversation of all is a series of lectures to each."[11]

Again, in the end the young adult is attracted to a social context that appears to be compatible with his or her inner truth, or at least with some very important part of that truth. Simply wanting to belong is no longer enough. The young adult self depends upon and responds to those individuals and groups that express patterns of meaning resonant with the experience and the new critical awareness of the still fragile, inner-dependent self. There is, however, profound receptiveness to any network of belonging that appears to promise a place of nurture for the potential self, even (and sometimes especially) if its forms are demanding, calling forth the new strength. A place that recognizes the gifts and potential competence of the young adult, and that requires only as much inner-dependent strength as the young adult yet has, meets the yearning for power and communion in their young adult forms.

A mentoring community does just that. It offers a network of belonging in which young adults feel recognized as who they really are, and as who they are becoming. It offers both challenge and support and thus offers good company for both the emerging strength and the distinctive vulnerability of the young adult.

Inevitably Ideological

As the young adult recomposes meaning with fresh, critical self-awareness, shifting from a tacit, interpersonal orientation to an explicit, systemic mode, a new "ideological" quality appears. This occurs because the new meaning that the young adult has the courage to compose and embrace is held with great tenacity, since the new meaning must ground an equally new and still fragile self. The very tentativeness and ambivalence of young adult meaning-making renders it inevitably ideological.

By *ideology* I mean structured and largely rational attempts to understand self and world and to prescribe directions and corrections. By this definition, it may, of course, be argued that all structures of meaning are ideological. Ideology, however, tends specifically to connote a cognitive, firm, and even rigid orientation. In the case of the young adult, this is inevitable, because here the self and system are still one. The young adult must sometimes hold new meanings most fiercely when working up the gumption to make the passage off a once-stalwart (but now seemingly leaking and inadequate) ship that has hitherto held the self, and onto a promising but unknown new shore.

The young adult most thrives when there is access to a network of belonging centered in the strength of worthy meanings that impart a sense of distance from the conventions of the young adult's past and from the larger society with which the young adult must still negotiate terms of entry. This is why Keniston described the affiliations of this period as having an over-against quality.[12] This quality is, however, distinguishable from the simple counterdependence described earlier. The young adult is over-against the world as it is, but in a mode that is more discerning and dialogical than simply pushing away from the dock.

This dialogue between self and society-world-other may initially take the form of a fairly strong dichotomy. As we have seen, when one begins to take responsibility for one's own meaning-making there are unavoidable tensions between competing values and life choices: freedom to travel versus getting ahead, carrying on family traditions versus going one's own way, guaranteed financial security versus a riskier option, stress versus leisure.

In contrast to the tested adult, the young adult does not yet have practice in holding the full range of complex feeling and thought that a mature adulthood requires. Hence the appeal of an ideological stance that offers a kind of certainty and purity of vision, whether the issues are large or small. But the character of this stance differs from the Authority-bound and dualistic mode of the previous era. It is precisely the awareness that all perspectives are relative that may energize a fierce, sometimes tenacious, reach for a place to stand within the anxiety of that reality. In a premature bid for confidence, the young adult is vulnerable to collapsing the tensions of felt dichotomies.

Shelly, who earlier described an integration of conflicting images of womanhood, suffered a very strong sense of irreconcilable tensions, which she described as:

parents	vs.	self
religion	vs.	agnosticism
sweet	vs.	sassy
sexism	vs.	feminism
God	vs.	empiricism
believer	vs.	psychologist
marriage	vs.	graduate school
helping others	vs.	materialism
men	vs.	career
values (control)	vs.	experience (emotion)

In the midst of these tensions she did, on numerous occasions, land on one side or the other. If the voice of a boyfriend prevailed, she abandoned her feminist perspective; if anxiety over her mother's health became too great, she tried to return to an earlier faith; if the study of behavioral psychology was compelling, she dismissed God for empiricism. Then she told us:

> I worked with [the dean] in an internship and we talked about religion . . . and . . . just lately people have been really reaching out to me. [A psychology professor] and I are in similar places. We really have trouble with empiricism and we're wrestling with it, so we've spent time talking . . . and so it's suddenly . . . again the hot issues and I'm open to being a believer but . . . I'm comfortable and aware now that whatever I come up with will not be the traditional, and that's OK. It can still be bona fide even though I know everyone doesn't agree with it . . . and I don't have to fit into a niche. So I'm sorting it through and it feels comfortable and it feels like it'll come.
>
> And also I always thought I would get married when I was twenty-three or, the latest, twenty-four. Well, right now I probably project to twenty-six or twenty-seven. It is helpful and it's also very freeing. . . . I am a deviant. I'm way off the scale as a deviant and I feel very good about that, in fact I'm . . . probably proud of it more than anything else, and I know I'll get flak from my parents. They've taken awhile to adjust to my being a Ph.D., which has not happened yet, but I'm on the road, and they know it. . . . They wanted me to get married, maybe get a master's degree but get married and then get pregnant right after that and start a family. . . .
>
> I want to go to an environment where I'll really be tested. It seems so often here that I haven't needed a God, and I think maybe in Chicago I'll need one.

In Shelly's description of this push-and-pull, there seems to be a good deal of pushing away from the dock. Yet when she describes her resolution of these tensions, she seems not to stand in a place of simple opposition. Rather, she seems to find a certain relief in describing herself as "deviant." It is a strong word, but it seems to reflect both the freedom of her emerging inner-dependence and the quality of over against the world as it is that marks the still fragile capacity to take responsibility for the relationship between self and world. The new self is able to accept, articulate, and affirm a sense of engaged choice and struggle. She strengthens this new emerging voice by seeking alliances with those who share this emerging stance.

In the company of good mentors, Shelly accepts deviance, tentativeness, and testing as a place to stand apart from previously held patterns of meaning and affiliation. She remains, as do the rest of us, in significant measure dependent upon the forms of belonging available in any given context. But now there is an enlarged awareness of "who I belong with," a diminished desire to fit in, no matter what, and less sense of being utterly at the mercy of the social expectations within which the self happens to be located.

In a similar fashion, we hear a young man with growing inner-dependent strength questioning earlier assumptions and, in the context of networks of belonging, recomposing his sense of self and faith:

> Until the end of high school, my experiences regarding faith and/or spirituality revolved primarily around what my family and my community had exposed me to—the Christian faith. Though many of my family's beliefs and practices closely resembled a Christian way of life, I wouldn't call myself or any one of my immediate family members practicing Christians. We celebrate Christmas and Easter and believe in the basic principles of the Ten Commandments, but we hardly ever went to church.
>
> When the subject of what religion/denomination I considered myself to be came up in junior high, I professed ignorance or told whoever was interested that I didn't really consider myself to be religious. During high school, I adopted my father's point of view and declared myself an atheist, stating (whenever asked), "I don't believe in God." With this type of attitude, I found myself in many discussions regarding religion and God—about its/his/her validity, purpose, and worth. So, by the end of high school I had been exposed to a fair number of different ideas and beliefs, but any actual experience with spirituality or faith was very limited. I spent most of my time arguing against the possibility of God instead of attempting to experience any kind of faith at all.
>
> In terms of religious faith, my first couple of years at the university were no different. I found myself in the same conversations about religion—agreeing with my fellow atheists about the absurdity of God, while challenging the believers about the possibility of God. It was not until a conversation with a close friend's father and sister that I altered my view on the topic of faith. I was visiting my friend and his family in Munich. Only because I didn't know them well enough to voice my opinion, I decided only to listen to a conversation they had about religion. There were three major players—the sister (religious/Christian type), the father (agnostic/philosopher type), and the friend's other

friend (violent atheist type). I listened long and hard. By the end, I realized how ridiculous I had been sounding. The father convinced me to
at least consider myself an agnostic, because when it came down to it,
I really didn't have any good proof that God *didn't* exist. I decided,
however, that the sister didn't have any solid evidence for the existence
of God either.

But this is when I promised myself that I would try and be more
open-minded. And this is what I practice now—open-mindedness with
a little bit of research.

So, when I was offered a job to plant trees for the summer with a
Christian group, I took it. This was another turning point. I attended
their church services regularly and did my best to open my mind fully
to the possibility of Jesus as a savior and the Christian faith on the
whole. I thought, "so many million people can't be wrong," so I
attempted to learn and accept. I remember wanting to believe in what
the rest of them believed in. They seemed so at peace, sure of themselves and sure of each other. I was envious of their comfort level. I
loved the sense of community—everyone helped everyone else, self-
ishness was at a minimum, and the general air of the camp was just so
positive.

By the end of the planting season, however, I decided that they were
too sure of themselves and of each other. And God was thrown around
too loosely—doing too many things for too many people. If he exists,
I felt they trivialized his existence. Their comfort level was too high
and their tolerance of nonbelievers was more like pity. . . . There was
not enough doubting for my liking. But I still do like the sense of community and cooperation they/we were able to establish—something I
still envy organized religion for. (I also learned from them a small sense
of global responsibility that has grown in me since that time.)

So! I came out thinking that Christianity by itself, and probably all
of the other religions by themselves, couldn't answer all of my questions on their own. So I continue to learn as much as I can.

Self-Selected Group

In the ongoing development of faith, such learning can over time settle
into tested adult faith. The tested adult can maintain the tension of earlier dichotomies, especially between self and the larger social world. As
one becomes more confident, having composed a meaning and a voice of
one's own that is less threatened by every competing point of view, fiercely
ideological and over-against modes can be relinquished. The world can

be readily engaged as well as critiqued. The form of community of this confident adult self is not the ideologically compatible and mentoring community upon which the young adult is dependent in a primary way. Rather, the tested adult values a self-selected class or group that shares the meanings that the adult authorizes within.[13]

This new capacity for a confident sense of authority within, and thus a relaxed engagement with others in the world as it is, is both strengthened and made vulnerable by a corresponding willingness to make pragmatic accommodations that no longer appear to threaten the essential integrity of the self. Adult faith can sustain respectful awareness of communities other than its own; and it can tolerate, if not embrace, the felt tensions between inevitable choices.

Yet even this form of faith has its limitations. The self-selected class or group that serves as the network of belonging for the tested adult confirms the adult's world, composed in a critical systemic mode, but confirms also the particular content. Thus, in this era of development, we may still remain tribal, keeping company with those like us (now more broadly defined). Hence, though one's new network of belonging may be much more diverse in some respects, its members may nevertheless hold similar political, religious, and philosophical views and values and share the loyalties of a particular economic class. Even the most cosmopolitan and liberal of mind often discover, upon close examination of their own network of belonging, that those who count are also of like mind.

Toward Greater Complexity and Inclusion

In his book *Beyond Our Tribal Gods,* Ronald Marstin was the first to forcefully elaborate the essential linkages between the development of faith and the capacity to move beyond provincial perceptions and narrowly tribal forms of community. He boldly affirmed that implicit in developmental theory is the perception that each succeeding stage, era, or form of consciousness *is* better in that each represents a capacity to account for more, to handle greater complexity, and thereby to provide the potential for greater inclusivity.[14] Marstin's boldness was not rooted in arrogant elitism but was rather a sober assessment of the competencies of mind and soul that social-environmental justice requires. In other words, if justice is a matter of who and what is included or excluded, then just as complex perspective taking is essential to adequate moral reasoning so too the character of one's composition of the whole of reality (one's faith) determines what one finds tolerable and intolerable.

Marstin understood that human beings develop "because we *need* to."[15] We recompose purpose, meaning, and faith when we encounter the other (other people, other knowledge, other experience) in such a way that "we are left with no other choice, short of blocking out what we can no longer block out with any degree of honesty."[16] When human development happens well, we embrace a new way of interpreting the world because it can account for things that the old way no longer could. We can acknowledge considerations previously ignored, take more facts into account, and extend hospitality to questions that earlier we could not entertain.

This developmental perspective celebrates the promise for human life inherent in a person's ongoing encounter with a world inhabited by other selves and other beings with their own needs, an encounter that requires incessant recomposing of what is true for the self in relationship to a world of others. As Marstin grasped, cognitive development surely requires relativizing the tribal gods—recognition of the limitations of one's provincial ultimacy and a subsequent recomposition of one's faith. He was, however, keenly aware that for many, leaving their tribal gods appears to lead only to adopting a new set of tribal gods. (This occurs, for example, whenever people settle into a self-selected class or group that offers an easy ecumenism, the leisure to experiment that shapes only a private truth—while those who suffer throughout the world remain unrecognized.)[17]

In other words, critical awareness that prompts movement to a self-selected class or group represents an adequate *structure* of knowing, but it may not necessarily represent an advance in the inclusiveness that fosters deeper reordering, which in turn leads to a greater measure of social or eco-justice. Those of critical but like mind may even represent diminished concern for others, if critical awareness leads only to forming a network of belonging marked by cynicism or a systemic view too narrowly drawn.

Open to the Other

Further transformation, however, may be prompted by a deepening receptivity to "otherness." If one continues to bump up against those who are significantly different, the inner-dependent self begins to discover in new depths how the most adequate intimations of truth emerge in dialogue with the other, both within and without. The fundamental yearning for a fitting belonging within the vast home we all share may finally yield a still more profound understanding and practice of inclusiveness, because it is truer. Ongoing meaning-making necessarily leads to challenging the system that protects some while neglecting others: "Issues of social [and environmental] justice are essentially about who is to be cared for and who neglected, who is to be included in our community of concern and who excluded, whose point of view is to be taken seriously and whose ignored. As faith grows, it challenges all the established [tribal, assumed, conventional, and even self-selected] answers to these questions."[18]

This challenge becomes embodied in a form of community that recognizes the other as "truly other," yet part of a complex and differentiated whole. This form of community appears in its strongest form in the post-midlife period. It is characterized by a longing for communion with those who are profoundly other than the self, not as a matter of mere political correctness, or ideology, or ethical commitment, but as a longing in the soul for an embodied faithfulness to the interdependence that we are.

The Value of Recognizing the Young Adult Era

By combining the three dimensions of development we have described—knowing, dependence, and community—we are able to portray the place and role of the young adult era in the development of a mature adult faith. This model suggests a series of transformations by which we may become fittingly at home in the universe, moving from Authority-bound forms of meaning-making anchored in conventional assumed community, through the wilderness of counterdependence and unqualified relativism, to a committed, inner-dependent mode of composing meaning. It challenges notions of adulthood that are cast in an Authority-bound form of faith by inviting attention to the possibility of further movement toward a still more mature faith—an engaged wisdom grounded in the conviction of interdependence, seeking communion with those who are profoundly other than the self.

This portrayal is, of course, but one way of telling a story that could be woven with other elements, other perspectives, and in other proportions—each conveying additional facets of human meaning-making. One of the most serious limitations of this model is the possible implication (and not infrequent charge) that the activity of faith is being represented as linear and fixed, rather than as the dynamic, multidimensional, creative process that it is in reality. A spiral model, for instance, might capture elements that this portrayal does not.

The critical feature this portrayal does reveal is a place of integrity in the journey toward mature adult faith that is distinctively characteristic of young adulthood. It brings into the foreground of our awareness a mode of meaning-making that existing theories and institutional structures still largely overlook. Accurate naming is an act of creation. Naming the power, vulnerability, and inherent ambivalence of young adult faith helps us recognize it when it arises in our midst. If we understand its articulate nature and special hunger for mentors and mentoring communities, we are better able to respond. There is much at stake—for young adults and for the life of the commons—in whether or not we do this well. Never before in the human life cycle (and never again) is there the same developmental readiness for asking big questions and forming worthy dreams. In every generation, the renewal of human life is dependent in significant measure upon the questions that are posed to us during this era in our meaning-making. The dreams those questions seed yield the promise of our shared future.

The alchemy by which powerful questions yield worthy dreams is the subject to which we now turn—the faithful imagination. Here we begin to shift from emphasis on the structure of young adult faith—its characteristic outlines—to the complementary issue of its content. What specific kinds of images find resonance in the young adult soul? How do the images around which worthy dreams coalesce come into being? The next chapter addresses the latter question by examining the dynamics of imagination. Then Chapter Eight, "The Gifts of a Mentoring Environment," suggests the kinds of images that effective mentoring communities may help cultivate into the stuff of worthy Dreams.

7

IMAGINATION

THE POWER OF ADULT FAITH

TWO YEARS out of college and talking with a friend, twenty-four-year-old Stacy reflects: "I believe that the universe is organized and interconnected. For me, it's not a question of God as a single entity running the whole show. I have a big problem with the personification of God. God is not human—and more importantly not male. The word 'God' seems to imply that Universal Presence has an ego, and I have a problematic relationship with that idea. I prefer 'The Force' or something that is egoless. I believe there is a plan or pattern, and the daily struggle for myself, and for people in general, is to figure out one's place in that plan. I don't know who it is or how it works, but people call that [conviction of a plan] 'God.'"

This young adult is making meaning and doing the hard work of theology: exploring, understanding, and naming self, world, and "God." Every person who is a young adult in the development of faith must begin to do this work, sorting out reality on the largest canvas he or she can conceive. It is an ongoing act of imagination—the highest power of the knowing mind. How young adults imagine and reimagine matters of ultimate significance as they move into the future takes on additional layers of meaning in a time of profound cultural transition, because our shared imagination of life determines (economically, politically, religiously) the ways in which we will—or will not—be able to dwell and flourish in the decades ahead.

Imagination: Power in Three Dimensions

There are three dimensions of the activity of imagination that are essential to understanding the formation of meaning and faith. First, imagination is a *process*. It is the power by which we move from faith to faith.

The transformations of the forms of faith that we have described (such as the movement from assumed Authority-bound faith to the emergence of an inner-dependent, probing commitment) occur by means of the trans-formative *process* of imagination.

Second, an act of imagination is an act of naming. By employing images, we name self and world and conceive the ideal, the worthy, the good—as well as all that is toxic and destructive. Images are the *content* that the underlying structures of thought hold. Images lend their form to name and hold our experience; thus they participate in giving form to faith. As Stacy recognizes, it makes a difference, for example, whether we name ultimate reality Father, or Mother, or Nothingness, or The Way, or a unified field, or The Force, or the Holy One, or the Abyss. It makes a difference whether one feels the universe is loving, indifferent, hostile, or however the reader might name it.

Third, by the power of imagination humans participate in the ongoing *creation* of life itself, for better and for worse birthing new realities into being. We create forms of political community and economic life, produce communication technologies, design new architectural expressions, develop religious ritual, envision medications, compose music, discern the-ories of the origins of the universe, and invent ways of playing and ways of making war. It is by means of the imagination that we entertain the great questions of our time and craft the dreams we live by.

Threshold Existence

As human beings, we find ourselves again and again on the thresholds of time, space, and the unseen. Despite the massive evidence of the mundane, the ugly, and the fearful in our experience, at the core of the human spirit lies an amazingly resilient intuition that there is more for us to live into, embrace, and be embraced by. We sense that we participate in possibili-ties wider and deeper than we have yet realized: the creative work of our own lives, a more profound ordering of justice, richer loving of life in its manifold forms. Time, the world as it is, and the world of space and sense awaken and beckon our longing for profound participation in a coherent and holy universe.

As we have begun to see, young adulthood is a critical period for becoming more conscious of this "threshold existence"[1]—awareness that we do not dwell in static assumptions but live always on the verge, on the borderland of something more. With abstract, hypothetical thought well established, and an inner-dependent sense of authority taking form, the young adult is ripe for developing an informed passion for the ideal. This is, then, the time for initiation into the powers of imagination and for learning to "self-superintend"[2] this power and its consequences.

Imagination: A Shaping and Composing Activity

At least since Immanuel Kant,[3] we have been aware that all of our knowing is a composing activity. The human mind does not receive the world as it is in itself. Rather, we act upon the world to compose reality (or better, we interact with it in a mutual composing). As Suzanne Langer expressed so well, the human mind is "not merely a great transmitter, a super switchboard [or computer]; it is better likened to a great transformer. The current of experience that passes through it undergoes a change in character, . . . [as] it is sucked into [a particular] stream of symbols which constitutes a human mind."[4]

Following on Kant, Samuel Taylor Coleridge also identified imagination as the composing activity of the mind, but he extended its significance. Coleridge was intrigued with the German word for imagination, *Einbildungskraft. Kraft* denotes power; *bildung,* shaping; and *ein,* one. Imagination: the power of shaping into one.[5] Coleridge made visible the indivisible bond between imagination and faith: understanding that faith is the place of experience and the imagination. Faith by means of the imagination is a shaping, unifying activity integral to being human and to discerning the character of "eternal truth" (ultimate reality).[6]

Imagination Versus Fantasy

In Western culture, imagination is usually equated with fantasy. Imagination and fantasy, however, are not the same thing. Imagination must be distinguished from mere fancy, fantasy, or the fanciful. *Fanciful* in its common usage connotes "the unreal." Indeed, Coleridge identified fancy as having a function quite other than the act of composing reality. Fancy, he explained, takes the images already in the memory and arranges and rearranges them associatively or aggregatively.[7] Fancy, for example, can associate talking and mice, composing a Mickey Mouse to reign over Fantasyland. This is not to say that fancy is necessarily trivial. Free association of fancy can play a significant role in exploring possibility in the quest for adequate truth, as demonstrated in psychoanalytic method. Fancy alone, however, cannot finally compose truth. By contrast, the task of the imagination, and particularly of the religious imagination, is *to compose the real.*[8]

Imagination: The Highest Power of the Knowing Mind

Coleridge described imagination as the highest power of Reason, which includes all of the powers of the mind (sense, perception, understanding, and so on). Coleridge's sense of Reason corresponds to Kant's "practical reason." Thus Reason can apprehend transcendent, moral truth. "Above all Reason is the integral *spirit* of the regenerated person. Reason constitutes the human relationship to the divine, . . . one only, yet manifold, overseeing all, and going through all understanding. . . ."[9] The power within Reason that can transcend the contradictions of understanding is imagination.

Thus for Coleridge, Reason constitutes the human relationship to the divine; it is the highest and most complete power of the mind, and its completing, unifying, transcending activity is wrought by means of the imagination. We reason by means of the imagination.[10] Since Reason is the regenerate Spirit in the human, imagination is the activity of Spirit—"the breath of the power of God." Reason is, if you will, the "animating essence." Thus for Coleridge, imagination—the power of shaping into one—is the power by which faith is composed.

In the same vein, contemporary philosophers Owen Barfield and David Abram compellingly argue that the human transformation of breath into speech participates in this ancient, immediate, ongoing creation of life.[11] The human participates in the activity of Spirit that in the biblical story of creation "hovered over the face of the waters" at the dawn of creation.

As we are keenly aware, however, the human imagination works for both good and ill. Thus a crucial insight for our purposes is the Enlightenment and postmodern insistence that if human beings are to awaken to the fulfillment of their own humanity, they must become aware of and responsible for the powers of imagination. The human being is most mature and true to his or her own nature when the powers of imagination are fully awake, alive to the presence of Spirit—the deep motion of the universe—and to the power of those who participate in this motion of life to create (and to distort) self and world.

We turn, therefore, to an exploration of the process of imagination, a process that those who mentor young adults join in powerful ways.

Imagination: Essentially Vital

Coleridge's most focused statement describing imagination is a brief, packed definition in his *Biographia Literaria*:

> The IMAGINATION then, I consider either as primary, or secondary. The primary IMAGINATION I hold to be the living Power and prime Agent of all human Perception, and as a repetition in the finite mind of the eternal act of creation in the infinite I AM. The secondary Imagination I consider as an echo of the former, coexisting with the conscious will, yet still as identical with the primary in the *kind* of its agency, and differing only in *degree,* and in the *mode* of its operation. It dissolves, diffuses, dissipates, in order to re-create; or where this process is rendered impossible, yet still at all events it struggles to idealize and to unify. It is essentially *vital.* . . .[12]

When Coleridge describes imagination as the primary power shaping all perception, this does not imply that people simply imagine the world into being, as though the world does not exist and the human imagination merely conjures it up. Rather, we compose that which we find.[13] The imagination thus orients perception (one notices and chooses certain details over countless others) and informs how one makes sense of discrete elements, forming a distinctive pattern. In other words, the imagination works as a filter and then a lens. It is in these ways that our perceptions are created by means of the imagination.

Moreover, although this process of imagination goes on without our conscious awareness, it can, to some degree, become conscious. We can reflect on our own experience of coming to know, and we can observe the process of imagination as it "dissolves to recreate" and "struggles to unify." We can feel that it is essentially alive and dynamic. In moments, we glimpse how the motion of creation moves in and through us—our imagination participating in the infinite "I AM"—the activity of Spirit in the ongoing life of creation.

A Paradigm

Coleridge was a powerful thinker, but not a systematic one. Nowhere did he lay out a comprehensive statement of his understanding of the imagination. Instead, he tucked his thoughts here and there into notebooks, elaborated upon them in poetry, and wove them into other writings as fleeting flashes of insight. We are assisted, therefore, by others whose reflections on imagination serve to order the thought of Coleridge.

The work of James Loder—an educator, clinical psychologist, and theologian—is useful. He describes a grammar of transformation that serves as a paradigm for how the process of imagination works. Loder identifies five critical elements in the process of imagination as they bear on human development. It is helpful to think of them as five "moments" within the act of imagination:

1. Conscious conflict (held in rapport)
2. Pause (or interlude for scanning)
3. Image (or insight)
4. Repatterning and release of energy
5. Interpretation or testimony (proving out)[14]

It is by moving through the ebb and flow of these five moments that we come to new horizons of insight, understanding, knowledge, and faith. Note, however, that this sequence of moments as they appear here does not presume that the process always begins with conscious conflict. It may begin, for example, with an image or insight. Regardless of where the process is entered, however, it drives toward completion.

Conscious Conflict

Whether or not we hold a formal theory of change and growth, we know from our own experience that new life, insight, and transformation often arise out of circumstances that may be, initially at least, somewhat uncomfortable. Or sometimes the conflict arises from an attraction, perhaps to beauty, awe, love, or wonder. In any case, the moment of conscious conflict occurs when something doesn't seem to fit and we are set at odds with our usual perceptions of things. Conflict may be present in an unconscious or preconscious sense, but it does not become available for recomposing meaning and for the transformation of faith until it becomes conscious.

Conscious conflict may foster doubt. Doubt is often viewed as a threat to faith. But viewed as a manifestation of conscious conflict, we may see it in quite a different light—doubt has power to serve the development of faith. Doubt may emerge in the form of increasing curiosity, a devastating shattering of assumptions, vague restlessness, intense weariness with things as they are, a body of broken expectations, interpersonal conflict, or the discovery of intellectual dissonance. In this moment, equilibrium is thrown off balance. From time to time, individuals (and sometimes whole communities and societies) experience such disequilibrium.

Conscious conflict spawns questions. The development of young adult faith is often precipitated by either the questions that arise from one's own life experience or those that are posed to the young adult by others. Young adult meaning making and faith is steeped in questions. Questions appear in many ways and forms; often they come unbidden and inconvenient, sometimes attracting and stimulating. Within the moment of disequilibrium that they create lies a threefold task. First, the conflict and the questions it awakens must be allowed, felt, and made fully conscious. Then it must be clarified: what is really amiss? Third, the conflict must be tolerated with openness to a solution—no matter how remote it seems. That is, the conflict must neither be glossed over nor otherwise suppressed, and it must be held in a sense of hope.

The conflict must also be wrestled with. The moment of conflict cannot serve the process of transformation so long as there is only a contradiction of vague generalities. One must enter into the particulars of the puzzlement, tugging unruly thoughts and feelings into view. The elements of the conflict need to be put at right distance—"putting the phenomenon, so to speak, out of gear with our practical, actual self" and thereby looking at it in a new way.[15]

This moment of conscious conflict requires rigorous and disciplined care for thought, and it may be exhilarating. It can be a feature of the vitalizing, intensifying nature of imagination, for in the moment of conscious conflict "everything comes alive when contradictions accumulate."[16] On the other hand, facing a new complexity and the specter of a new truth may sometimes also require a measure of courage.

PERILS. Thus the perils of this moment of conscious conflict are two: overdistancing and overwhelming anxiety. Overdistancing—separating oneself too far from the task—breaks the connection with one's own field of receptivity, with affective grounding, and with Spirit. It breaks the felt tension of conscious conflict by dividing the conflicted self from the rest of the self, at the cost of a broken spirit and the emptying out of all that is vital. The essence of the self becomes disengaged and unaffected.

One young woman, for example, described how in high school she "was not afraid to love. Then in college there was getting my heart broken and deciding never to be that hurt again. This was a conscious decision to put in check anyone ever seeming to get power over me. It was an act of self-preservation." She coped by overdistancing herself from the conflict arising from new experience.

If the conflict is allowed to nourish development of meaning and faith, it is experienced to varying degrees as a baffling struggle with irreconcilable factors. Questions of faith ("Who and what can I trust and depend upon? Who and what matters?") are rarely small—or if they begin so, they tend to balloon and appear increasingly irresolvable. Whatever the factors may be, they generally represent a tension between established meaning—deeply rooted in mind and heart—and new experience, which appears to be in conflict with established meaning. Echoes of the yearnings described earlier are embedded in this tension: longing for both preservation and transformation, continuity and new life, familiar comfort and truth. This is, therefore, typically the moment of trying to figure out and to name what's wrong, while at the same time feeling some resistance to finding out. The young adult is particularly vulnerable to escaping the conflict either in false security ("I'll never get that hurt again") or in facing the polarity of the conflict in its starkness ("Loving is wonderful—but I'll get hurt"). Having had little experience of hope in the face of radical uncertainty (whether personal or professional), the young adult may assume the conflict is ultimate—a recipe for armoring, despair, and depression.

Overdistancing occurs also when intellectual engagement with significant issues becomes mere academic swordplay, alienating the student from learning. Overdistancing is manifest when managerial policy loses touch with the realities of employees' lives, and when the promise of domestic life disintegrates into domestic violence. This same dynamic feeds the erosion of political passion, turning it into the mere exercise of power.

We separate to distinguish, never to divide. It was Coleridge's great conviction that this moment of conscious conflict must not lead to ultimate separation. To distinguish is to clarify. To divide is to destroy the underlying and ultimate unity. Thus thought distinguishes but is essentially connective.[17]

Hence, rather than splitting the soul apart, the moment of conscious conflict that serves to recompose meaning in more adequate forms invites enlarging clarification, encourages enlivening restlessness, and suggests new possibility. At the same time, it is also the location of much of the suffering dimension of faith, and the temptation to avoid this moment is understandable.

"A CONTEXT OF RAPPORT." For this reason, Loder insists that the moment of conscious conflict must be held in a "context of rapport" if one is not to fall into excessive distancing, overwhelming anxiety, sheer avoidance.[18] When faith itself is being reordered, when meaning at the level of ultimacy is disordered and under review, a community of rapport is especially crucial.

If disequilibrium is to be tolerated and sustained in the hope of a solution that can be embraced with integrity, there must be a sustaining sociality: for instance, a friendship, or a mentoring relationship. The most significant conflicts are best held through participation in a community that can include, sustain, and even encourage constructive conflict—intellectual, emotional, spiritual. Communities that remain resilient in the face of both doubt and wonder can profoundly serve the processes of imagination and the development of faith. These communities embody an informed hope, and young adults appropriately require them.

We can hear the young adult's conscious awareness of this need in an account by Scott Russell Sanders in *Hunting for Hope: A Father's Journeys*. Trying to break his son's sullen silence following a quarrel, as they bounced along a rutted road on what was supposed to be a father-and-son hiking trip, Scott demanded of his son:

"So what are my hang-ups? . . . How do I ruin everything?"

"You don't want to know," he said.

"I want to know. . . ."

"You wouldn't understand," he said.

"Try me."

He cut a look at me, shrugged, then stared back through the windshield. "You're just so out of touch."

"With what?"

"With my whole world. You hate everything that's fun. You hate television and movies and video games. You hate my music."

"I like some of your music. I just don't like it loud."

"You hate advertising," he said quickly, rolling now. "You hate billboards and lotteries and developers and logging companies and big corporations. You hate snowmobiles and jet skis. You hate malls and fashions and cars."

"You're still on my case because I won't buy a Jeep?" I said, harking back to another old argument.

"Forget Jeeps. You look at any car and all you think is pollution, traffic, roadside crap. You say fast-food's poisoning our bodies and TV's poisoning our minds. You think the Internet is just another scam for selling stuff. You think business is a conspiracy to rape the earth."

"None of that bothers you?"

"Of course it does. But that's the *world*. That's where we've got to live. It's not going to go away just because you don't approve. What's the good of spitting on it?"

"I don't spit on it. I grieve over it."

He was still for a moment, then resumed quietly. "What's the good of grieving if you can't change anything?"

"Who says you can't change anything?"

"*You* do. Maybe not with your mouth, but with your eyes. . . . Your view of things is totally dark. It bums me out. You make me feel the planet's dying and people are to blame and nothing can be done about it. There's no room for hope. Maybe you can get by without hope, but I can't. I've got a lot of living still to do. I have to believe there's a way we can get out of this mess. Otherwise what's the point? Why study, why work—why do anything if it's all going to hell?"[19]

What this son is aching for is a context of rapport, some form of community that can share his despair and at the same time buoy his hope. This motion at the heart of life is the essence of hope and can carry us toward a more adequate truth if it is sustained in a network of belonging that can face wonder, uncertainty, anxiety, and grief in the bonds of a shared promise of life. Such holding environments honor the inner momentum that arises from conscious conflict and drives toward resolution. Momentum of this kind can be ignored, thwarted, or submerged only at the great cost of betraying and diminishing the potential self and consequently impoverishing the human community.

Pause

Once the nature of the conflict has been clarified, it is no longer fruitful to try to keep sorting it out or otherwise work at it. Rather, it is time for the second moment in the recomposing process of imagination, the moment of *pause* or incubation, an "interlude for scanning."[20] One puts the conflict out of consciousness, but not out of mind. This moment is one not of escape, but of relaxed attention. In the moment of pause the conscious mind remains passive, or better, permissive. Here, the mind is asleep, but "the soul keeps watch with no tension, calmed and active."[21] Coleridge described this moment of intellection with the images of the waterbug and the snake—images incorporating pause as a factor of locomotion.[22]

Coleridge also described consciousness as "connected with master-currents below the surface."[23] In the moment of pause, these master currents are at work. The activity beneath the calm surface may be likened to scanning for integrative patterns—some of which may already be present, others of which have yet to be composed from emerging experience.

Humankind has formalized modes of giving itself over to the deep master currents of the soul. The essential and powerful nature of pause is embodied in all contemplative traditions. One finds it, for example, in the great tradition of Buddhist contemplation practices and the practice of

Quaker silence. Contemplative pause is integral to the intellectual life, to the formation of trustworthy meaning, and to the life of faith. Yet the contemplative moment is under siege in contemporary society, where life is shaped by the unexamined demands of an economy running on digital and brittle time. The deep need of the spirit for pause relentlessly makes its claim, nevertheless, sometimes in mundane forms. We discover ourselves lingering, even when we feel we should be speeding on our way. Something shifts in us, even as we are waiting for the bathtub to fill, or for the line we are standing in to wind its way to the ticket booth up ahead. "Let me put it on the back burner for a while," we say, or "I'll sleep on it."

Recounting the experience of Barbara McClintock, a pioneering genetic biologist and a Nobel prize recipient, Evelyn Fox Keller describes the experience of pause in the intellectual life:

> By her own account, her confidence had begun to fail. . . . "I was really quite petrified that maybe I was taking on more than I could really do." She went, set up the microscope, and proceeded to work, but after about three days, found she wasn't getting anywhere. "I got very discouraged—something was quite seriously wrong. I wasn't seeing things, I wasn't integrating, I wasn't getting things right at all. I was lost." Realizing she had to "do something" with herself, she set out for a walk.
>
> A long winding driveway on the Stanford campus is framed by two rows of giant eucalyptus trees. Beneath these trees, she found a bench where she could sit and think. She sat for half an hour. "Suddenly I jumped up, I couldn't wait to get back to the laboratory. I knew I was going to solve it—everything was going to be all right."
>
> She doesn't know quite what she did as she sat under those trees. She remembers she "let the tears roll a little," but mainly, "I must have done this very intense, subconscious thinking. And suddenly I knew everything was going to be just fine." It was. In five days, she had everything solved. . . .
>
> Her principal success lay in being able to pick out the chromosomes clearly enough to track them through the entire meiotic cycle. . . . Seven days after coming out from under the eucalyptus trees, she gave a seminar on the meiotic cycle of *Neurospora*. In addition to the five days of actual work, many years of experience went into those observations. But above all, she felt it was "what happened under the eucalyptus trees" that was crucial. She had brought about a change in

herself that enabled her to see more clearly, "reorienting" herself in such a way that she could immediately "integrate" what she saw.

That experience taught her an important lesson. "The point is that when these things happen—when you get desperate about something and you have to solve it. . . . You find out what's wrong, why you are failing—but you don't ask yourself that. I don't know what I asked myself; all I knew was that I had to go out under those eucalyptus tress and solve what was causing me to fail."[24]

This moment of pause may require only a few seconds, or many years. But if young adults are going to learn to self-superintend the power of imagination, they need to be initiated into the power and practice of pause—particularly since our present society seems to offer such a toxic combination of demands and distractions. Recognizing this, when a new foundation was recently created to support young adults as they seek to test their commitments by working among the poor in inner cities, in emerging nations, or on behalf of the environment, they gave to those they had selected for financial assistance an additional gift: a book about the importance of honoring "Sabbath time" in their lives.[25] They were recognizing that a good mentoring environment in today's world initiates young adults into ways of life that encourage them to build pause into the emerging patterns of their adult lives.[26]

The gift of pause in the process of imagination and the reformation of faith is a unifying image or insight, a gift that, no matter how intense the struggle that precedes it, always "takes awareness by surprise."[27]

Image (or Insight)

The moment of pause has completed its work once it gives rise to an image or insight that simplifies and unifies all that seems to be irreconcilably disparate and complex. The image recasts the conflict into a single unified whole, thereby repatterning it into a coherent form. This is the moment of insight, of "Ah-ha!" Seemingly unrelated frames of reference converge to create a wholly new outlook, a new take on reality.

The image that works creatively simplifies and unifies the disarray of the conflict, shaping it into one. The image is in itself simply an object or act of the sensible world. In the service of the imagination, it becomes an "outward form that carries an inward sense."[28] That is, when we wish to express a thought, emotion, or intuition that cannot be simply pointed to or physically demonstrated, we must use objects and acts of the sensible world as mediators. To convey our meaning, we point to an object or act of the sensible world, not as a one-to-one correspondence but as metaphor. The image then loses its own gross material quality, so to speak, and lends its form as a vehicle to convey inner life or spirit.

For instance, the word *sincerity* is rooted in "*sine,* without, and *cera,* wax; the practice of the Roman potters was to rub wax into the flaws of their unsound vessels when they sent them to market. A sincere (without-wax) vessel was the same as a sound vessel, one that had no . . . flaw."[29] To take another example, the word *spirit* in many cultures is rooted in words such as "breath" or "wind" or "air in motion," suggesting a power that moves unseen.

Thus, as Bushnell saw, "the soul that is struggling to utter itself, flies to whatever signs and instruments it can find in the visible world, calling them in to act as interpreters, naming them at the same time, to stand, ever after, as interpreters in sound, when they are themselves out of sight."[30] Objects and acts of the sensible world serve as forms for thought. "Thinking . . . is the handling of thoughts by their forms."[31]

IMAGE AS SYMBOL. Whether as mathematicians, physicists, sociologists, philosophers, biologists, theologians, or historians, human beings give form to their meaning-making with images. If the image serves as a key to a whole pattern of relationships, the image becomes a symbol. Meaning is anchored and expressed by symbols. Because the task of faith is to shape into one the whole force field of life, whenever an image functions to give form to meaning at the level of faith, it necessarily engages a degree of complexity held only by symbol. Its form may be a concept (God created the universe), an event (Passover), a person (Muhammad), things (bread and wine), or a gesture (kneeling). The function of the symbol is to grasp and shape into one a fitting conviction of reality.[32]

Langer asserts that the distinctive activity of the human being is this act of symbolization. She writes: "I believe there is a primary need in human beings which other creatures probably do not have, and which accentuates all . . . apparently unzoological aims, . . . wistful fancies, . . . consciousness of value, . . . utterly impractical enthusiasms, and . . . awareness of a 'Beyond' filled with holiness. . . . This basic need, which certainly is obvious in any person, is the need of *symbolization.*"[33]

For example, every nonutilitarian act of humankind—including ritual, art, laughter, weeping, love talk, superstition, dreaming, and some aspects of scientific genius—is the transformation of experiential data into symbolic forms. Such symbolic transformation has no purpose in the sensible world apart from the human need for meaning, which transcends, per-meates, and shapes into one the whole of being. Symbols serve as the architecture of our thoughts and affections.[34]

Listen to a young athlete, writing an essay for a college application, reveal how "an act of the sensible world"—in this case, running—serves as a symbol, a key to a whole pattern of meaning, anchoring her sense of being at home in the universe:

> The cold crisp air strains our lungs as we surge forward into the wan-ing November afternoon. Today was made for running: the sky is dull blue and the autumn leaves make a satisfying crunch under our well-worn Nike tennis shoes. Cross-country has ended for the year and yet we still gather in twos and threes to enjoy the camaraderie of a late afternoon run behind the high school. For me these runs are no longer about training. For now, each run is a sort of reconciliation, a time when I can come to terms with the thought of leaving this place and these people who have shaped me into the person that I am today. As my body falls into the reassuring rhythm of speed next to my sister, Megan, my mind is free to wander. Here, on the trails I know so well, it is hardly necessary for me to look at the ground. Each turn is antic-ipated, each dip as natural to me as cracks in the sidewalk are to city-dwellers. It was here that I first started running and it is on these trails that I still feel the most at home.
>
> Running always seems to intensify the connection that I feel to my Island dwelling place and today is no exception. Here, surrounded by fir trees and wild huckleberries, time warps; I no longer need to worry about work schedules, term papers, or scholarship applications. For a brief moment each day I am free to merely exist. Each breath is invig-orating, each step healing. Even the musty smell of the forest comforts me. It promises the continual cycle of the seasons and stability in my ever-evolving existence. On these trails I can believe in myself like nowhere else in the world. Here, any dream seems within my reach and there is a solution to every problem. I know that eventually these trails will be nothing more than a haunt of my youth, but today they are everything to me. Today these trails are my home.
>
> As we crest the last hill of today's loop, Megan and I are running completely in synch. Step for step we glide through this evergreen par-adise, elevated beyond the petty jealousy of sisterhood to a place of total equality. Here, in the pristine silence of the forest, we are both a part of each other and a part of nature. All barriers are broken and our conversation flows at the same easy pace at which we are running.

We speak of life and the world, of the inconsequential details of daily life. Nothing is too grand a topic for this place, nothing too slight. The words drip off our tongues like juice off popsicle sticks in the summer. Our relationship as sisters is secure.

It is at moments like this that I know I am truly blessed. I won't always be able to run these trails while I discuss life with my sister and let the cool breeze play with my dreams, yet the essence of this place will remain with me always. In every corner of the world I will be able to believe in dreams and solve impossible problems by merely letting my mind wander while my feet find the familiar rhythm of speed. And I know that no matter how far I stray from the waters surrounding Whidbey Island, I will always be able to come home with no more than a pair of Nike tennis shoes, a dirt trail, and a healthy batch of nostalgia.[35]

IMAGE AS REVELATION. We are now prepared to recognize that images function religiously when they serve as symbols orienting us to the whole of life. Religion, at its best, provides a dynamic distillation of images (symbols, stories, smells, sounds, songs, and gestures—what Tom Beaudoin describes functioning in many young adult lives as "sacramentals"[36]) powerful enough to shape into one the chaos of existence—powerful enough to name a community's conviction of the character of the whole of reality that its members experience as both ultimate and intimate. The religions of the world survive only when countless people are able to confirm, "Yes, life is like that."

The moment of image and insight in the process of imagination is, in religious experience, the moment of revelation. Revelation is that part of the inner experience of a people that "illuminates the rest of it."[37] Revelation is the event that offers an integrative, unifying image of meaning. H. Richard Niebuhr wrote:

> By revelation in our history . . . we mean that special occasion which provides us with an image by means of which all the occasions of personal and common life become intelligible. What concerns us at this point is not the fact that the revelatory moment shines by its own light and is intelligible in itself but rather that it illuminates other events and enables us to understand them. Whatever else revelation means it does mean an event in our history which brings rationality and wholeness into the confused joys and sorrows of personal existence and allows us to discern order in the brawl of communal histories.[38]

Niebuhr likens such revelatory images to a luminous sentence in a difficult book, "from which we can go forward and backward and so attain some understanding of the whole."[39] The new image or insight enables us to see the whole of life in ways that previously eluded us. Occasions of just such revelatory insight are the motivating purpose of all truly liberal education, and it is this moment in which the purposes of education and the formation of faith are most inextricably linked. As Niebuhr expressed it, "When we speak of revelation we mean that moment when we are given a new faith."[40] This is what Whitehead understood when he wrote that the essence of all true education is religious.[41] The formation of young adult faith is nourished by abundant revelatory moments.

STRENGTHS AND LIMITS OF IMAGES. Images can carry us into communion with the sublime, and they can also get us into trouble. Understanding the power of image in its use as metaphor and symbol leads us to the critical insight that every image functioning as a bearer of inner life and insight is at once true and untrue. Since the image only gives *form* to the truth it attempts to convey, it can only *represent* that truth; it cannot fully reproduce or embody it. Consequently, the image is simultaneously like and unlike the intuition, concept, or feeling it mediates. This is always the case, if for no other reason than that the image gives form to what is without form. Thus, there is inevitably some distortion in every image, and therefore in every expression of truth.

All images, as well as the words, concepts, symbols, stories, and rituals that derive from them, are merely forms we employ to handle reality. Insofar as they convey some essential aspect of truth, they are faithful to that truth. Their deception—their untruth—lies partly in their tendency, as earthen vessels in which truth is borne, to offer their mere pottery as being truth itself. If the earthen vessel is regarded as truth itself (rather than as a participant in conveying truth), we lapse into idolatry.

Such idolatry is deepened when we fail to recognize that any image employed to grasp, name, and give form to unseen reality is always peculiar to the individual or group that selects it. Every image, therefore, carries particular associations—social, political, and psychological. Thus the same image may bear quite another meaning—or no meaning—for another person, or for a different group. This is true even of those images that have become sacred.

This awareness of the strengths and limits of images, and of the words that spring from them, enabled Horace Bushnell (perhaps overstating the point) to assert that there are few creeds one could not affirm if one were to return to the standpoint of those who originally made the creed and were to receive it in its "most interior and real meaning." Conversely, he also notes that, given the fluctuations of language and its ongoing "peculiar" appropriation of images, over time "we cannot see the same truths in the same forms. It may even become necessary to change the forms to hold us in the same truths."[42]

If the image that appears to simplify and unify the earlier conflict emerges and creates a new window into reality, we move into the next moment in the process of imagination: repatterning and release of energy.

Repatterning and Release of Energy

A repatterning of reality is required in light of the new image or insight; new energy is released for this task by the relaxation of the earlier conflict. New energy is made available because the mind and heart have found an easier way to hold all the aspects of the conflict.[43]

In this moment, vast reaches of one's knowing and being may be reordered in light of the new insight, as there is a repatterning of the connections among things. From the point of the insight, there is a rippling effect that recomposes the former pattern into a new way of seeing the whole. Whether the insight is dramatic or subtle, reordering *any* particular repatterns the whole, in at least some measure. This moment in the imagination process requires its own time.

For Barbara McClintock, it took five days of intense work to lay out the new pattern of connections that arose from a single insight. For others, it may require a period that feels like ongoing reflection, a debriefing in which the new experience and insight is plumbed for its meaning. How does it fittingly connect with previous experience? How does it change one's understanding of self, world, truth? It requires us to turn back to see where we have been and to live into where we are now arriving. It may be understood in part as the process of composing a new home place for the intellect, for the soul. One young adult who had recently "found faith" said that "finding faith is not enough. The key is to find connections between faith and life. My period of revelations was a honeymoon period. Now it's figuring out how to make things work—period."

Educators sometimes describe this moment as "teaching for transference." This happens, for example, when one assists another in seeing that what is now known in one arena of life also pertains to another aspect of one's world. Making fitting connections deepens associations and enriches awareness, making new power available. The consequence is a feeling of enlargement and a new quality of openness to self and world.

Repatterning makes possible a "freshness of sensation" that Coleridge described as a "seeing with new eyes as on the morning of the first day of creation."[44]

This moment contributes to the vitalizing power of the imagination. The reflective process required for the work of repatterning keeps meaning-making pliant and spares us from brittle faith. New vision combined with the gift of new energy recomposes and exhilarates the soul and affectively grounds a sense of confidence, assurance, and new strength. Above all, there is a sense of having achieved a more adequate orientation to reality. Imagination, therefore, is the power of realization: to make real.[45]

Thus faith as the activity of realization is indeed something quite other than wishful thinking or mere assent to irrelevant dogma. But if the image that gives form to faith is to serve the composing of truth, no matter how compelling the image and the pattern it constellates may appear, before the act of imagination is complete it must be tested. The testing of the new "reality" is the next and final moment in the act of imagination.

Interpretation: Testimony and Confirmation

Transformation of our knowing and trusting is not complete until the new insight comes to voice and finds a place of confirmation within a wider public life.

TESTIMONY. We do not seem to fully grasp the new insight, and we are not entirely at ease with it, until we express it in our own terms. What was once inchoate now wants to be given form. We are drawn into an act of creation.

In this act, we become dependent upon a community of others for completing and anchoring our new composition of reality. As social beings, we seek assurance of a correspondence, coherence, and connection between the original conflict, the new image, and a concerned or interested public before the new insight can take up full residence within us. Sometimes we do this through verbal or written communication, but the new insight may also be demonstrated through scientific experiment and replication or artistic expression. Whatever the form of testimony may be, bringing our insight to voice in ways that relate our new knowing to a wider communal life is crucial to the formation of our inner confidence in what we have come to see.

What we are describing here is a way of understanding the deep motion of life, a process that is integral to knowing, development, creativity, transformation, and the spiritual life. As physicist Arthur Zajonc has stated it, "Knowledge is an event, not an object. . . . Once we appreciate knowing as personal epiphany, the way is opened up for a reconciliation between facts and values, between science and spirituality."[46]

STRONG AND PRECARIOUS. Examining this process of imagination by which we formulate our knowledge and our ultimate trust, we cannot help but recognize both how strong and powerful a process it is and at the same time how precarious. That so much depends on the search for fitting and right images and that our access to images is so conditioned by context should give us pause. Northrop Frye has said that the use of metaphor can seem "like crossing a deep gorge on a rope bridge: we may put all our trust in its ability to get us across, but there will be moments when we wish we hadn't."[47]

We most wish we hadn't when haunted by questions such as "How do I know I'm not just making all this up?" or "How do I know I'm not crazy?" Once we have developed the capacity for critical thought, we know that sometimes even the most attracting images and insights nevertheless seriously distort and lead away from truth.

Images may be held, for example, with deep feeling, but depth is no guarantor of truth. Loder has observed the "seduction of the depths." The depths are as "capable of error and distortion, seduction, and corruption as are the routinized patterns of behavior that others use to keep them from ever exploring matters of depth. The creative process surely *has* a depth dimension but is not validated thereby."[48]

If we compose our knowing and are formed in faith by means of the imagination, how do we account for, and how are we saved from, what H. Richard Niebuhr describes as the "evil imaginations of the heart"?[49] Is it not the case that though we have been following Coleridge's perception of imagination as the act of Reason—the divine in the human— nevertheless imagination persists in common usage as a "slippery term designating a power that penetrates the inner meaning of reality but also a power that creates substitutes for reality"?[50]

Indeed, Coleridge also recognized an evil imagination. He understood it to be the isolated imagination, divided from the unity of the "One Life" and therefore cut off from its Source.[51] Thus if the imagination of an individual, a small group, a community, or a nation becomes isolated, whether as a result of ignorance or arrogance, oppression or depression, that imagination becomes vulnerable to the distorting features of its own metaphors.

Communities of Confirmation and Contradiction

All images must, therefore, be brought to the test of "repeated, critical, and common experience."[52] The only way of saving us from the distortions of our own subjectivity is within a community of others who are also seeking truth. Hence, formally or informally, we test our knowledge with the knowledge of others. The interpretive moment of testimony is essential, not simply as the completion of an inner process but also as participation in the forum of common experience that alone can confirm or refute the capacity of the image to grasp the real, since "which 'gods' [images of defining and unifying power] are dependable, which of them can be counted on day after day and which are idols—products of an erroneous imagination—cannot be known save through the experiences of . . . history."[53] This is to say that a community must serve as a community of *confirmation* and also, when necessary, as a community of *contradiction*. Emancipation from narrow faith and from distorting subjectivity may occur only in a community that distinguishes between evil images—those that separate, distort, and diminish selves and communities—and life-bearing, truthful, vital images.

We must not, however, too easily endorse the power of finite communities to serve the search for truth. It must be acknowledged that even a cursory review of the history of human communities, including those of religious faith, abounds with examples of abuse of the process in which spirits and images or symbols are discerned. Too often, inadequate images are greeted with acclaim, whereas the true prophet is rarely popular. Moreover, in today's world, so riddled with new media technologies dispensing vast streams of images into the everyday environment of all of us, every finite community of discernment is in some measure overwhelmed. The adequacy of communities of confirmation and contradiction must be assessed in the context of the long-term historical experience (past and future) of both particular communities and, increasingly, the whole earth community.

Imagination and the Moral Life

Having recognized that all images are finite, and now acknowledging that the process of imagination itself is fragile and vulnerable to distortion, how can we have confidence at all in any meaning, truth, or faith? Doesn't awareness of the imaginative process lead us into the cul-de-sac of unqualified relativism, a vulnerability increasingly apparent in the postmodern world?[54] Yet as H. Richard Niebuhr saw so clearly, "the heart must reason," and "the participating self cannot escape the necessity of looking for pattern and meaning in its life and relations. It cannot make a choice between reason and imagination but only between reasoning on the basis of adequate images and thinking with the aid of evil imaginations." Thus "anyone who affirms the irrationality of the moral and religious life simply abandons the effort to discipline this life, to find right images by means of which to understand oneself, one's sorrows and joys."[55]

The search for "right images" is a powerful way of thinking about the formation of young adult faith in a rapidly changing world. Today's young adults must swim in an unprecedented and vast sea of images (visual of course, but also aural, tactile, and kinesthetic) calculated to recruit their allegiance—and in many cases to numb their souls. One of the perils of an advertising-saturated society is that so many false images are offered in highly sophisticated ways to resolve questions of meaning, purpose, and significance.[56] There are too few networks of belonging in which young adults are encouraged to critically reflect on the primary images, symbols, and stories-ideologies-myths that shape their souls and their society. A strong, empathic, moral imagination—not just on behalf of the self but on behalf of the other as well—is increasingly critical to the practice of citizenship and the vocation of a faithful adulthood in a world marked by social diversity and the awareness of suffering on a global scale.

To Mend a World

Graduating as a master's student in religion, Mary Moschella gave a baccalaureate address, excerpts of which illustrate the process of imagination as the power of shaping into one—the underlying grammar of faith, a primary power of adult faith:

> Many of us might admit that we . . . were drawn to this place by the modest desire to learn to see everything clearly. Though it sounds presumptuous, we who have spent two or more years here, dissecting holy Scriptures, comparing world religions, constructing and deconstructing the concept of God, cannot pretend any lack of ambition. We did not come here to satisfy cool academic curiosities, but rather to learn how to see everything—the whole picture of life—clearly. We came to explore the very mysteries of God, to expand our view of the world, and to discern what it is that the universe demands of us.
>
> After being here for a while, we have discovered that the process of learning to see religiously is a difficult, if not overwhelming, endeavor.

For in delving into questions of ultimate meaning, we have learned how blurred is our vision, how tentative and partial our . . . insight. In this, we are like the blind man from Bethsaida, who even with a miracle, could only slowly and gradually learn how to see. . . .

Our studies and our common life have bombarded us with more . . . than we know how to manage. For our study . . . has caused us to examine our own faith and values: To decide what it is that we treasure . . . and what is essential to human be-ing.

Thus we have been involved in the process of naming our Gods. This process has demanded not only that we clarify issues of personal faith and belief, but also that we regard anew some of the global issues of human struggle. It is not that horrors such as world hunger have just recently come into being. But somehow before we hadn't quite seen (or faced) the magnitude of suffering involved, or the ethical challenges that such suffering present.

So in the process of naming the gods, we have been naming some demons too. We have seen and named the terrifying demons of militarism, racism, and sexism in our world. These appear to us as horrifying patches of darkness, frightening shadows that make us want to shut our eyes tightly and return to the comforts of our former blindness. . . .

Last summer I was in Israel, working on an archaeological dig. At the site of the ancient city of Dor, each day as I swung my pick into the age-old soil, I was inwardly chipping away at just these sorts of issues. I expended a good deal of energy cursing the facts of human suffering in the world, and trying to imagine some kind of hope of restoration.

Excavating at the level of the Iron Age can be rather tedious; only rarely did we turn up any precious small finds. Most of the time was spent staring at dirt walls and broken pottery shards. In my square, not even one whole vessel was uncovered all season—just so many broken pieces, scraps of ancient civilization. All of the brokenness appeared to me as an accurate metaphor for understanding the world. Broken and crushed, every piece of it; broken with small personal pains, as well as with overwhelmingly large human struggles. Yet as the summer went on, and I kept staring at the pottery, I slowly started to notice something more than just the brokenness. Some of the pieces of clay, however broken, were really quite beautiful.

Later in the summer, I found out about the business of pottery mending. This tedious work goes on year-round in a cathedral-like building not far from the tel. Here ancient vessels have been slowly and carefully reconstructed. I remember being completely amazed at seeing those huge restored jugs for the first time. How could anyone have possibly managed to piece together so many small nondescript chips of clay?

Seeing those restored vessels encouraged me to imagine perhaps that at least some of the world's brokenness could be overcome. I began to picture myself in a kind of vocation of mending, of repairing some of the world's brokenness.

To mend the world. To proclaim a radical vision of social transformation that would prevent future brokenness from occurring. These are the tasks that I perceived the world to be demanding of me.[57]

Robert Lifton has written that "human existence itself can be understood as a quest for vitalizing images."[58] In Moschella's account, we hear the power and process by which imagination grasps through an adequate enough image (broken shards) something of the truth of the world as it is. We also hear the power of imagination to envision possibility: a mended world, social transformation "that would prevent future brokenness from occurring." Finally, we hear the emergent self-aware reflection, the conscious, self-superintending imagination of the young adult.

Not simply to the study of religion but to every discipline, professional school, corporation, or other workplace, the young adult comes seeking initiation into the powers of the imagination and into vitalizing, fitting, and right images by which to name self, other, world, and "God." The young adult has a unique capacity to receive images that can form the dreams and fire the passions of a generation to heal and transform a world. It is the vocation of a culture—including every institution that shapes the formation of young adult faith—to inform and nurture the young adult imagination. By intention or default, the environments in which young adults dwell become communities of imagination, mentoring environments with the power to shape or misshape the promise of young adult faith. A positive mentoring environment is a gift to the young adult imagination.

THE GIFTS OF A
MENTORING ENVIRONMENT

MENTORING, IN ITS CLASSIC SENSE, is an intentional, mutually demanding, and meaningful relationship between two individuals, a young adult and an older, wiser figure who assists the younger person in learning the ways of life. In the Harvard Assessment Seminars, however, students reported that their most positive learning experiences were *not only* in one-on-one learning contexts, where, for example, an individual student might work with a professor in an office or laboratory setting. The students indicated that often their most valued learning occurred with a teacher and a *small group* of students.[1]

This is good news for faculty and other potential mentors, in an age when mentoring has reappeared as an important—and scarce—relationship. Many professionals, pressured by the growing demands of institutions increasingly shaped by economic stressors, understandably wilt when the call to be a mentor is added to a long list of musts. Thus, it is vital to recognize that a network of belonging that serves young adults as a *mentoring environment* may offer a powerful milieu and a critical set of gifts in the formation of meaning, purpose, and faith.

Mentors

Mentor is a venerable term, grounded in Homer's *Odyssey* and laden with expectations of a tradition of guiding wisdom. It has been popularly captured in the figures of Obi-Wan Kenobi and Yoda in George Lucas's *Star Wars* film trilogy. Interestingly, it is said that while George Lucas allows a good deal of exploitation of other characters for commercial purposes, there are special protections on Yoda. Apparently there is some recognition that a good deal is at stake in the little wizened figure of faithful wisdom—an anchoring center that has to hold even amid the feeding frenzy of global media economics.

Indeed, good mentors help to anchor the promise of the future. As young adults are beginning to think critically about self and world, mentors give them crucial forms of recognition, support, and challenge. There is more. Mentors care about your soul. Whatever the immediate challenge or subject matter, good mentors know that all knowledge has a moral dimension, and learning that matters is ultimately a spiritual, transforming activity, intimately linked with the whole of life.

Mentors convey inspiration for the long haul. They do not simply recruit people to serve their own agenda. Though true mentors are never perfect, they know that the young adult has a future beyond the imagination of the mentor, and they try to hold their own commitments and the promise of the young adult life in fruitful tension.

Mentors offer good company as young adults cross the threshold of critical thought into new questions and possibilities. They respect the competency of the young adult, and at the same time they are prepared to be present in ways that invite more learning and becoming. Mentors are willing to be part of the young adult's initiation into a practical and worthy adult imagination of self, other, world, and "God."

Overuse of the Term Mentor

Reaching for this much-needed moral dimension in all helping relationships, popular usage has begun to use the mentor figure to evoke a sense of genuinely caring and educative relationships across the entire life span (that is, with children, adolescents, and sometimes very mature adults), where other terms may apply more appropriately: parent, teacher, sponsor, role model, hero or heroine, counselor, coach, companion, supervisor, guide, colleague, or helpful friend. The term *mentor* is best reserved for a distinctive role in the story of human becoming.

Mentors are those who are appropriately depended upon for authoritative guidance at the time of the development of critical thought and the formation of an informed, adult, and committed faith. As we have seen, this may occur in the young person's twenties, but it may also occur a bit earlier or later—or never.[2]

Recognition

If we want to learn about the formation of a person's life, a helpful question to pose is "Who recognized you?" or "Who saw you?" As human beings, we all have a need to be "seen." This is important—in differing ways—at every place in the life span. One young woman in her early twenties was living away from home, still sketching her sense of her future. In a phone call home, she shared how wonderful it was to have a couple who had been family friends for many years declare, credibly and thoughtfully, that she was very smart and capable, and that she could be—and already was—worthy of respect in her chosen field. Although her parents responded that they already thought of her in the same way, she said, "But you're my parents, and of course you think of me that way."

Clearly, parents can play aspects of the mentoring role, but quite understandably the young adult seeks recognition in a wider world of adult roles and responsibilities. Important as a respected voice from *beyond* the parental sphere, the mentor recognizes in practical terms *the promise and the vulnerability* of the young adult life.

Support

One way in which mentoring recognition is practiced is in forms of support. Supportive mentors are well known in the world of adult work: in corporations, in the professions and the arts, and in other organizations and fields of practical skill. As a young adult is moving into the labyrinth of the corporation, through a combination of showing and telling mentors may assist the protégé in finding his or her way into the arenas of power and finally up the corporate ladder. This is not merely a matter of the protégé doing what he or she is told or merely copying the mentor's own pattern. The good mentor simply recognizes that the young adult is still dependent in substantial ways upon authority outside the self, while at the same time the mentor is a champion of the competence and potential the young life represents.

Thus the mentor extends support, in part by consistent recognition and affirmation of every manifestation of that potential. One young woman, reflecting on her experience of having a mentor in a business context, said simply, "I had to live up to being terrific!"[3] Mentors are supportive in a host of ways, including serving as an advocate, a guide to resources, a source of comfort, and sometimes a source of healing.

Mentors sometimes function unawares. A campus minister spoke movingly of a young woman in her second year of college who came from a city two thousand miles away. She had been abused and neglected by her family, but she had a good therapist who helped her make her way to college. There, on the therapist's advice, she sought out a campus minister, who in turn, referred her to a therapist nearby. The young woman had no other meaningful relationships in her life. Staying in regular contact with both the therapist and the campus minister, she took classes. She did well—especially demonstrating real intellectual talent in philosophy—yet every day, she was asking herself, "Do I want to live, or do I want to die?"

I will always remember the way the campus minister looked directly at me across the lunch table and quietly said, "The faculty in the philosophy department have no idea what a vital gift they are giving this young woman every time they tell her that she is doing excellent work and has great promise."

Challenge

Mentors dance an intricate two-step, because they practice the art of supporting and challenging more or less simultaneously. While giving the well-timed push into a new area of potential competence, the mentor may also provide essential counsel when a protégé is in well over his head. All the while, the mentor assures him that there is solid, challenging, and meaningful work to do—adult work that invites and tests the emerging strength of the young adult. The art of mentoring is located, in part, in assessing the readiness of the protégé to recognize and creatively respond to heretofore unseen opportunities, ideas, dangers, relationships, and solutions. Good mentors almost always practice a kind of tough love.

You may notice and may resist an implied hierarchy in the mentor-protégé relationship. But it must be remembered that mentors do not necessarily represent a hierarchical relationship as generally conceived. Sometimes the mentor is decidedly senior, but often mentors are peers with a bit more experience or insight in a particular domain; as suggested here, many mentors of whatever age or gender have the capacity to work shoulder to shoulder with the young adult. This capacity is often a distinguishing feature of the mentor's strength because it is so honoring of the gifts and promise of the young adult. Thus, although a mentor brings some larger realm of experience or talent to the relationship, great mentors nevertheless also learn from their protégés through a process of mutual challenge and discovery. Mentoring relationships are most alive when both the mentor and protégé are working on the edge of new knowing and possibility.

Inspiration

Above all, the mentor is conscious of the growing challenges that confront the young adult in the process of learning to practice critical thought in a complex world, and to stand outside or apart from things as they are on behalf of strengthening perception, understanding, and potential insight, opening into a wider horizon of possibility and faithfulness. In the midst of this sometimes rocky, sometimes exhilarating learning, the mentor serves as a steady, inspiring point of orientation, beckoning toward the possibility of meaningful commitment on the other side of the achievement of relativized and critical thought. To varying degrees and in differing forms, mentors worthy of the name embody and inspire the possibility of committed and meaningful adulthood. On the other side of the formation of critical awareness, a good mentor is an antidote to mere cynicism.

In Dialogue

Embedded, therefore, within the supporting, challenging, and inspiring role of the mentor, there is a subtext. The mentor becomes significant only if he or she "makes sense" in terms of the young adult's own experience. Although the protégé is still appropriately dependent upon the authority of the mentor, she discovers that her own voice is increasingly included in the arena of authority. The good mentor is recruited to (but not overwhelmed by) the young adult's dialogue between fear and trust, power and powerlessness, alienation and belonging, doubt and belief, as she becomes more at home in a larger world.

The task at hand is to search for ways to strengthen and confirm the still fragile young adult self and its integrity, while the young adult finds a place of participation, contribution, and significance in the world of adult work and relationships, freedoms and responsibilities. The dialogue between mentors and protégés is marked by mutual respect, and, as Buber saw, it is in the dialogue between an I and a Thou that reality is recomposed in more adequate terms.[4] At their best, mentors keep finding ways to call forth the kind of dialogue in which the protégé's experience and the distinctive voice it may birth can learn to speak with integrity and power in the force field of life. In a festschrift to his mentor, Gary Whited writes candidly about this hard learning:

> I remember many afternoons sitting with Henry [Bugbee] while he guided me through my study of Marcel's . . . *The Mystery of Being.* . . . We would begin with whatever end of a thread presented itself to us, and follow where it led, weaving in and out of war stories, fishing stories, reflections on other philosophers' writing, and often hearkening back to the *Bhagavad Gita* or *The Book of Tao,* from our earlier work together. As I look back on these conversations now, I see that I was being mentored. . . . I was being initiated into a style of philosophic reflection grounded in experience, in recollection, and in trust. . . .

I learned a hard lesson about trusting my own voice when . . . I went to graduate school in the East. I was drawn to the work of the pre-Socratics, Parmenides and Heraclitus in particular. The sense that all things are interconnected, often in ways invisible to us, but nonetheless always so, grew directly out of my prairie experience—and it is this sense that drew me to the central theme of unity in Parmenides' poem. The first draft of my dissertation was in design a dialogue between Parmenides' poem and a phenomenology of my early experience on the prairie. In the course of rewriting, however, I lost faith in the enterprise. Perhaps I was too self-conscious to use all that recollected material from my past, or perhaps I thought I needed to speak in a more acceptable "philosophical" voice. In any case, in the final draft, I dropped most of the recollections, which I believe Henry had liked very much in his reading of the first draft.

Shortly after Henry read the final version, I returned to the University of Montana to teach. I'll never forget that first meeting upon my return. Henry was standing in his home office holding my dissertation in his hand, the usual smoking pipe clasped between his teeth. In a pensive tone he asked simply, "What happened?"

At the time I do not think I took in the full import of Henry's short question. Over the years what he meant has slowly, and somewhat painfully, dawned on me. What Henry saw was that I had suppressed my own voice, and with it, my trust in the ground I stood on as a source for philosophic reflection.[5]

Mentors are like that: posing questions that go straight to the heart and the heart of the matter. Their power lies in the protégé's growing awareness that the mentor knows that each life has a distinctive contribution to make to our common life, and if this contribution is not made, a life is diminished and the commons is impoverished.

This does not mean that the mentor regards everything that comes from the protégé as golden. Rather, the mentor is allied with the potential of the young adult life and, as we see in Henry Bugbee, works to develop within the protégé the capacity for discerning what is true, worthy, and life-bearing.

Mentoring relationships do not always take the form of face-to-face relationships sustained over time. Sometimes mentors are quite mindful of their role; other times, they play a powerful role with little or no awareness that their life is being watched and "speaking volumes."[6] There are people who perform some elements of what mentors do, while failing altogether in other elements. There are "mentoring moments": brief yet powerful encounters that make a difference. Sometimes a mentor is a favorite author or historical figure, known only from afar. One young adult put it simply: "Books can be good mentors." Long ago, Coleridge wrote that the writings of George Fox, Jacob Behmen, and William Law "during my wanderings through the wilderness of doubt, . . . enabled me to skirt, without crossing, the sandy deserts of utter unbelief."[7]

Today we wonder whether and how digital technologies may serve the young adult searching for a mentor; there is a compelling logic that argues that if books can be good mentors, so can the Internet. It appears that digital technologies can indeed serve as a source of exploration and a vehicle for some aspects of a mentoring dialogue. But just as a book that is a good mentor offers to the imagination something far more than information alone, contemporary technologies serve the potential of the mentoring relationship only to the degree that they mediate the central gifts of mentoring, beginning with recognition, support, challenge, and inspiration. Because the functions of mentoring occur both through words or images and through grand and subtle gestures, as well as the elusive quality we call presence, the mentoring function appears to occur best when digital communication functions to augment rather than replace face-to-face encounter.

Mentors and Clay Feet

No matter what the mentor may offer in various forms of recognition, support, challenge, and inspiration, in the alchemy of mentoring the talents, smarts, skills, and best intuitions of the protégé combine with the mentor's wisdom to forge new realities that neither could create alone. Although initially either may seek out the other, the relationship comes about finally through mutual attraction toward similar aims. When the relationship works, the meaning and satisfactions that it yields are gifts to both the protégé and the mentor.

As important and laudable as the role of the mentor is, however, few mentors manage to get it right all the time. A mentor is in every case a finite human being, and the relationship can go awry. The false mentor may attract the engagement of young adults for any number of self-aggrandizing reasons.[8] Mentors are sometimes threatened by the growing competence of the protégé, or in other ways allow shadow factors the upper hand. Precisely because good mentors bring a quality of commitment and passion to the work, they are vulnerable to assimilating the protégé's vision and potential into their own vision rather than honoring the distinct gifts and callings of the protégé.

One woman, now a pediatrician working with infants born to mothers addicted to crack, revealed how the mentoring relationship may be costly to both: "We've maintained a close relationship even though I didn't follow the path that she [the mentor] would have liked. She would have liked to see me in research. She respects what I do, particularly now that I've had some successes. But when I first started out, it wasn't OK. I think she was very disappointed."

A form of mentoring that can dissipate some of these pitfalls while offering strategic formative power is the mentoring community.

Mentoring Communities

If a young adult is going to be initiated into a profession, organization, or corporation as it is presently defined and practiced, a mentor who guides the way is enough. But if one is going to be initiated into a profession, organization, or corporation and the societies they serve *as they could become,* then only a mentoring community will do.

Because we are social beings, if each new generation is to contribute to the ongoing creation and renewal of life and culture, young adults need more than to be challenged individually to realize their full potential. They need to know they will not be alone—or alone with "just my mentor." If they are going to have the courage to take the road less traveled because it represents a more worthy truth, then they must discover that in doing so they will encounter a new sociality: a trustworthy network of belonging. Ideas and possibilities take hold in the imagination of the young adult in the most profound ways when he or she is met by more than a mentor alone—by a mentoring community.

Mentoring communities include a mentor who functions in the terms just described, providing recognition, support, challenge, and inspiration. But the mentor may or may not be devoted to or sustain a dialogue with a single protégé alone. Rather, the mentor, or a team of mentors, create a mentoring environment: a context in which a new, more adequate imagination of life and work can be composed, anchored in a sense of *we.* Mary Jo Bona, Jane Rinehart, and Rose Mary Volbrecht have elegantly described the special benefits of *co-mentoring,* by which they mean the formation of a learning environment in which the leadership team members model mutual support and challenge among each other. This evokes comparable relationships among the students, creating a mentoring environment that is characterized by a heightened degree of trust and enhanced capacity for engaging and challenging everyone.[9]

In the study for *Common Fire*, it became apparent that although people in later adult life may appear to sustain significant commitments to the common good with little or no support, courageously going against the tide, in fact they carry within them a deep sense of *we*. This conviction is often forged in the young adult years in association with a group of others around inspiring ways of thinking and working in the world. Even if they have not necessarily maintained direct contact with the others who shared their experience of a young adult mentoring community, the confidence of participation in a commonwealth of aspiration and commitment is sustained.[10]

Mentoring communities are particularly essential to the formation of adult faith. Since young adulthood is a time of critically recomposing a sense of self and world and the nature of the ultimate-intimate reality that holds both, the young adult imagination is appropriately dependent upon a network of belonging that can confirm a worthy, "owned" faith. When necessary, the same community must contradict the composing of a weaker faith, one unable to stand up to the challenges of the diverse and morally complex world in which today's young adults will live out their adulthood.[11]

Features of a Mentoring Environment

Mentoring communities play an essential role in the formation of a faith that can ground ongoing meaning and purpose throughout adulthood. They do so by incorporating certain features that distinctively honor and animate the potential of young adult lives and nourish the renewal of culture for the common good. These include a network of belonging, big-enough questions, encounters with otherness, important habits of mind, worthy dreams, access to key images, concepts (content), and practices that mediate these gifts of a mentoring community.

A Network of Belonging

A mentoring community is a network of belonging that constitutes a spacious home for the potential and vulnerability of the young adult imagination in practical, tangible terms. It offers a sociality that works (at least well enough) physically, emotionally, intellectually, and spiritually as the young adult becomes more fully at home in the universe. A mentoring network of belonging may be sustained for only a relatively brief but influential period of time, or it may extend for many years.

While the young adult is reimagining self and world on the other side of critical thought, a trustworthy network of belonging serves as the community of confirmation and contradiction that is so essential to the practice of a faithful imagination. Jonathan, a young adult, participates in an annual summer program for college students that intentionally builds an interfaith mentoring community to serve the formation of faith and commitment to the common good. Upon his return to the program the second summer, he described this aspect of his experience:

> Over this past year, any time I had a problem or something that I didn't think that any of my friends at college would understand, I knew I could always sit down at the computer and send someone a long e-mail . . . and they would reply back. And I knew that even though we weren't all together, I still had the support system—it was just a little bit further away. . . . But it was still the same people, and I knew that they would understand, and that they could help me through it, or give me a suggestion, or at least say, "You're crazy, don't make such a big deal of it, or whatever. It was very reassuring."

Another young adult in the same program said, "We had this great experience, and then everyone leaves, but you know that there's some kind of web or connection out there. You don't just leave it behind. You stretch it out. So that gives me hope, and actually it gives everyone else hope."

The way this works was captured by still another young adult, who said:

> I could kind of like put [this community] in a little box, and if something wasn't going right, or if a program I was putting together just didn't seem like it was happening, then I could look back, and it was an inner strength in a lot of ways. I know someone else in this program who's doing something like what I'm doing, and we made a commitment to each other to do this together, and I can't let my part of the commitment down, so I need to step up and be strong here. Just knowing that there are a bunch of people out around the U.S. getting the message out, it made it feel a lot less lonely, and it was definitely like a strength."[12]

In these accounts, we can glimpse how it is that a mentoring community that is a meaningful network of belonging serves both to reassure and to encourage the development of inner-dependence, honoring both the potential and the vulnerability of the young adult.

Big-Enough Questions

Mentoring communities that serve to recompose meaning and faith in the young adult years are particularly powerful in their capacity to extend hospitality to big questions. If the process of imagination and ongoing development is partially prompted by conscious conflict, then big questions play an important role.

Why big? Since faith is the dynamic composing of meaning in the most comprehensive dimensions, questions of little consequence or those that only skim the surface of things can distract and preoccupy us while a larger field of potential consciousness remains assumed, unexamined, or neglected. Over time, it can become stagnant and insufficient, and even begin to disintegrate. In contrast, big questions stretch us. They reveal the gaps in our knowledge, in our social arrangements, in our ambitions and aspirations. Big questions are meaning-full questions, ones that ultimately matter.

What are some of the big questions young adults ask?

Who do I really want to become?

How do I work toward something when I don't even know what it is?

Am I lovable?

Who will be there for me?

Why is suffering so pervasive?

What are the values and limitations of my culture?

Who am I as a sexual being?

Do my actions make any real difference in the bigger scheme of things?

Do I want friendship, partnership, marriage? If so, why? With whom?

What is my society, or life, or God, asking of me? Anything?

What is the meaning of money? How much is enough?

Is there a master plan?

Am I wasting time I'll regret later?

What constitutes meaningful work?

How have I been wounded? Will I ever really heal?

What do I want the future to look like—for me, for others, for my planet?

What is my religion? Do I need one?

What are my real talents, preferences, skills, and longings?

When do I feel most alive?

Where can I be creative?

What am I vulnerable to?

What are my fears?

How am I complicit in patterns of injustice?

Will I always be stereotyped?

What do I really want to learn?

Do I want to bring children into the world?

How do I discern what is trustworthy?

Where do I want to put my stake in the ground and invest my life?

These are questions of meaning, purpose, and faith; they are rightly asked in every generation, in young adulthood and throughout adult life.

There are also big questions particular to our time in history, or to particular domains of inquiry. For example, Why is there a growing gap between the haves and have-nots? Why is the prison population growing in the United States? Why are antidepressants being prescribed for increasing numbers of children? What are the reasons for climate change? Why is the nature of the economic-political process—nationally and globally—a matter of increasing complexity and concern?

All of these questions are about the relationship of self and world. When we are younger, we can defer these questions to others, but becoming adult means increasing capability and responsibility for our own participation in the life of the commons and our own knowledge and action. These are questions of consequence that can't be simply ducked as irrelevant or "not my concern."

Yet it is my observation that many young adults, even those who are regarded as privileged, are often being cheated in a primary way. *They are not being asked big-enough questions.* They are not being invited to entertain the greatest questions of their own lives or their times.

Some are swept up in what I have described elsewhere as the flow of success. Apparently perpetually willing simply to jump the next hurdle, they are at once highly sophisticated in their capacity to calculate certain opportunity costs, while remaining naïve about the wider context in which their career choices, for example, are being made. As a consequence, they seek power but have little awareness of the reach of their own agency in truly shaping their lives and their world. They are functioning within various systems upon which they have very little if any critical purchase. That is, they may have the capacity for critical thought, but they use it only within certain limited frames—unable to question the frame itself.[13]

A very bright young businessperson, asked to comment on an investment decision by a health care chain, suggested that certain risks were acceptable "because a community hospital is, after all, simply a piece of real estate that could be liquidated if necessary." This young adult had not been initiated into the complex social, political, and moral terrain of the commons and the big questions that lurk there.

These and other less-privileged young adults are, like the rest of us, increasingly distracted by the lures of an entertained, consumerist, and anxious society, making their way as best they can, enjoying what life has to offer, and keeping up. For many, the big questions somehow just don't come up, get set aside, or are more or less not worth it since the experts seem to disagree on what the questions are. Or (more cynically), as one young man put it, "It is better not to care than to care and have to deal with the fact that others don't."

In a mentoring environment that nourishes the formation of adult faith, others do care. There is a place for asking the questions that begin to arise in the imagination of the young adult, from the inside, from that emerging inner authority. There is a willingness to tolerate the conflict (along with both the zest and the anguish) that such questions may raise, in the trust that it may lead to a more faithful imagination. In return, mentoring environments pose questions that the young adult would otherwise not have the privilege of engaging. The mix of questions arising from within and posed from without can create great questions that launch the worthy investment of a lifetime.

Encounters with Otherness

In the interviews that informed *Common Fire,* we discovered that encounters with otherness are the most powerful sources of vital, transforming questions that open into ways of making meaning that can form and sustain commitment to the common good, even if one is not naïve about the complexity of contemporary life. By *otherness* we mean encounters with those outside one's own tribe, those generally regarded as *them* instead of *us*.[14]

It has been said that in the life of faith, "God is always revising our boundaries outward."[15] A primary way this occurs is through an encounter with the other, in which an empathic bond is established that transcends *us* and *them,* creating a new *we*. This grounds commitment to the *common* good, rather than just to me and mine.

In a constructive encounter with otherness, an empathic bond arises from recognizing that the other suffers in the same way as we, having the same capacity for hope, longing, love, joy, and pain. These are the under-girding features of our humanity that link us with the vast commonwealth of being. The ability to imagine the experience of the other by drawing upon our own well of experience, blending it with the particular features of the other's experience, makes it possible to see through another's eyes, to feel through another's heart, to know something of another's under-standing. What one knows of another's experience is always partial. But one of the most significant features of the human adventure is the capac-ity to take the perspective of another and to be compelled thereby to recompose one's own perspective, one's own faith.

This kind of perspective taking gives rise to compassion (the capacity to suffer with). Compassion in turn gives rise to a conviction of possibil-ity, the sense that there has to be a better way. This conviction of possi-bility fosters the courage to risk on behalf of more than mere self-interest, recognition that my well-being and the well-being of the other are linked.

Young adulthood is a time of special readiness for this expansion of soul. Loosening the bonds of conventional belonging (which is fostered by critical thought) and developing inner-dependence (with a consequent openness to wonder and exploration) both conspire to set in place a ripeness for meeting and hearing the other.

Just home for the Christmas holiday, a freshman reflected on her expe-rience during a camping trip in college orientation week. She remembered especially meeting other freshmen "who were into the 'hard-core alter-native scene' and in high school I would have thought of them as just that. But on the camping trip, there we were, all coping with the rain and the mud, and I discovered that one of them had a cat they hated to leave behind and another had a mom he liked to cook with. I learned to see them for who they are, not what they are."

This doesn't mean that it is necessarily automatic or easier for young adults to entertain unpopular and challenging perspectives within a field of study, or amid the realities of growing diversity in our society. Young adult inner-dependence is fragile, and authority—though more chosen—remains located outside the self. Young adults remain vulnerable to needs for recognition and inclusion in terms that are normative within the net-works of belonging to which they have access.[16]

Nevertheless, it is not happenstance that in this society and elsewhere we are expecting colleges and universities (and in some measure, the military)—

institutions with young adult populations—to be primary testing grounds for discovering how we will all learn to dwell together within the small planet home we share. In both large and smaller institutions, we bring into close proximity multiple points of view embodied in young adult lives and representing a very broad range of social-cultural perspectives. We expect that they can manage it—and to some degree they often can, precisely because of the young adult readiness I have described. When we must bridge vast cultural differences, there is power in proximity, but proximity alone is often not enough.[17]

I remember talking with a young man who graduated from a prestigious university and was embarking on a master's degree in business. I asked him if he could tell me when, if ever, he had significant encounters with people different from himself. He felt he had not, but hoped it would happen in the school in which he was now enrolled, where there was an obvious diversity of American ethnic and international students. He recalled, "At the university where I was an undergraduate, there were a lot of different people, but we all sat in our own section of the dining hall." This experience is common, as all of us tend to seek out our own comfort zone, our own tribe. In a related fashion, some faculty report that increasing numbers of young adults, even the bright and informed, are reluctant to disagree openly with one another, whether in informal or classroom contexts, because the terms of belonging (increasingly fragile in our society as a whole) appear to be set too much at risk by the free exploration of ideas around matters of real consequence.

Constructive, transforming encounters with otherness and true exchange of ideas are facilitated in mentoring communities, where hospitality to otherness is prized and practiced. This can be created in the workplace, in the living space, in the classroom, and on the playing field. In most social environments today, there are many forms of otherness in addition to ethnicity, culture, gender, sexual orientation, and economic class. In almost every environment, it is useful to take an "otherness inventory" to assess the many divides waiting for creative abrasion. Constructive encounters across any significant divide set at the soul's core an experience of knowing that every assumption may be potentially transformed by an encounter with otherness. Thus the soul becomes more open, expectant, and available to ongoing learning and transformation. Faith develops at the boundary with otherness, when one becomes vulnerable to the consciousness of another, and thus vulnerable to reimagining self, other, world, and "God."

This quality of engagement with otherness is dependent, however, upon the practice of key habits of mind.[18] One of the gifts of a mentoring context is initiation into the habits of mind that make it possible for young adults to hold diversity and complexity, and to wrestle with moral ambiguity, developing deeper wells of meaning and purpose and larger and stronger faith.

Habits of Mind

A mentoring environment that prepares young adults for today's world appropriately can and necessarily must assist in creating norms of discourse and inclusion that invite genuine dialogue, strengthen critical thought, encourage connective-holistic awareness, and develop the contemplative mind.

DIALOGUE. Dialogue is not just talk. It is a way of being in conversation with others that involves a good deal of listening, desire to understand, and willingness to be affected—to be moved and informed, and to change one's mind. In a sound-bite world, the art and practice of dialogue is relentlessly at risk. Dialogue requires time and space, and it has to be learned.

Diana Eck, a professor and director of the Pluralism Project at Harvard University, is providing significant leadership in opening pathways into the multireligious reality of today's societies. She has written: "Dialogue in which we listen as well as speak may seem so commonsensical it is scarcely worth making a fuss over. And yet dialogue, whether between women and men, black and white, Christian and Hindu, has not been our common practice as an approach to bridging differences with understanding. Power and prestige make some voices louder, give some more airtime, and give the powerful the privilege of setting the terms for communication. . . . Today the language of dialogue has come to express the kind of two-way discourse that is essential to relationship, not domination. One might call it mutual witness. . . ."[19]

Unless they have become armored and cynical, young adults are particularly open to cultivating the art of dialogue because it is a satisfying means of honoring one's growing curiosity about self and world. When one speaks and then is heard—but not quite, and therefore tries to speak yet more clearly—and then listens to the other—and understands, but not quite, and listens again—one becomes actively engaged in sorting out what is true and dependable within oneself and about one's world. How one makes meaning is composed and recomposed in this process. This can occur in a wide variety of contexts when mentors embody and establish norms of discourse that foster genuine encounter and engagement.

Where models and expectations of this kind of conversation are nourished and there is support for learning its forms and rhythms, more than dialogue can be learned. Dialogue tills the soil for the growth of critical thought.

CRITICAL THOUGHT. As described earlier, critical thought is the capacity to step outside of one's own thought and reflect upon it as object, to recognize multiple perspectives and the relativized character of one's own experience and assumptions. One becomes a young adult in faith when one can begin to reflect critically on one's own ways of making meaning at the level of ultimacy. Mentoring environments that serve the formation of adult faith extend hospitality to critical thought and invite its further development.

Nourished by compelling questions, critical thought also flourishes if young adults are invited to test their responses (their mental and practical powers) in a supportive and challenging milieu of differing perspectives that awaken more adequate means of seeing and being. But to lead to viable commitment rather than mere combative individualism, relativism, or cynicism, when this occurs it must be met in ways that sustain a deepening, refining dialogue. Renee Lertzman has written:

> It was the day after our professor, Carlos Norena, lectured on Kant that I felt something slipping away from me. I was in my dorm room, looking out the window at the redwoods, and the view of the Pacific Ocean beyond the knoll. I suddenly had the sense that I had no idea what was real and what wasn't and how to tell the difference. Under this new gaze, the chair, the table, the cup, all became questionable entities in the universe, each containing their own subjectivity, truth, and meaning. Coherency was elusive and beyond my grasp. How was I to know what was going on here? How could I continue to live—buy groceries, run errands, call friends—if I did not know?
>
> I went to Carlos' office that day, and told him, "I don't know what is real and what isn't. I am thinking of dropping out of school to do organic farming. At least I know that growing carrots is real. . . ." He laughed and said to me in his thick Spanish accent, "Let's not do anything too drastic here. I suggest you take up swimming."
>
> Since that day in my freshman year in college, I have felt a sort of "waking up" from sleepwalking through life. . . . I was perplexed by my own catapult into wanting to know what life was about. . . . Why was no one talking about this?
>
> It was when I left college midway for an eight-week field study in the Sierra Nevada Mountains studying "nature philosophy and religion"

that I began to locate this inquiry in the larger context of how we live among others—humans and non-human species. For two months, we lived in various wilderness areas. We walked between worlds; drinking the cold clear waters of the mountains while making plans to return to the streets, lamps, steel and glass. To step into wilderness is to see how complex our relationship with the ecological world is, and to see more clearly what we have determined as "meaningful." . . .

The questions I was asking that first year in college did not go away; they only deepened, found new contexts and arenas. I had a professor once who jokingly called me "ontologically insecure" like the people on the Star Trek holodeck. It is as if to question reality and living deeply . . . can actually unhinge one's attachment to normative reality, so as to occupy a space of "always looking in." This sense of being ontologically insecure, I have come to see, is where I draw my strength; . . . I have also come to see that to question and investigate life, on the deepest levels possible, is to walk on a rim of sorts. . . . For me, the life worth living is to have the courage to be on the rim, and tolerate the space of not knowing, and honor what is known.

The people I look to as role models and teachers are those who live contemplatively, ask keen questions, and tolerate uncertainty. They thrive on the rim. Their minds are like diamonds, glittering with inquiry and beauty . . . deeply engaged with the world of the living.[20]

CONNECTIVE-SYSTEMIC-HOLISTIC THOUGHT. In an increasingly diverse and complex world, however, critical thought alone is insufficient for the tasks of citizenship and faith. The capacity to see distinctions and difference must be combined with the capacity to discover the fitting connections among things, to recognize how the vast tissue of life is dynamically and interdependently composed. This is a critical feature of the composing of an adult faith that can stand the test of time and support lasting commitments and effective action.

An international student, making the transition from Authority-bound ways of knowing to a critical-systemic perspective in a graduate school master's program, described his experience this way:

I don't know whether it's good or bad, but the way my brain works now has changed a lot. It's like a large flywheel which has been spun, and you can't stop it anymore. Before it was kind of an unstructured approach to the surrounding environment. You saw facts around you, but you weren't able to select and structure them—just to place them on a kind of shelf in your brain. But now it's more like you are inclined just to analyze all the facts of life and try to structure them and place them on different tiers in your brain. This actually is my concern because now there is a brain inclination of using the tools [systemic ways of seeing and new theoretical perspectives in his profession] maybe not on relevant events in my life, even on the way the world is working. It's a stress . . . because you can't do it; you can't apply this to the *whole* world around you.

What we hear in the reflection of this young adult is the capacity for critical thought; he can think about his own thinking. In addition, we hear the capacity for connective-systemic thought: the ability to structure the facts, placing them in relationship to one another. We hear also a question of faith: "Can I apply this to the whole world?" His answer seems to be no. Theories that may interpret some aspects of life, though powerful and compelling, may not be adequate to interpret the whole of life. Mentoring environments that serve the formation of an adequate faith not only attend to discrete aspects of life but also welcome and encourage grappling with ways of seeing the whole of life. This is the kind of big question that young adults are ready to ask.

A CONTEMPLATIVE MIND. Big questions, prompted by dialogue with otherness and the critical thought it nourishes, activate the reimagination of meaning and faith, thus repatterning the connections among things. For this to happen in strong and trustworthy ways requires, as we have seen, the moment of pause—contemplation. Particularly because the phenomenon of busy-ness has become so pervasive, contemplative pause is increasingly crowded out of our experience. Mentoring contexts that most profoundly serve the formation of adult faith provide an initiation into the power of pause.

The Contemplative Mind in Society, a nonprofit organization initially sponsored by two foundations, has been developed in response to the recognition that we are in real peril when decision makers and others do not have time for, and are unpracticed in the power of, contemplation. This organization, among others, fosters the opening of new pathways for contemplative practice in a wide range of contexts where young adults are ripe for learning the power of pause, in undergraduate education, in professional schools, and even in prisons.

Pause is powerful for young adults because it encourages cultivation of the inner life, honors the emerging inner authority of the young adult, and activates the awareness that he or she participates in the motion of life that transcends one's own efforts to manage and control, a reality larger than the scope of one's ego. The place of pause in the process of imagination is the place where each of us must go with the apparently irreconcilable tensions that constitute life's biggest questions. Initiation into the power of pause at once strengthens and chastens the imagination of the young adult and can be one of the greatest gifts of a mentoring environment.

Worthy Dreams

Powerful dialogues with otherness, critical and connective thought, and the practice of contemplation can yield the gift of a worthy dream. A worthy dream is an imagination of self as adult in a world that honors the potential of the young adult soul. Daniel Levinson was the first developmental theorist to recognize the power of the Dream, and that the "novice" phase of adulthood is the crucial time for forming a Dream for one's life. With Judy Levinson, he recently contended that the most crucial function of a mentoring relationship is to develop and articulate the dream.[21]

The Dream, with a capital D, is something more than night dreams, casual daydreams, pure fantasy, or a fully designed plan. This Dream has a quality of vision.[22] It is an imagined possibility that orients meaning, purpose, and aspiration. The formation of a worthy Dream is the critical task of young adult faith.

A REACH FOR THE IDEAL. Dreams come in all shapes and sizes, from conventional to radical. But the Dreams that most profoundly serve the composing of a faith to live by stem for the most part from a particular capacity of the young adult: the capacity to envision the ideal.

Because the threshold of young adulthood is marked by the emergence of critical thought, young adults have the ability to critique self and world and also to imagine how it might become. Thus, although young adults are often accused of youthful idealism, we might better understand young adulthood as the birthplace of adult vision.

The young adult has struggled to push away from the safe but constraining harbor of conventional knowing in order to achieve an initial sense of self-aware integrity. On the other hand, the young adult is not yet embedded in the full range of adult commitments. These circumstances create a certain freedom, and a unique capacity to critically conceptualize the ideal. By *ideal* the young adult means that which is pure, consistent, authentic, and congruent. The young adult's search for the ideal is a potent element in the search for what will most adequately ground and orient the integrity, commitment, and investment of the emerging self.

Carol Gilligan's classic analysis of students who took Kohlberg's course on moral and political choice elegantly captures conditions that give rise to the quest for the ideal.[23] Among those she studied were students who seemed to be dealing seriously with real experience, such as starvation in Biafra, competing obligations, and the reality of human pain and suffering. Wrestling with the complexity of reality seemed to have the power "to undo the most principled moral understanding."[24] Students questioned the principles in their practical construction, that is, in their application to the reality of the actual moral dilemma, to what one student called "the dilemma of the fact."[25] According to Gilligan, "the assumption of 'all other things being equal' tangled with the awareness that in reality they never were."[26] As a consequence, these students came to see that "reason had outstripped morality, as Kant and Dostoevski had seen, and, in the absence of knowledge, moral judgment became a matter not of logic but of faith."[27]

One student Gilligan described experienced a period of extreme relativism, beginning at the end of his sophomore year in college, when he "came to" the conclusion that "morality was by and large, a lot of bunk, that there were no right or wrong answers whatsoever." This had marked for him the end of "huge theoretical moral constructs and systems."[28] (We might say that this marked the shipwreck of the hopeful assumption that the logic of Authority could lead to certainty.) "He now believed that 'what we think is very much a part of how we live' and that in detaching thought from life he had been 'building a castle in the air.' Still the moral problem remains, . . . because 'human beings come in contact with each other's lives.' Moral values are human constructions, conventions of thought that inevitably are tied to the conditions in which people live and in which they must act."[29]

The voice of the student continues in the search for the ideal:

> A truly moral experience, if there is such a thing, [would be] relating to any person one comes across, not as a means, but as an end in himself and essentially as a human being and nothing more and nothing less, not as my client, not as my waiter. When one is "beyond good and evil," you talk about human beings vis-à-vis other human beings rather than talking about right or wrong. . . . I guess to me the *ideal* societal situation is where everybody related to everybody like that and did not worry about right or wrong, because then moral dilemmas might not exist or might not arise.

Gilligan observes that though the students' ideologies ranged from the New Left to the New Right, the quality of the ideal laced through the various moral postures. Gilligan poignantly noted: "When the injustices of conventional morality were apparent and there seemed no alternative way to judge, . . . then the flexibility of . . . thought made anything seem possible. Given a morality that appeared both absurd and hypocritical, a matter more of rationalization than of reason, [for a few] hedonism returned as at least an 'authentic' basis for choice."[30]

This observation alerts us to the sobering fact that once the young person has seen relativism and seeks a new integrity in which to stand, even hedonism or a comparable variant may appear as a viable faith. In other words, whatever content (or ideology) appears to be at least consistent and authentic may appear to fit the young adult's hunger for the ideal, so long as it is liberated from the "hypocrisy" of the conventional (and the inconsistent).

Gilligan also observed, however, that those students most able to develop a capacity to grapple effectively and responsibly with moral issues seemed to be those "whose concept of morality . . . entailed an 'obligation to relieve human misery and suffering if possible.'"[31] This sense of obligation arises from recognizing the connections among things; it can give rise, in turn, to a sense of vocation.

VOCATION. Note that the Dream understood through the eyes of the great traditions of faith across time is more than imagining a job or career or profession narrowly understood. The Dream in its fullest and most spiritual sense is a sense of vocation. *Vocation* conveys "calling" and meaningful purpose. It is a relational sensibility in which I recognize that what I do with my time, talents, and treasure is most meaningfully conceived not as a matter of mere personal passion and preference but in relationship to the whole of life. Vocation arises from a deepening understanding of both self and world, which gives rise to moments of power when self and purpose become aligned with eternity. Vocation is the place where the heart's deep gladness meets the world's deep hunger.[32]

Access to Images

Forming a worthy dream depends, in significant measure, on access to fitting, vital images. There are types of images that are especially important in the formation of young adult faith. Mentoring communities gift the imagination of the young adult with images of truth, transformation, positive images of self and of the other, and images of interrelatedness.

IMAGES OF TRUTH: A WORLD OF SUFFERING AND WONDER. Forming a viable faith depends upon serious engagement with the truth of the world, the universe as it is, including "things that should not be so."[33]

This means that though we can never fully comprehend Truth, the young adult may learn to apprehend something of the wholeness of life—the infinite complexity of the social and more-than-human world in the dimensions of both suffering and wonder.

It is not surprising that one of the most ancient and venerable stories about the formation of human faith concerns a young person who went into a wider world and discovered the realities of suffering. Just as the Buddha came to grapple with suffering as a feature of enlightenment, any adult faith must do the same in some form. Young adulthood can be a time of coming to terms with suffering, often one's own and sometimes that of others who suffer far more than the young adult may heretofore have imagined.[34] As the quest for truth sharpens, young adults grow increasingly vulnerable to a raw awareness of the stark and tragic dimensions of suffering. The injustice of some forms of suffering and the pervasiveness of suffering as a primary feature of the fabric of life itself are among the irreducible facts of life that mature faith must be able to embrace.

The paradox is that as integral to life as suffering is, it is matched by wonder. By wonder I mean the awe and gratitude invoked in those moments when we come alive to the intricate luminosity, beauty, power, and vast grandeur of the universe (or some tiny part of it) and the amazement we feel that we are in any measure privileged to behold it. By wonder I mean also the sense of Mystery that cannot be exhausted even by our most magnificent forms of knowing, including the awe-full ambiguity that arises from any reasonable assessment of the complex, dynamic, and confounding character of life. Young adults have a readiness for soaking up such wonder, especially if it is distinguished from the various forms of artificial high that exploit this readiness. This dimension of wonder, too, is a fact that any worthy faith must be able to enfold.

Ironically, contemporary life also offers a good many ways to be insulated from truth—both the scope of suffering and the opportunities for wonder. A good mentoring environment, however, provides an initiation into both. When the young adult is invited into both suffering and wonder, then contradiction and dissonance proliferate, raising big questions and activating the imagination in its search for meaning and faith. I recall how Joan Baez once said, "I do not know whether it is worse to bring a child into this world and submit him or her to the disease we call society, or to refuse to bring a child into this world and thus rob him or her of one glorious red sunset." If young adults are steeped in images that grasp both the suffering and wonder of their time, they may gain faith that can be sustained because it cannot be in a certain sense surprised. A great mentoring environment skirts neither suffering nor wonder; rather, it holds them in a dynamic paradox.

IMAGES OF TRANSFORMATION: HOPE FOR RENEWING THE WORLD.
Suffering and wonder, faithfully conceived, appear to be disparate, if not,
opposing realities. They are resolved in the human soul only in the sensibility we call hope. Authentic hope is no mere bromide. It is grounded in
the facts of things as they are, taking into account all that is known and
unknown. If young adults have learned in some measure the nature and
scope of suffering and wonder, the images that capture their imagination
promise a fitting embrace of the heights and depths of the human condition and are in this sense ideal.

Therefore, if young adults are to be initiated into a conversation with
truth that leads toward mature adult faith, they must be offered images
dynamic enough to grasp the complex and composing character of the
motion of life and its transformations. Young adults must be met in their
dialogue with promise: the dialogue between despair and hope, shipwreck
and gladness, bondage and freedom, death and life, stasis and the incessant transformation of all things. Accordingly, mentors serve well when
giving access to an imaginal complex of integrating symbols that grasp
the dynamic of dissolution and recomposition. A recognition of the finite
nature of all constructions of knowledge *and* the possibility of their ongoing reconstruction toward more adequate knowing is a crucial feature of
the initiation of young adults into an adult knowing that fosters hope.
This dynamic may be revealed in a wide range of contexts.

Rosemary Radford Ruether, a noted Roman Catholic theologian, recounts her discovery of this central dynamic through the teaching of
Robert Palmer, a classicist:

> Palmer was . . . more than faintly contemptuous of Christianity. . . .
> [It was] Palmer, the believing pagan, who first taught me to think the-
> ologically or, as he would have called it, "mythopoetically." Through
> him I discovered the meaning of religious symbols, not as intrinsic doc-
> trines, but as living metaphors of human existence. I still remember
> the great excitement I felt in freshman Humanities when he said some-
> thing that made me realize that "death and resurrection" was not some
> peculiar statement about something that was supposed to have hap-
> pened to someone 2,000 years ago, with no particular connection to
> anyone else's life. Rather it was a metaphor for inner transformation
> and rebirth, the mystery of renewed life. He happened to be talking
> about Attis or Dionysos, not about Jesus. For the first time I under-
> stood a new orientation to Christian symbols that eleven years of
> Catholic education had never suggested to me. That was the beginning
> of my being interested in religious ideas in a new way.[35]

If young adults discover this dynamic of dissolution and recomposition at the core of life, they become attuned to the motion at the heart of the universe and the activity of spirit and Spirit, which may be expressed in religious/spiritual or secular terms.

POSITIVE IMAGES OF SELF. Forming a worthy dream also depends on access to positive images of self linked with a compelling sense of possibility and aspiration.[36] Although this can happen through awards and grades, it is most profound when the young adult is affirmed in ways that convey a faithful correspondence between his or her own aspirations and positive reflection in the eyes of another whom the young adult values and trusts. This is the power of confirmation that mentoring communities hold.

Reminding us that mentoring can be practiced by those who are still young adults themselves, a young Kenyan, Moses, tells a story. After completing a Jesuit education in Kenya, he came to the United States for study in a small college. Unprepared for the racism in this culture, he came close to despair and almost shut down as a way of coping. Then a Caucasian American student whom he admired, Krista, only slightly older than himself, said to him one day, "It isn't your problem that they have a problem with you, it's their problem." It was a turning point. It was an insight that made sense of his experience, and it suggested an alternative, positive image of himself. In time, he became the first international student to be elected as student body president in that college, and today he is in graduate school, preparing himself for religious leadership.

Young adults hunger for images of self that promise authenticity and a mix of competence, excellence, and the finest qualities of life, without minimizing the struggle inherent in claiming these qualities, a struggle of which the young adult now has the capacity to be acutely aware. One young woman reflected:

> I had one really terrific coach. He was my coach for track. He was much more interested in personal bests and the effort produced than actual placings. I wanted to train really hard to prove to myself and to him what I was capable of. This desire came out of a set of personal goals rather than feeling overpressured from him. He helped me keep the goals realistic and always provided positive feedback. After both years of track season, there were other athletes that set outstanding records. I accomplished good performances and was above average but did not have these same outstanding overall results. And yet, after both seasons, I was the one awarded the female track MVP by my track coach, based on the personal achievements, extensive improvements,

and intensive training and effort that I had put in on a daily basis. The qualities and characteristics he most respected in an athlete were ones that he suggested through his attitude and words, that I had developed to a fair extent, and many of those qualities were further strengthened in me because of his apparent respect for such characteristics.

Images of self that encourage high aspiration and excellence in meaningful terms (in contrast to mere success) enable the young adult to see beyond self and world as they presently are and to discern a vision of the potential of life: the world as it ought to be and the self as it might become.

IMAGES OF THE OTHER AS BOTH SIMILAR AND UNIQUE. In the search for a knowing of oneself that can be meaningfully sustained, our images of the other make an enormous difference. How we construe the other is an elemental ingredient in composing self and world and in the formation of faith: who and what we trust, who *we* are and who *they* are, and what we consider worth our time and trouble. Richard R. Niebuhr has suggested that a key element of the reflective activity by which we participate in the moral society of conscious life is the awareness that as selves we are a synthesis of other and "same"—"a living synthesis of opposites." He writes: "There can be no I without a You, no You without an I, and no I and You without a He, She, They and Those. We cannot become *one* in the sense that *persons* are *one* without also becoming manifold, without also becoming, as it were, the other life-forms that sustain us. It is a *moral* process of apprehending and striving to comprehend, of going forth and returning, expanding and contracting as the heart does, a process of diastolic and systolic development."[37]

This synthesis of opposites is dependent upon images that fittingly name the other in ways that in turn will more fittingly define the self. For example, a young African American who had grown up in an suburb of a major American midwestern city recalled that through his high school years he assumed that any young person of color in this society who worked hard could have the same access to the privileges and comforts of upper-middle-class society that he had. It was not until he was in college and began to tutor a young African American boy in the inner city that he had his first conscious encounter with otherness. He discovered that without the same resources and encouragement that he had known, it would be much more difficult than he presumed. As the living image of the young boy in the inner city took up lodging in his imagination, he had to recompose both self and other, becoming a different I because of a reconfigured You. This deepening of the relationship between self and other, self and world, forms the double-strand helix of the DNA in the seed of vocation.

IMAGES OF INTERRELATEDNESS AND WHOLENESS: INSTITUTIONS THAT WORK. The faithful moral imagination is increasingly dependent upon recognizing the interrelatedness of all of creation. As we emerge into a more profound ecological and global consciousness spurred in part by new technologies that daily destroy any illusion that our actions in one place do not have unexpected consequences everywhere else, we can feel overwhelmed and powerless. We have discovered, however, that consciousness of "our small part" can become a positive source of power and confidence if that part is seen as participating in, and thus affecting, the larger whole. Thus the search for right images in our time needs to include images that enable us to grasp an intuitive sense of the whole, in ways that link the particular and the universal, holding each accountable to the other.[38]

In their appropriate dependence upon the images available to them in their environment, young adults are vulnerable to partialities. By confusing a part with the whole, they may move toward a faith that consequently works "here" but not "there." One young adult commented: "You have to remember that I have lived in a different environment every year for six years. So have most people I know. Nothing is stable and we switch between worlds all the time. We go from having money to being broke to having money again, from being surrounded by friends to being lonely to having friends again in a matter of a few months. Those kinds of major transitions would make anyone refigure the way they think about the world, especially if they are already grappling with issues of identity, career, life-goals, etc."

Access to images, symbols, stories, insights, and theories that create durable, widening, and open-ended patterns, systems, and networks of connection and meaning enlarge the mind and expand the heart. They enable young adults to compose and anchor an increasingly trustworthy faith that, in spite of immediate circumstances, makes it possible to become at home in the universe.

Organizations and institutions that can serve as images of a meaningful wholeness and interrelatedness are the soil in which the seed of vocation may grow. Young adults seek places where they can roll up their sleeves and pitch in. In today's complex societies, big questions are likely to spawn worthy dreams that require working closely and cooperatively with many others. Increasingly, the world's deep hungers can only be adequately met with the collective wisdom and passion of a host of inspired hearts and minds. Thus, young adults depend on finding meaningful places within organizations and institutions, places where they can contribute their part as an element of a larger effort than the self alone can achieve.

In reflecting on the formation of people who can sustain commitment to the common good, we have come to believe that most had the opportunity during their formative years to be part of some workable, effective institution. Participating in an organization that successfully enacts a worthy purpose gives flesh to the intuition that one is part of a larger and meaningful whole—and that one's own power is amplified when set in resonance with that of others who seek a common goal. This sensibility is at risk if cynicism regarding virtually every form of institutional life abounds. Yet almost every organization has the opportunity, as a mentoring environment, to gift the young adult imagination with an experience of an organization that works. Though the young adult may not find the same again, the conviction takes root that it is possible to take on ambitious dreams in a complex, interdependent world. Given such an experience, one learns the power of participation in something larger than oneself and knows that viable modes of shared action can be effective and transforming.

As institutions that work, mentoring communities embody possibility— a gift to the young adult imagination. A primary form of this embodiment is found in practices that serve the formation of faith.

Communities of Practice

Mentoring environments are communities of imagination *and practice*. Humanizing practices, as we use the term here, are ways of life, things that people do with and for each other to make and keep life human.[39] Among the many that might be identified as important to forming meaning, purpose, and faith in the young adult years, there are three in particular that all mentoring environments might strategically recover to serve the formation of young adult faith: the practices of hearth, table, and commons.

THE PRACTICE OF HEARTH. Hearth places have the power to draw and hold us, for they are places of equilibrium offering an exquisite balance of stability and motion. Hearth places are where we are warmed in both body and soul, are made comfortable, and tend to linger. Indoors or out, hearth places invite pause, reflection, and conversation: the ocean shore, a wooded sanctuary, a bench set amidst an active park or plaza. These are places for lingering.

Hearth places invite reflection within and among. As we have seen, young adult faith is forged in an ongoing dialogue that occurs both within the self and among an available network of belonging in interaction with the wider world. The dialogue of which we speak—for example, between power and powerlessness, success and failure, alienation and belonging, right and wrong, despair and hope—cannot usually be accomplished in fleeting sound bites. It requires something more like a hearthside conversation.

Dialogue does not mean two people talking, but rather "talking through." Time and places for talking through are essential in forming critically aware, inner-dependent, and worthily committed faith. An understanding of the courage and costs in the formation of young adult faith asks educator-mentors and their institutions to acknowledge in their everyday practices that when truth is being recomposed in the most comprehensive dimensions of self, world, and "God," then necessarily the soul suffers disequilibrium in the service of a larger, more adequate knowing. If a new equilibrium is to take form, there must be ways of being that are consistently present in the environment to support and nourish a new imagination.

Young adult shipwreck and the search for a new shore occur often in inconvenient, untimely forms: trauma in a romantic relationship, raising fundamental questions about the nature and worthiness of the self; a tumble into issues of social justice, disordering one's notions of the character of the world; an unwanted pregnancy, a divorce, or a death that shatters expectations of both past and future; or an encounter with "the books," leading to an intellectual impasse that swamps an earlier faith and its hope, replacing them with a sense of futility that no lecture can cure but that an afternoon with a mentoring professor might comfort and inform. These are hearth-sized conversations.

In some colleges, business settings, and elsewhere, one can still find vestiges of the traditional hearthside. Interestingly, they are reappearing in some new educational and corporate structures, though often in rather cold forms designed more to create an elegant ambiance than to invite lingering conversation. Students do not want simply more office hours. Coworkers and colleagues do not want an appointment. There is a hunger, however, for hearth and for conversation that begins as it happens and concludes whenever.

The practice of the hearth place can be recovered in a variety of forms and throughout a wide range of organizations and institutions. We know the difference between offices and homes that are at least sometimes willing to run on hearth time, and those that cannot or will not. Mentoring environments find a way to practice hearth time.

THE PRACTICE OF THE TABLE. It has been said that the table is a place where you know there will be a place for you, where what is on the table will be shared, and where you will be placed under obligation. In every culture, human beings have eaten together. The practice of the table prepares us for *civitas*. In the practice of the table we learn to share, to wait, to accommodate, to be grateful. The table is emblematic of economic, political, and spiritual realities. At the table, we learn delayed gratification, belonging, commitment, and ritual. Table is another kind of hearth place; likewise, it is a place where we may share conversation and become practiced in dialogue. It has served many as a place for learning how we can disagree yet remain deeply aware of our common bonds.

In an overindividualized, consumerist culture, however, the microwave oven easily becomes a primary saboteur of the family dinner, ensuring warm food for all whether or not they are home for dinner "on time." We are not only consumers of "fast food," but there are "stand-up gourmet restaurants" in which people eat sophisticated cuisine on the run and alone. The typical cafeteria design serving young adults in schools or workplaces focuses more on infinite individual options than upon arrangements and aesthetics that encourage shared, lingering conversation. The practice of the table shrinks under the pressures of efficiencies and choice.

Yet we hunger; yet we eat. Young adults are drawn to those places that nourish them: places that in very practical terms recognize that the body, the heart, and the intellect are intimately interrelated and the whole is nourished. Because today's young adults have in many cases not had the practice of the table, there is a good deal at stake in whether or not mentoring communities incorporate a table practice as an elemental feature of common life.

It has been said also that a group has become a community when someone brings food to the meeting. The practice of the table may play a significant role in preparing faithful adults who can impart leadership in reweaving a civil and flourishing society. The practice of the table foreshadows the practice of the commons.

THE PRACTICE OF THE COMMONS. Just as the table serves as a micro expression of *civitas,* so does the practice of the commons. The commons, as we discussed in Chapter One, is the image that stands behind the concept of the common good. It is a place where people meet by happenstance and intention and have a sense of a shared, interdependent life within a manageable frame. The commons affords practices of interrelatedness, belonging, and learning how to stand—and stand with—each other over time.

Many organizations and communities have a commons: the common room, the quad, the lunch place, the volleyball court, the park, the place of shared meditation or worship. Whether the commons is inside or out, an active practice of the commons can bring together in fruitful tension and celebration the disparate elements of the community. It is a place within which to confirm a common, connected life, and in combination with various forms of story and ritual it can become the center of shared faith and grounded hope. A practice of the commons sets at the heart's core an imagination of *we* and weaves a way of life that conveys meaning and orients purpose and commitment.

When parking lots create a centrifugal pull away from the center, when there is no common time for gathering, when common space is shaped exclusively by commercial interests (as in a shopping mall), the commons ceases to serve as an integral image of community and becomes fragmented into special and parochial interests, used only serially by various tribes, if at all. Young adults become vulnerable to dreams that represent only the interest of self and tribe rather than building Dreams that embrace and serve a wider life.

I am persuaded that if young adults are going to become at home in the universe in ways that prepare them for citizenship on what has now become a global commons, they need to be grounded in faith shaped, in part, by a micro experience of the commons—an embodied image and practice that nourishes an imagination of the possibility of shared participation in creating the common good. As faith is the place of experience and the imagination, the lived practice of hearth, table, and commons is a threefold gift by which a mentoring environment may nourish the young adult imagination of faith in a changing, complex, and diverse world.

Gaston Bachelard has written that the chief function of the house is to protect the dreamer.[40] It is the purpose of mentoring environments to provide a place within which young adults may discover themselves becoming more at home in the universe. Through many means, including the practices of hearth, table, and commons, mentoring environments create a context of recognition, support, challenge, and inspiration. They foster dialogue, critical and connective thought, and initiation into the power of the contemplative life. As networks of belonging, they convey the promise of a sociality within which big questions may be asked and worthy Dreams may be formed. Mentoring environments are communities of imagination that distinctively serve young adult meaning-making and the formation of vocation and faith.

9

MENTORING COMMUNITIES

HIGHER EDUCATION ○ PROFESSIONAL
EDUCATION AND THE PROFESSIONS
○ THE WORKPLACE ○ TRAVEL
○ THE NATURAL ENVIRONMENT ○ FAMILIES
○ RELIGIOUS FAITH COMMUNITIES

AS BEARERS OF THE GIFTS described in the previous chapter, mentoring environments may take form within a wide range of contexts. Each context has particular opportunities to honor and participate in the young adult's search for mentors, meaning, purpose, and faith. The seven we focus on here are somewhat arbitrarily chosen, but with an eye toward identifying places that typically represent the power of mentoring communities in young adult lives. They are higher education, professional education, workplaces, travel, the natural environment, families, and religion.

HIGHER EDUCATION:
A COMMUNITY OF IMAGINATION

For several important reasons, higher education can serve as a central institution for young adults in today's world. As society becomes more complex, extended education becomes increasingly necessary to meet the needs of the workplace, and an informed, broad, multicultural perspective combined with the capacity for critical, connected, and contemplative thought becomes increasingly vital for the functioning of democratic societies.

At its best, higher education is distinctive in its capacity to serve as a mentoring environment in the formation of critical adult faith. It does so most profoundly when it functions with clear consciousness of its role as a mentoring environment composed of multiple mentoring communities. These communities may take form within or across academic departments, a particular course or program of study, a laboratory research team, an athletic team, an arts group, a residence hall, programs of service learning, campus religious life, or the newspaper office.

When we speak of the academy as a place for the formation of faith, this may appear to run counter to the commitments of the academy, as well as to speak of a domain beyond the academy's purposes and responsibility. Yet if we recognize faith as meaning-making in its most comprehensive dimensions, higher education inevitably functions, at least to some degree, as a mentoring community for those who are young adults in faith (at whatever age[1]), even if only by default. It is primarily to this institution that young (and older) adults come to be initiated into critical thought and must make meaning in new ways on the other side of that discovery. Thus every institution of higher education serves in at least some measure as a community of imagination in which every professor is potentially a spiritual guide and every syllabus a confession of faith.

Epistemological Assumptions

Before proceeding, however, it is important to acknowledge and reflect upon the epistemological assumptions of the academy.

Since the nineteenth century, and particularly with the development of the research university, higher education has been increasingly dominated by a particular interpretation of academic objectivity that over time has appeared to preclude a self-conscious search for value and meaning. As a result, commitment to the true has been divorced from the question of the good. Responsible teaching has seemed to require dispassionate presentation of value-neutral fact, or the mere presentation of multiple points of view. Teachers, individually and collectively, are more inclined to say "The data show . . ." than "I have found . . . ," "We contend . . . ," or "I believe. . . ."[2]

Recently, this stance has been challenged by voices at the margins of the academy who in varying ways make the claim for perspectives outside the privileged norms. These perspectives, many rooted in the particulars of place, ethnicity, gender, sexual orientation, and economic class, are typically grounded in personal or communal experience, both immediate and historical. In its adjudication of these claims, the academy finds it difficult to respond and yet maintain the established canons of objectivity.

Correspondingly, the academy tends to perceive students either as independent thinkers prepared to make objective judgments among competing alternatives or as conventional, dependent neophytes in need of being awakened to the complex and relative character of all knowledge. These assumptions and this ambivalence have extended to residence hall and extracurricular life, where *in loco parentis* once prevailed but where, on the one hand, students are now regarded as adult (read: rational) and, on the other hand, presumed to be in a process of cognitive-affective-social-moral development. If, however, these aspects of development are recognized, in many instances they are no longer seen as the direct concern of the faculty per se; nor are they regarded as central to the purposes of the college or university.

These norms of academic life are rooted in Western epistemology, and its assumptions about what we can know and how we come to know it. The nineteenth-century influence of a Kantian perspective (discussed in Chapter Seven) still pervades today's academy. Like the academy itself, its members register considerable discomfort in engaging subjects that cannot be submitted to empirical investigation. That is, following Kant, we sharply distinguish the knowing of the empirical world (pure reason) from the world of meaning or ultimate truth (practical reason). This distinction has had considerable power to limit the discourse of the academy and to determine the focus of our collective attention. The academy is dedicated to knowledge. The phenomenal can be known, but noumenal reality cannot. And if it cannot, the reasoning goes, then questions of meaning, morality, ultimacy, and faith—although surely important—stand outside the realm of "knowledge" and are beyond (or irrelevant to) the work of the academy.

To state the case most sharply, the domain of knowledge has been reduced to the domain of objective reality (understood as empirical fact and theoretical analysis abstracted from fact, standing in contrast to ultimate reality). This divorced the knowledge of the object that is known from its relationship to the subject who knows, thus diminishing the significance of emotion, intuition, the personal, the moral, and full engagement with the complexity emerging from the practice of lived experience, for all of these are difficult to apprehend empirically. Reason and knowledge, thus defined, are reduced to those processes that can be analyzed and replicated—in short, produced and controlled.

As a consequence, whether one traces the origins of the academy to the monastery or to Athens, the academy's complex relationship to truth has been diminished. Wilfred Cantwell Smith described this shift as follows:

I would submit that one of the central and most consequential developments in intellectual life . . . especially [in] the academic West, has been the lowering of the idea of truth and knowledge from something higher than human beings to something lower than we. Traditionally, and essentially, universities were what they were and uncontrivedly had the allegiance and respect that they deserved to have—because they were in pursuit of a truth that is above us all. Because it was above us, transcended us, it freely won our loyalty and—not so freely—our behavior: we strove to live (not merely to think) rationally, in the sense of conforming our wills to an intellectual order higher than our individual persons; something that could be attained at times only at great cost, and never without firm discipline—but worth it. . . .

These ideals were approximated to in actuality, of course, only partially . . . and at times hypocrisy was substituted for even a distant loyalty. Nonetheless the vision informed and sustained academia for centuries; . . . many persons . . . were touched by it and in some small or large degree transformed. Ideally, education consisted in that transformation.

The shift in recent times has been from this notion of truth that we serve, to a different notion of it as something that serves us. . . . We manufacture knowledge as we manufacture cars, and with similar objectives: to increase our power, pleasure, or profit—or if we are altruistic, to offer it to others that they may increase theirs. The university has been becoming "the knowledge industry," its products ours to command (to buy and sell).[3]

This shift in our claims for knowledge was initially a great relief. A more adequate recognition of the limits of the human mind required a more modest stance in relationship to claims of ultimate truth. The academy relinquished some forms of hypocrisy, elite moralism, and unself-critical assertions of truth. Scholarship has made important progress as a result of its now more self-conscious methodologies.

Still, wherever a strict dichotomy between the objective and the subjective has been practiced, we have become vulnerable to exchanging wisdom for knowledge and moral commitment for method. Moreover, professors have been vulnerable to functioning as less-than-whole persons, the vocation of higher education has been impoverished, and young adults searching for a fitting orientation to ultimate reality—a faith to live by—have been abandoned by faculty and others in the academy who are distinctively positioned to serve the formation of a critical and worthy faith. Accordingly, young adults are bereft of mentors they need, professors are too often mere technicians of knowledge, higher education can articulate no orienting vision or offer leadership toward a coherent unity, and discrete academic disciplines disclose only isolated (and thus distorted) aspects of truth. As a consequence, some of the most important questions of the contemporary world are difficult to address within the prevailing rubrics of the academy.

In light of the relative character of all knowledge, how might the academy maintain its commitment to truth, proceed with integrity, serve the formation of young adult faith, and extend leadership toward an integral vision on behalf of the wider society and culture? Is there an alternative epistemology—a more adequate way of perceiving the relationship of human understanding to the apprehension of the whole of reality?

George Rupp, president of Columbia University, has argued the inadequacy of both a stance that claims to be immune to relativism (the stance, for example, of some religious and some political communities) and one that accepts unqualified relativism as unavoidable (the perceived stance of the academy, especially when exacerbated by the cultural complexity and social diversity in the postmodern academy). Rupp contends that there is a sense in which both of these positions presuppose a Kantian epistemology. On the basis of a Hegelian critique, he asserts that a strict dichotomy between phenomenal knowledge and noumenal reality is untenable. It is, writes Rupp, "useful and even necessary to distinguish between the object as it is in the consciousness [the imagination] of the knower and the thing in itself. But while the intention of this distinction is to call attention to the limitations of a given claim to knowledge, its effect is [also] to drive the knower toward more adequate comprehension."[4]

This epistemology recognizes that every perspective is relative to particular personal, social, and cultural conditions. Yet because each incomplete perspective is, nevertheless, an attempt to comprehend the one reality there is, it is possible to make judgments about their validity, as multiple perspectives mutually inform and correct each other. (The interaction of subject and object upon which this epistemology depends is consistent with Piaget, and as a critique of Kant it presses in the same direction as Coleridge.)

This model renders the boundary between the knower and "the one reality there is" permeable, setting in its place an ongoing, dynamic process between the knower and the real, between the whole knower and the whole of life—the process Coleridge identified as Reason, with imagination as its highest power.

This way of understanding our search for truth recomposes the relationship of the academy to issues of transcendent meaning. The reified boundary between empirical truth and questions of value, meaning, and faith that has characterized (if not tyrannized) the academy is, in principle, dismantled, and the whole of reality becomes the concern of the academy in its commitment to truth. It invites faculty and students to bring the competence of contemporary scholarship to the search for critically composed and worthy forms of faith within a relativized world.

Certainly this perspective does not negate the responsibility of the academy to facilitate the learner's encounter with the relative character of all knowledge; indeed, it affirms that responsibility. But this perspective also frees the academy first to recognize that a value-free course has yet to be taught, and second to serve young adults by assisting in composing critically aware and worthy commitments to self and society within a relativized world. For if in the end all knowing is one; if truth is not adequately grasped by discrete, compartmentalized domains of knowledge (as not only theology but the new physics and ecological perspectives suggest is indeed the case); and if all knowing is inevitably also a valuing, then any absolute value neutrality is, in any case, in any field, spurious.

The academy's commitment to truth requires engagement with the whole of truth, the full scope of reality. In sum, a critical appraisal of the epistemological assumptions of the academy itself points toward a new reordering of the relationship among the academy, the young adult's search for faith, and the relationship between the academy and society.

In a wide range of settings throughout the academy, there is growing evidence of considerable interest in exploring alternative epistemologies that give voice not just to ethnic, gendered, and class perspectives that have been marginalized by the prevailing norms but also to perspectives that contend with questions of value and incorporate a recognition of the spiritual dimensions of knowing.[5] This coincides with a profound reordering of the academy taking place as a consequence of the development of new technologies, and with growing concern about how the academy has become more beholden to corporate and other economic interests and reflects the careerism of students, regarding them as mere consumers.

This set of conditions means that on the one hand there is a fresh opening within the academy to big questions of purpose, personal meaning, and social concern, but on the other hand an erosion of the relative freedom of the academy to grapple with such questions on behalf of the wider culture. As a consequence, we are seeing bright young adults who have had so-called privileged educations yet have not been initiated into some of the great questions of this time in our cultural history. It is within this complex milieu that faculty, therefore and nevertheless, have significant opportunities to create mentoring communities.[6]

The Syllabus: A Confession of Faith

Harvey Cox has observed:

> When I ask my students to read something for a class, they want to know *why*. And when they ask why, they want me to tell them about the person who wrote it, why he or she wrote it and, most of all, why I find it important. They want especially to know what in *my* experience leads me to think they should bother to read it.
>
> Students will not sit still anymore while I argue that anyone who wants to be familiar with the "field" should know this book. They are drowning in things they "ought to know," as we all are. They sense already what it took me years to discover—that they will *never* know all the things somebody thinks they ought to know. Like me, they stagger under the daily surfeit of words we call the "information overload crisis." They wisely suspect that much of what they are supposed to "know" is useless information that has been magically transformed into awesome lore by those who control educational institutions and career advancement. But they do not want lore, they want testimony. . . .
>
> What my students are saying, sometimes incoherently, is, "I don't want to master a field, nor do I want to leave all the decisions to experts and pros. What will help me survive, choose, fight back, grow, learn, keep alive? That I'll read or think about: anything else can wait."
>
> These sentiments are not those of mere intellectual vagabonds growing up to be dilettantes. We are evolving a new way of organizing the life of the mind, and contrary to the criticisms, it does have a principle of selection and order. These students want to learn whatever will help them make sense of the world as they experience it and enable them to work for the changes they believe are needed. They will also gladly read something they know has made a real difference to someone they respect, be he or she faculty, student or anyone else.[7]

Cox wrote this in 1973. If it sounds current, it is because early on he was attuned to the realities of information overload and to the careerism that increasingly shapes the expectations of students in higher education and reorients the student's search for meaning in the curriculum. It has often been the case that some students, seemingly motivated only by utilitarian concerns, simply never consider or abandon the hope of finding meaning and purpose that is truly satisfying. They need initiation into critical thought, in part so that they may reflect upon the careerism to which they have become subject. For others, the question looms large: "Can self and world be composed into a meaningful and viable future?"

Once we recognize that the academy is by intention or default a community of imagination in recomposing knowledge and faith, it appropriately follows that a syllabus functions as a professor's "testimony," as a "confession of faith." In preparing a syllabus, educators declare what they believe to be of value: questions, images, insights, concepts, theories, sources, and methods of inquiry that they have found to lead toward a worthy apprehension of truth. In an interdependent universe in which all aspects of knowledge participate in the one reality there is, we may say that each theory, course, and discipline discloses some aspect of this one reality. Nancy Malone, a Roman Catholic educator, writes that "in a sacramental universe, to teach and study mathematics can be, and in fact is, as holy as to teach and study the Bible."[8]

It does not surprise me that, in my experience, the most effective educators are those who engage in their discipline (or administrative responsibilities) because in the work that they do they have found at least some access to transcendent meaning. In a world in which there is evidence in almost every news broadcast that matters of scientific fact are also matters of moral concern, reflective learners are intrigued by and grateful for access to the connections professors have seen between the subjects they teach and life lived in the complexity, wonder, and terror of the everyday world.

Students may rightly intuit that it is not typically by mere happenstance that educators have given the energy of their lives to the particular discipline they teach. They have done so because, to some significant degree, they find their discipline to be a worthy place of investment in their own composing of meaning—even in the composing of faith. Thus, the syllabus reflects only a portion of the professor's truth if it includes nothing more than a confession of some *aspect* of meaning (such as particular technical aspects of study) and fails to include the educator's understanding of the relationships among the technique, the discipline, and the quest for meaning and purpose in a complex world.

Big-Enough Questions

Every generation of scholars, therefore, must wonder: To what questions do we lend our intellect and discipline? What is the work of the academy in today's world? Do we serve the formation and practice of adequate truth? This is not to suggest that the academy exists for merely pragmatic purposes narrowly defined. Rather, it draws our attention to the moral power of the academy to teach critical thought, awaken the imagination, and encourage development of the inner authority and the potential leadership of young adults—in part by creating conscious conflict and pulling together a livable tension of restless opposites. The academy may bring together with real power and seriousness those subjects that are at the present time thought to be major aspects of reality, no matter how threatening their mutual contradiction.

In a time of dramatic social and technological transition, the art of the syllabus and the curriculum as a whole dwells in composing the questions that give them life. For example: in today's world, should students be able to graduate from a university if they have not learned to live with those around them?[9] Do we have a functional cosmology—a "common sense"— by which we can hold in common a sense of reality and purpose that respects insights from the new sciences, appropriately assesses new technologies, and addresses our radically changing circumstances? Do we need a new economic imagination? Can we continue to prepare people to extend human dominion over the more-than-human world without preparing them for intimate presence and responsible participation within it?[10] Can the resources of the university become increasingly sophisticated, while the neighborhoods on the university's doorstep deteriorate? Such questions can stretch the imagination of all and reorder the syllabus and the wider curriculum. Questions of this kind invite the academy to reexamine its own faith and vocation in the service of becoming a still more powerful mentoring community.

The Professor as Spiritual Guide

Mentoring communities are composed of more than mentors, but apart from mentors they do not exist. Many people within the academy may serve in mentoring roles: administrators, residence hall, other professional and technical staff, and often students themselves. It is, however, the faculty-student relationship that forms the backbone of any educational institution, and it may be said that the true professor serves, inevitably, as a spiritual guide.

Again, we must acknowledge that to speak of the professor as a spiritual guide may well make any number of teachers and administrators uneasy. It is an especially problematic concept for public institutions in a culture committed to "separation of church and state." I use this image, however, not to violate an appropriate distinction between political and religious influence but to emancipate professors from an inappropriate separation of self from truth.

The professor is an educator (from *educare*, meaning to lead out or draw out), one who has the responsibility of guiding toward right imagination—toward truth. The practice of right imagination is, as Coleridge saw, participation in the motion of life itself, the activity of Spirit, a process that faculty do not ultimately control, but that they can participate in and guide. Further, since the young adult (in whatever field of study or endeavor) is still appropriately dependent upon authority outside the self, one way in which the professor leads out is by beckoning the spirit—the animating essence—of the student. Hence the encounter of student and teacher that serves a recomposing of truth at the level of ultimacy is a meeting of spirit with spirit.

We are assisted in seeing how this is so by reexamining the word *professor*. A professor (at an earlier time, this meant "church member") is, in the primary definition, a person who professes something, especially one who openly declares his or her sentiments, religious belief, subject, and so on. Therefore, an educator-professor is one who leads out toward truth by professing his or her intuitions, apprehensions, and convictions of truth, in a manner that encourages dialogue with the emerging inner authority of the student.

Cheryl Keen, a professor at a leading progressive university, has recognized the vital role that such professing can play in the learning process. A competent student first asked for a more challenging assignment and then for more time to complete the paper. When she did arrive, with a completed paper describing her own educational philosophy, the student didn't feel it was finished. There were kernels of ideas drawn from the student's recent teaching experience in the community, but she was in pain because writing the paper had reminded her of how critical she was of the present school system, and she was questioning whether or not she could be a teacher anyway. Keen writes:

> In the face of her frustration, I can feel myself shift to a deeper plane. I want to be honest, to partner with her as she asks essential questions. She is pulling from me the best I have to offer. I'm surprised it has taken this long for me to share explicitly my own philosophy of education. I tell her, "I try to speak to that of God in every person. I work to make my classrooms, my assignments, and my conversations with students reflect this approach. I trust that our relationships matter a great deal. I worry just as much about the whole learning environment

we are working in as I do about my own classroom. This means I want to know people as individuals, . . . to design assignments that provoke thought and connections between ideas and with the 'other' . . . and to give the other person the benefit of the doubt, trusting that people are trying to do their best and hoping to give them the space their inner spirit requires. I have to listen closely and pay attention or I may not see the flickering of a hopeful spirit or an awakening mind. Time has taught me to trust my intuitions. I assume that class discussions, conversations, and counseling sessions . . . help . . . toward a sense of what really matters and, ultimately toward their vocation."

The gratitude of the student confirmed in Keen a sense of that meeting of spirit with spirit.[11]

This is not to suggest in any way that the educator is given license to impose idiosyncratic or private truth upon the student. Scholarship is a disciplined engagement with sources that both include and go beyond one's own immediate personal experience and perspective. An intellectual community not only consists of its living members but extends to include its forebears and a critical reappraisal of their legacies. Thus, the responsible professor is, among other things, a bearer of tradition, participating with the student in a community's ongoing composing of wisdom. Goethe said that a tradition is not inherited; rather, one must earn it. It is earned if tradition is set in rigorous dialogue with the living community, both as known in the present and as anticipated in the future.

The mentoring professor, therefore, must convene and mediate among multiple perspectives, composing a trustworthy community of imagination— a community of confirmation and contradiction. This disciplined wrestling with multiple perspectives is the practice of objectivity in a reformed sense: that is, a community's commitment to the shared discernment of truth, understood as that upon which all minds can agree. A graduating master's student reflected on the process this way: "I think probably 30 percent of the learning in the first year was done in preparation for class, and 70 percent came out of the discussion, because there was a lot of controversy, a lot of different perspectives that I hadn't even dreamed of."

Passion

For the young adult to be drawn into full participation in the academy as a community of imagination, he or she must be led out by scholarship that is animated by passion. Coleridge grasped this dynamic in describing the poetic imagination. He recognized that the image that potentially grasps truth remains a fixed, dead object (in the human mind) until it is infused with the poet's own passion, the poet's own spirit. Only then does the imagination become vital—full of life—and awaken those truths "that lie slumbering in the dormitory of the soul." The poet remains "faithful to nature" (honoring objectivity) while, at the same time, employing images and modifying them by a "predominant passion"—the poet's own spirit and apprehension of truth.[12]

This understanding of the poetic imagination suggests that all educators are in this sense poets, who, by the guidance of their own passion (spirit), represent familiar objects so as to awaken them in the minds of others. Coleridge contended that "to contemplate the *Ancient* of days . . . with feelings as fresh, as if all had sprang forth at the first creative fiat, characterizes the mind that feels the riddle of the world and may help to unravel it."[13]

If the vocation of higher education is to feel "the riddle of the world and to help to unravel it," mentoring educators are invited to serve as poets—awakeners of imagination, professors whose spirits so infuse their subject matter that the spirit of the student is beckoned out and finds fitting forms in which to dwell.

Images become fitting forms when they are resonant with the experience and spirit of the one who imagines. An image that can shape a new faith must fit the truth of both mind and heart. This is to say that truth for anyone, at least ultimate truth, is only that which engages his or her whole being. If an image is going to anchor the composing of a new reality, it must resonate in the feelings, history, and anticipated future of the young adult; it must have the capacity to affect, to touch, and finally to lock into the being of the person. This asks the educator to draw on the reservoir of images already planted in the experience of the learner, or to give the learner an experience of an image that brings the whole person into an encounter with the images the educator deems worthy. Jacques Barzun has stated it well:

> How do you pour a little bit of what you feel and think and know into another's mind? In the act of teaching it is done by raising the ghost of an object, idea, or fact, and holding it in full view of the class, turning it this way and that, describing it—demonstrating it like a new car or a vacuum cleaner. The public has an excellent name for this: "making the subject come to life." The student must see the point, must re-create Lincoln, must feel like Wordsworth at Tintern Abbey, must visualize the pressure of the atmosphere on a column of mercury. The

"subject" should become an "object" present before the class, halfway
between them and the teacher, concrete, convincing, unforgettable.
This is why teachers tend so naturally to use physical devices—maps,
charts, diagrams. They write words on the board, they gesture, admon-
ish, and orate. Hence the fatigue and hence the rule which I heard a
Dean enunciate, that good teaching is a matter of basal metabolism.[14]

The vitalization of both the act of teaching and the curriculum itself is
being addressed by voices arising from many quarters. All seek new or
renewed passion, authenticity, and wholeness in the dialogue among
teachers and learners in a search for truth that honors the fullness of what
is at stake in terms of the meaning, purpose, and the vocation of higher
education itself.[15] Keniston observed, however, that wholesome passion
is rare in American life:

> Passion is usually placed "out there"—in others, in the movies, in
> uncivilized countries, or even "out there" in some far corner of our
> psyches for which we feel neither kinship nor responsibility. . . . The
> changed meaning of the word "passion" itself illustrates this dis-
> avowal: in colloquial speech, "passion" has become virtually synony-
> mous with sexual excitation, and rarely means deep or ennobling
> feeling.
>   Of all the forces of human life, however, passion . . . is the least
> amenable to repression and the most prone to reassert itself in some
> other form. Pushed down, it springs up; denied in one form, it reap-
> pears in disguise; refused, it still makes its claim and exacts its price.
> When denied a central and conscious place alongside of intelligence,
> it becomes ugly and degenerates into mere instinct.[16]

Some instructors do not share their passion and commitment, because
in their own formation as educators their vision was so disallowed that it
has lost its voice. Others conscientiously resist having "too much influence," yet in so doing they shrink from the power inherent in professor-
ship. Indeed, the responsible professor does not seek a cult following built
around his or her personality. Rather, and again, the young adult (in contrast to the adolescent) does not seek a hero but a mentor, and in the mentoring relationship it is the passion and the potential of the student that
is finally what the relationship is all about. In the mentoring relationship,
the tested commitments of the educator and the potential, emerging commitments of the protégé coincide—at least for a while.

Listen to how three people describe mentoring professors who invited
them to deepen their own sense of inner authority, encouraged their power

to question, and helped them develop their own sense of participation in important work.

A freshman reflecting on one of her "best classes" said of a mentoring professor: "It is actually a lecture course, but somehow he keeps it a dialogue. He's always asking questions. He's more interested in an opinion than an answer. He is willing to talk about himself and doesn't distance himself from the subject. He is willing to say 'from my experience' or 'from my perspective.' He's not saying that his is the 'right one,' but he is willing to share it with us. Once when we happened to bring up a particular film in class discussion, he responded by showing it the next day in class."

A woman well into her professional life in public health remembered:

> I had a philosophy teacher whose whole approach was not to teach about philosophers but to teach different ways of thinking. She would teach about Plato, but then in the test not ask you anything at all about Plato. She'd ask you to talk about your own life experience from a Platonic perspective. And then there was my biology teacher, otherwise known as The Ace. She was young—maybe only ten years older than me—and dynamic. It was her enthusiasm that drew me. She was clearly brilliant and very dedicated to her own field of research. . . . I've always been attracted to people who are up on what they do. I didn't have that many classes with her, but what she did for me was serve as a sounding board.

A man who became a successful sociologist and executive said: "There isn't any question that one of the greatest things that we do for anyone else is to show enough confidence to ask them to do something which is important—important to them, important to you. . . . I've had people around me . . . teachers, advisers . . . all of whom have done that. They came and asked me to do things that both of us agreed were important and I was willing. I found out the joy of that as well as the duty of it. These people saw their role, rightly I think, as cultivators of talents and opportunities for young people."

The Courage and Costs of the Intellectual Life

Many thoughtful professors are soberly aware that teaching of this sort has consequences that can touch the whole life of a student. Patricia O'Connell Killen has written:

> Developing more complex ways of thinking and knowing, of perceiving and constructing experience and its meanings, changes our students irrevocably. This is the kind of knowing that cannot be un-known. For

our students this is a process of reconstituting themselves as human
beings . . . for some welcome, for others not. For all, however, it . . .
usually involves . . . a sense of tension and even betrayal of family, peer
group, social class, ethnic community, religious denomination, or political ideology. . . . Anyone who has had occasion to listen to freshmen
students talk in an unguarded manner during January term about being
at home over Christmas break after their first semester . . . gets a glim-
mer of the human costs of education. To have an idea and to know one
has an idea can be a fearsome thing. . . . To formulate a question and
to know that one's question is good is at once exhilarating and terrifying. To be able to articulate why one's question is good is to have
passed a point of no return. In all of these acts a new and more complex consciousness emerges in a person, a consciousness that offers both
promise and peril. The promise includes richer, more nuanced relationships to whoever and whatever is, including oneself. . . . The peril
includes loss of the comfort of a host of absolute certitudes; the burden
of self-responsibility; . . . and the realization that one's actions, motivated by the best of intentions, cause harm. The wager of the humanities has been and still is that the promise outweighs the peril.[17]

As this quality of awareness conveys, when educators fulfill their deepest
vocation, leading out the next generation by addressing these larger dimensions of knowing, they do not have to be on an ego trip. One can so teach
simply out of a humble recognition that "one generation owes the next the
strength by which it can come to face ultimate concerns in its own way."[18]
One twenty-five-year-old university student, obviously overstating the point
for emphasis, put it this way: "You are not going to remember . . . any of
the thirty classes, but I guarantee you that you will remember the one time
a professor took ten minutes . . . to tell you about struggles they had . . . or
how to go about learning this material, or what to think about—who gave
you some . . . insight into this program, into life, into their subject, into being
a scholar. . . ."
    In manifold ways, higher education serves—consciously or uncon-
sciously—as a mentoring environment for the re-formation of meaning
and faith. If higher education is to serve formation of faithful citizenship
in a complex world, attention needs to be given to the myriad opportunities in the context of higher education to recover the practices of hearth,
table, and commons, to reclaim the art and duty of contemplation, and
to create safe spaces for constructive encounters with otherness. Moreover, higher education will reclaim its role as a community of imagination
and a primary setting not only for preparing for a career but for planting
the seeds of profession and vocation.

PROFESSIONAL EDUCATION
AND THE PROFESSIONS

There is an increasingly permeable boundary between higher and professional education and the professions themselves in terms of their influence in the formation of young adult lives. There are two reasons.

First, young adulthood takes time. The transformation from conventional faith knowing, through the formation of young adult faith, to a tested adult faith requires living through a series of transformations over time. Though the initiation into critical thought and the unfolding of its substantial implications may begin in the undergraduate years (or earlier), they typically extend through the process of further schooling and into the domain of first professional position or positions, or other adult roles and responsibilities.

Second, and consequently, for many the journey into adulthood wends its way through an ecology of institutions. At any juncture, formal study may be suspended for a work opportunity, resumed, laid down in order to gain experience in the field, and picked up again. Service learning, internships, residencies, and the like blur the boundaries between formal study and the practice of the profession itself.

At the same time, stronger linkages between the academy and other institutions are being forged, often motivated by economic drivers coupled with the quest for talent. Among other examples that could be named, there is an intimate relationship between the professional schools of law, medicine, and business and these professions themselves.

Thus when we turn our attention to professional education, it is useful to see a complex of institutions constituting a mentoring ecology. Then, we may ask, does this ecology of institutions as a whole serve as a mentoring environment for forming a worthy sense of faith and vocation to ground a viable adulthood? Are the objectives of these related but differing institutions well aligned for the formation of the young professional? Does one institution undermine or enhance the contribution of another? Do the protégées have consistent access to mentoring professors and to syllabi that offer worthy "confessions of faith"? Is there collective commitment to the full potential of young adults, or are they vulnerable to being exploited for purposes too small to match the promise of their lives?

Within most professional schools, for example, there is renewed attention to the ethical questions and dilemmas that are integral to professional life. Some believe that this is prompted only by scandals of various kinds that have tarnished the professions. A closer look, however, reveals that this turn to ethics arises from a deeper cause. Everyone now works within a dramatically changing world; we stand on new moral and ethical frontiers.

Many of the canons of yesterday that provided guidance through established professional custom no longer suffice or even pertain.

Yet no matter what the curriculum for ethical reflection may be, it is not compelling in the young adult imagination unless it corresponds with the perceived requirements of the profession as young adults believe they will be asked to practice it. Moreover, whenever "ethics" (issues of right and wrong, legal compliance, fairness, justice, compassion, meaning, and purpose) is made into something that has a circumscribed place as a special subject rather than being an integral part of every aspect of the practice of the profession (business, law, social work, engineering, medicine, religion, and so on), ethics becomes marginal in the minds of young adults who are so acutely attuned to the real terms of participation in the world of adult work.[19] This is even more the case when matters of conscience, meaning, and the wider welfare are defined as "externals," or worse, "soft" in contrast to "hard."

What this means in yet larger terms is that there are some who question whether there is any purpose in teaching ethics to young adults. They assume that the conscience has already been formed long ago, at the mother's knee, but this is decidedly not the case. As the young adult is engaged in "the wary probe," seeking a place of viable commitment in a relativized and complex world, the young adult conscience is ripe for orientation and ongoing formation.

In today's cultural climate, however, no matter which profession a young adult enters, there is a growing perception that all professions are becoming businesses, and that the goal of professional practice is to succeed primarily in monetary terms. It has been remarked by some young adults themselves that "what they believe in most is money because anything else is too risky."[20] Although an element of economic pragmatism serves one's own life and the life of any profession, what is at stake here is the young adult's capacity for idealism, which orients and powers both the Dream of the young adult and the potential renewal of the profession in every generation. What is at stake is a sense of vocation and the quality of life in the commons.

The Future of Callings

Interestingly, at a recent symposium titled the Future of Callings, across a wide range of professions there was shared concern that something has been lost in the education of professionals.[21] What emerged in the critical dialogue of this event was the recognition that we have lost the sense that one does not enter a profession simply to have a career and a means of livelihood for oneself, nor does one serve as a professional simply on behalf of one's individual clients alone. What is now appearing is a reappreciation of the role of each profession in contributing to the quality, strength, and vitality of our common life—a consciousness of the commons. This sense of working on behalf of our common life—a sense of calling—has traditionally been a central strength of the professions. This sensibility is rooted in awareness of the needs and opportunities of one's society and the motivation to invest mind and passion in something that transcends both the self and the profession: the public good. The symposium on the future of callings bore witness to "the unanimity of agreement regarding the common vocation of the professions to address the inter-connected and multi-layered issues of society within the confines of daily work."[22]

An Interpersonal Versus a Systemic Ethic

I have observed that many young adults, despite other forms of obvious sophistication, enter professional education with only an interpersonal ethical frame.[23] They have not yet been initiated into a critically aware and systemic way of seeing that would yield a more comprehensive understanding of the power of their chosen profession and the broad, systemic reach of their own actions. When asked to think about who or what they might hurt across the years of their professional life, they typically hoped they "wouldn't hurt anyone." Upon further time for reflection, they sometimes recognized that they might have to hurt their families because of the demands on their time, or perhaps they might have to "fire someone." They did not yet recognize that they aspired to positions in which they would inevitably have to make complex decisions that affect, for both good and ill, people whom they would never know.

Part of the work of professional education is to deepen and broaden the scope of meaning-making on the basis of which young professionals will make critical choices. When big questions are raised and honored within the process of professional education, the learning that ensues can foster real transformation in the life and direction of young adults. After being asked to grapple with a number of situations common to business, a young man in an M.B.A. program that taught ethical reflection as an integral feature of business practice pondered the consequences of dealing with big questions as part of being initiated into critical and connected thought: "I find that I have more flexibility in viewing things . . . whereas I used to have basically one way of grasping things, which was the way I'd been taught. The thing this program really does for you is that you suddenly hear somebody approach an issue from a totally different viewpoint. The next time you have two viewpoints from which to approach the issues, the next time four, six. Today I will very quickly look at things not only from my perspective, but also from the shareholder's perspective, what the press says, and I think that's really enriched the way I look at issues."

Another commented: It "has changed the way I was viewing the role of a businessman. It enhanced my sensibility as a business leader—being a part of a much broader system which includes countries, cities, local communities and understanding that whatever decision I make can have an impact which can go much further than just increasing the bottom line."

Mentoring communities within the professions can evoke big questions, crack open unexamined assumptions, awaken the imagination of young adults, and birth worthy Dreams. Graduate and professional education at its best lends itself to the practices of contemplation, hearth, table, and commons, which can rekindle the calling and art of each profession—the creative imagination upon which the evolution of culture and civilization depends.[24]

Many Mentors

Once the value of a mentor is recognized, there are varying ways in which the quest for a mentor in the professions can lead to discovering a mentoring community. I spoke with an international student who came to the United States from Latin America for graduate study in business administration. He was twenty-six and prepared to use the program well. He was highly intentional about his search for "*the* person" so that "we can work together on a short-term and medium-term business plan for my company." Yet when I spoke with him two years later, he had found not one mentor but five: "[Professor A] has been involved from the beginning, and he liked the challenge. He visited the company and we've continued it until right now. [Professor B] has been very, very helpful in giving me a broad picture of where the industry's going, who should I talk to, what kinds of things I should think of. And then [Professor C], he gave me very good advice, more on the personal side. And then [Professor D] was also very helpful. Also [Professor E.]" This young man created a modest mentoring community around his Dream.[25]

A woman who is now a research physician remembers a particular professor who created a mentoring community for her students in medical school through the practices of hearth and commons:

Dr. Sagov would run weekly research seminars where everybody would sit around a room and literally shoot the breeze—every idea you could think of. She could generate enough questions in an hour or two of conversation that the rest of us could go out and research for the next three years. What she taught me to do was ask the question, "Why?" and how to try to get at the answer. She taught me how to form the question in the scientific field, because once you can form the question, you can begin to generate a way to answer it. During the course of my residency she held Friday afternoon sherries in her office and all the residents would show up. She was a real mentor in that not only would she help career development and help in the learning process, she also would help with any personal issues. Her door was always open. . . .

In a currently unfolding example, a young engineer in England, Michael Lynch, is having notable success developing a computer model that can deal with a larger measure of uncertainty, conflicting truths, static, and frustratingly incomplete information. It appears to offer a closer fit with the world we live in than do present models. Lynch says his mentor's (Peter Rayner's) insistence on (real) problem solving as opposed to "hand-waving, headline-grabbing rubbish" encouraged him to think of innovative and practical applications. Interestingly, though Lynch is an exceptional student, this is not simply a one-to-one mentoring relationship; as *Wired* magazine reported, "It was over morning coffee with Rayner and other graduate students that Lynch first considered applying a 250-year-old theorem to the task of training computers to recognize patterns of 'meaning.'"[26] In a mentoring community, commitment to one's discipline and the promise of one's students can be held together in the practice of the table.

Becoming a Mentor

When professional education happens well, young professionals become mentors themselves early on and create mentoring communities in the course of their emerging work. Susan Bratton remembers how, when she was still doing her doctoral work in biology, she went to Costa Rica for more training. She took an undergrad student with her, although she had only seven hundred dollars for the both of them. "Mentoring," she says, "isn't something you do 'later.'" Across the years she has developed the fine art of conducting her field research in the company of her students.[27]

Apprenticeship

In the same conference on the future of callings, it was observed that a significant shift in the development of the professions is the loss of the apprenticeship. As professional education has moved into the academy and been affected by the rupture between faith and knowledge, the relationship between "master and apprentice" as well as a shared sense of the common good have been eroded. Brian Johnson makes the point clear:

> [This is] not to suggest that the professions were taught better in another day—though they might have been—or that apprenticeships were without fault—which they were not. What is being proposed, however, is that as a change in pattern occurred that favored an emphasis on learning and acquiring knowledge as a . . . scientific endeavor, the other . . . contributions cultivated in the relationships between master and apprentice were lost. Once this trajectory began, the professions lost their sense of themselves as an art. It was then simply a matter of time before individual students filled this vacuum with an emphasis on success and achievement, while the relationship with the public good [and a sense of vocation] became overlooked or was at least attended to after "work was done."[28]

What might it mean to prepare professionals for practicing the profession as an art? In the fine arts as well as in some other contexts, the time-honored practice of the master-apprentice relationship can still be found. The apprentice chooses a master in the presence of whom he believes there is an opportunity to become not only skilled but "master-full"—meaning that more is learned than the skill narrowly defined. The work of the head, the heart, and the hand is transformed into a larger consciousness, into new ways of seeing, being, knowing, and acting in the world.

This happens most profoundly if the "master" is committed to the flourishing of the "apprentice"—that is, if the master is a mentor, and better yet, if the master creates a mentoring community. This quality of engagement and investment is conveyed in an account of an apprentice working with a master fiber artist:

> Nell . . . would go home and ponder her pupils, she would meditate on them. Then she would come in and say something right into what you were agonizing over in a piece and didn't want to face. She would say, "Here it is—do it." There were about eight of us working with her that summer in a huge barnlike studio. I had a deadline on my first

appliqué piece. I had been working on it for at least three weeks and I was stuck. It wouldn't go. It wasn't resolved. She came up to me and said, "Where are your scissors?" I gave them to her and she said, "Let's see, suppose you just sort of cut into this," and she cut it and handed me a piece, "and then, you see, there's an opening here—oh, and let's cut over there. . . ." This went on for about fifteen minutes. I was standing there in absolute shock. She cut my piece to ribbons. The room got very quiet. Everybody stopped and watched. She turned to me and said, "Well now, see what you can do with that." I turned around with this stuff in my hands, and everybody was looking at me. I wanted to cry. . . . [Then] John smiled at me and said, "Don't feel too bad. The first time she did that to me she didn't hand the pieces to me. She dropped them on the floor."

That was a whole new way for me to live. Nell taught me that if I'm not ready to cut my piece to smithereens I can quit. If I'm stuck on a piece, or if I'm stuck in my life, I can look at something I'm protecting, something I feel I must have, something that is my favorite, a fabric I've fallen in love with. If I can identify what it is that I'm protecting and take it out, then it just goes, everything opens up.[29]

Here, in the vortex of the master-apprentice relationship set in the context of a small mentoring community, we can see a complex mix of recognition, challenge, support, and inspiration, opening into a whole new way of life and vocation. If the promise of young adult lives is not met by this quality of excellence and commitment, professional education may be reduced to the acquisition of training and credentials.

Every generation of young adults represents a readiness—either conscious or inchoate—for the formation of a Dream, and for the potential of a true profession. Roberto Unger addressed the betrayal of this trust in the contemporary academy at a critical legal studies conference attended by law faculty from throughout the United States. After he had brilliantly described the post-Enlightenment divorce of legal method from a transcendent ethical vision and called for a reformulation of that linkage, he closed, as I recall, by simply saying to his colleagues: the task is large and there are so few of us. But we know that we came to the study of law committed to the linkage between the practice of law and moral values. We found institutions prepared to flatter our vanity at the price of our self-respect. It is as though we found a priesthood that had lost its faith, tediously worshiping at cold altars. We find our intellectual work in the heart's revenge.[30]

THE WORKPLACE

When young adults go directly into the full-time workforce after finishing high school or college, their ripe hunger for a mentoring environment is no less than for those who immediately or eventually go from college to professional schools. In every workplace where young adults are present, there is both the need and the potential for developing a mentoring community. As young adults begin to take up adult responsibilities, they ask implicitly if not explicitly: Who am I as a worker? What is the reality within which I must find my place? What and who is trustworthy? What is going to really matter?

In workplaces, fundamental patterns of life and images of leadership are being laid down in a primary way; the quality of the workplace as a mentoring environment can have far-reaching consequences, for both the individual and society as a whole.

Eric Wallen, a computer engineer turned construction worker, describes his first day on the job:

> I awkwardly join the crew with my newly purchased light-brown leather carpenter's tool belt. Its untarnished color and stiffness betrays the inexperience of its wearer. My father's old rubber-handled hammer hangs loosely in the appropriate loop at my right hip; a twenty-five-foot heavy-duty Craftsman tape measure is wedged securely in its nest at my belt buckle. Other assorted items inhabiting this foreign object on my hips include a pencil, a utility knife, and a carpenter's square. . . . I nervously and inconspicuously examine the waists of the other guys, only to discover that I was a bit over-equipped to begin the day.
>
> Within a few minutes of arriving, my boss, the architect and builder of the awe-inspiring house that was being built, asked me to climb to the top of the scaffolding to perform a simple task. . . . I eagerly leapt to attention for my first assignment. . . . I had no fear at all of heights, so I confidently marched to the giant metal skeleton perched beside the twenty-five-foot column to perform my duty. The next thing I recall is the loud crashing of my hammer hitting the two-by-ten planks below me, and then falling an additional twenty feet to the ground, landing roughly two feet from [someone's] head.
>
> Is "embarrassed" a strong enough word? How about "mortified?" . . . The rest of the day is a blur, save for later that afternoon, when my tape measure, not to be outdone by the hammer, leapt from its cozy nest in my belt to plummet ten feet to the floor.

My boss had patience with my seemingly non-existent common sense during my first two months working in construction, while I tried to learn the arts of carpentry and good old-fashioned thorough thinking. I've been chewed out on more than one occasion for having my head in the clouds when it should have been on the ground. . . .

"Mindful" is my boss's favorite word out on the site. He continually urges us to pay attention to what we're doing, to think things through while keeping the big picture in mind. The shocking and revealing thing about it is that I thought I was already "mindful." . . . I was wrong.

The wonderful—and sometimes frightening—thing about this type of work is that the results of my thought processes and actions have immediate physical manifestations. This feedback stares me in the face as I look upon an uneven cut or a poorly filled-in hole. . . .

The work I do is a direct reflection of the type of person I am. I want to be a person who does things well, but I am only that person sometimes, in some situations, and not in others. Unlike construction work, mistakes or shoddy performances in some white collar jobs can sometimes be temporarily ignored or hidden. The in-your-face confrontation of construction has made me realize that I have spent far too much time and energy trying to rationalize away the inconsistencies in my life, rather than simply doing things right the first time. . . .

And gradually, I am at last curing my own disease of self-deception, and becoming the kind of person who genuinely cares about his work.[31]

Mentors

Supervisors, coworkers, and colleagues can individually and together serve as mentoring models and guides. One young man, after having become an effective captain in the Coast Guard, attributed his success in part to his first captain, who was a powerful mentoring figure. He watched as this captain, unlike many others, spent time up on the deck talking with his crew. The patterns of presence and communication that he observed became a powerful and orienting image, a template, which he has subsequently carried into other contexts, seeing every organization as in some measure a boat with a crew. Since then, working in educational and then corporate settings, he has demonstrated a distinctive though quiet commitment to succeed in "the mission" in ways that include the survival and achievement of all.

Deep Purpose

It is critical to remember, however, that one can be mentored into the Mafia as well as into work that is morally responsible. The content or deep purpose of the mentoring work environment has great influence in shaping the imagination of the young adult. Looking back on his early work experiences, another man, now a successful administrator and social commentator, realized how integral they were to developing his Dream and his commitment to the common good: "It's interesting, I was always in work environments where there was an ethic around working for the common good. And the friendships . . . that grew out of that were with people that I worked with who shared that value system. So there was peer support as well. That's interesting. Every single job that I've been in, if there was a community of people—staff, board, volunteers—what they were doing had a greater good involved."

This period of initiation into the world of adult work sets in place an image of what *work* means. Whether in the for-profit, governmental, or nonprofit sector, what the enterprise means is formed in the mind and heart of the young adult worker by the character of the workplace in its conscious or unconscious role as a mentoring community. How the enterprise is undertaken; how its purposes are named; who matters; how moral choices are or are not recognized, engaged, and decided—all affect the formation of the young adult's sense of self and world and structure major features of the young adult's meaning-making. If, as we have seen, a central task of young adulthood is finding a place in the world of adult work, workplaces play a central role in forming meaning, purpose, and faith in young adult lives.

Recognition as an Adult Worker

The importance of giving young adults opportunity for genuine adult work and a felt sense that they are recognized as having the capacity to share shoulder-to-shoulder work with other adults cannot be overestimated. A young woman, twenty-four, teaching general education and adult literacy in a community college setting for students from very diverse backgrounds and often considerably older than herself, described what mentoring recognition and support feels like from the inside:

> In general I get excellent support from all the other teachers in that they listen to my theories and ideas as much as to each other's even though I have, in some cases, ten or more years less experience than

they do. My boss comes to me for ideas, shares his ideas with me, and
has on occasion used my worksheets with his class. He has really made
me feel like a peer, even though I am closer to his children's age than
his. He and I are teaching the same level class right now, in the same
time slot, so we entered this semester trying to figure out some curriculum we could work on jointly. It sort of fell through because the
students' reading level was so low, but we both ended up teaching a
book I remembered from when I was in about fifth grade. He hasn't
even read the whole thing yet, but he agreed to teach it based on my
advice. His support is really, really encouraging and has made me feel
very welcome at the school. He has prepared me to lead my classes,
backed me up when I'm frustrated—basically, it's like being a real part
of the team. I guess the very nature of that interaction makes me feel
like an adult.

I would sort of half expect to be treated in ways that set my inex-
perience between me and credibility, but neither of my bosses treat me
like that at all. I had a recent situation with my class in which a few
of the younger students were giving me a hard time, and when I com-
plained in frustration, I was given only support and the benefit of the
doubt. . . . That kind of belief in me as a teacher and leader in a classroom, from someone who I really respect, makes me feel like a capable teacher and an adult.

This engagement in adult work that matters can serve the kind of faith
development that is so critical in the young adult years, because it builds
a sense of trust and a sense of one's own power and agency. Reflecting
how engagement in real work in a mentoring community helped to teach
both a sense of power and a systemic perspective, an African American
religious leader who was very active in community development recalled:

If the black teachers and professionals in my community saw a young
person who had talent and ability, they wouldn't let you stop. From
them I learned the role of black professionals and intellectuals in the
struggle. I saw the importance of having people who could strategize,
who could see the larger picture, the institutional relationships. . . . I
actually got to sit in on some of the strategy sessions where they were
analyzing the political situation, seeing whose interests were at stake,
and looking at the black community to see where we could engender
support. I asked to be allowed to do it, and I was encouraged. It was
just so important to be there, because I had to know that somewhere
people weren't just being beaten down and just taking it on the chin.
There was a thinking group that looked ahead and said, "This is what

we've got to do next." I had to be part of that for my own sanity. One began to see that there was a cadre of leaders and thinkers who saw far beyond Dallas and connected us with what was going on around the world and around the United States, so one didn't feel so powerless.

The Power of Hope

Mentoring communities that are engaged in good work can mediate hope when young adults are learning to critically assess how complicated and severe some of the central challenges of our times are. Charlie Murphy, who today codirects the Power of Hope, an extraordinary program for teens who want to make a difference, recalls that in his twenties he was beginning his work as a performing artist. He was deeply involved in political movements, was keenly aware of the injustices of his society, and had an emerging awareness of environmental degradation. "I was politically informed, engaged, and in despair," he says, "when I came across an article by Joanna Macy, who understood the potential relationship between grief and empowerment." He called her up. "Joanna helped me see potential in the despair—the possibility that if people are able to move through the despair it can be a part of the path to empowerment, and a part of the work of our time. And I realized it did fit my own experience." He also believes that the fact that he was living at the time with a group of people who were all working on behalf of social change enabled him to hear Macy's message.[32] It became a turning point into a new faith.

One of the primary questions of young adulthood is, "How do I find my place and contribution in the world of adult work?" As a consequence, workplaces are critical mentoring environments for testing the relationship of self and world and discovering a grounded hope.

TRAVEL

As young adults begin to develop a sense of inner-dependence and a yearning to know for oneself, there is new readiness for exploration and adventure. Accordingly, travel becomes a context that can serve as a mentoring environment for young adults. It is difficult to underestimate the potential significance of travel in the formation of faith during the young adult years. Transformative travel experiences do not necessarily require the young adult to cross oceans and continents. Across town or down the hall is sometimes enough to prompt a reimagination of self and world. Whatever the distance, travel can be a powerful means of becoming more at home in the universe.

Critical and Connected Thought

First and foremost, travel may encourage emergence of critical thought as one steps out of the context of one's own tribe and encounters the other. One's familiar experience is cast in a new light, and new questions emerge about self and world. Most obviously, international travel can evoke deepened recognition of connection and interdependence. As one young woman from Vermont, who had spent the fall term of her junior year in college in Ghana, remarked to those who felt she had gone "so far away," "It's only seven hours away, you know." Her world had become enlarged, but she also discovered a far closer relationship to another continent.[33]

Many people, however, travel and return essentially unchanged. Transformative travel does not happen simply by means of a shift in geographical location. Some simply coast through the time, armored with unexamined assumptions, insulated within a tribe of their own kind.

Providing provocative pathways and hospitality that is both welcoming and challenging for young adult travelers and explorers can be a critical mentoring function. This may take the very practical forms of a place at the table, a bed to sleep in, or a conversation that lingers into the night. It also may take on the formal nature of extending service learning opportunities, internships, short-term employment, and ways of getting off the beaten track of one's own assumptions into places that awaken curiosity, evoke awe, deepen compassion, inform the mind, and open possibilities.

A significant part of the power of programs such as the Peace Corps is the combination of travel combined with good adult work. This kind of opportunity also permits encounters with otherness and a mentoring community of peers and advisers that can become a community of reflection and learning. Creating mentoring communities in contexts that initiate young adults into seeing alternative ways of life can reshape the imagination for a lifetime. For example, one man who is now an executive and an educator offering leadership in securing funding for nonprofit organizations has described the lifelong influence of his travel to Pakistan when he was a young adult:

> Even though I had grown up in Manhattan, I had really led a very class-sheltered existence. . . . We were in a work camp of Canadians, Americans, and Pakistanis that I found I really liked. It really fed me. . . . The combination of being overseas in a whole new exciting experience and being part of a group twenty-four hours a day for eight weeks really kind of charged me up on a whole host of levels. I came back a very changed person. I made a commitment that I should learn more about

this country, particularly the poor people here. The next summer, I enrolled in a summer VISTA program. . . . So it really made me a socially concerned and active person.

Such mentoring environments often feature powerful life-shaping images for the young adult imagination to work with over time, grist for the ongoing formation of meaning, purpose, and faith. For example, Todd Daloz still harbors this set of images from a trip he took to Nicaragua two years ago with the Bridges program, to assist in building a new health clinic:[34]

We arrived in a town made up of a few brick buildings and a lot of cardboard/plywood/pressboard shacks with tin roofs that were tied on with wire or held down with stones. The night we arrived, we stepped off the buses into teeming masses of children—most of whom had no fathers because of the Contra War. We hurried into the cinderblock church where we were to stay. Most of us were blown away by the poverty and the dirt and the children and the place in which we found ourselves. We all slept on the floor, *gringos* complaining about how cold it was and most not realizing that the forty of us had brought more stuff with us to live here for three weeks than the people in the village had, period.

Once inside the church, we weren't alone. The windows were open but had bars on them, and the kids would jump up and hang on the bars and yell things to/at us. One kid loved to yell "my lob jew" (I love you) and someone also taught him "jew ahr a cra-sie mon-kie," which was pretty hilarious, but it was also an invasion of our space. It was mid-rainy season and everywhere there were tons of cicadas (which means "hopes" or "waits" because they only hatch every few years). The kids would take these and throw them inside the church onto people and these big (perhaps three-inch-long) glowing green bugs, who no doubt were absolutely terrified by being plucked off the ground and hurled through the air, were almost as frightened as the people they landed on. The *gringos* (myself included) jumped and screamed and ran about as we were pelted by these bugs. Eventually it calmed down as some village elder pulled the children away.

The cicada tossing began a cycle of how we felt and acted toward this mass of kids. As people got more tired and worn out by the long days of construction work and the stress of connecting our affluent life in the States to the life we were experiencing in Nicaragua, the kids were pushed further away. People got more and more protective of privacy and of what they saw as theirs (the church floor), when the kids were just curious about who we were and what we had.

In the last few days before we left, all the kids wanted *memorias,* gifts of remembrance, otherwise, they threatened, they would not remember us. There was one kid I had hung out with quite a bit, his name was Lenin. As we were leaving, he wouldn't stop bugging me about giving him a "memory." I knew he had more money than other kids and didn't "need" anything, and initially I refused. Finally, I gave him my hat and he ran off with it—I thought I would never see him again. "Greedy little kid," I thought, "our communication didn't mean anything. He gained nothing from meeting me, and all he wanted was that hat."

Well, I remember saying goodbye to him, and he was crying, and perhaps it was as touching as I remember it to be. The realization I came to was that I was being overly materialistic and morally way too heavy-handed in my thinking. He was a kid. He was eleven or so and he just wanted a hat with a Nike symbol on it. It didn't hurt me at all to give it to him. If anything, my refusal to give it to him had hurt our friendship more.

As we left there was relief for a lot of us, but also a sadness. I still remember the faces, always dirty, hanging at the windows, yelling to us to come outside to play with them. So many times we refused because we were scared or tired. I have a sense of a lost opportunity, of a duty that I skipped out on or didn't try hard enough to achieve. What I gained from it the most, something that Mom told me, was that the real connection that you make with people of such different cultural and economic backgrounds is that no matter how different someone seems or in fact is, there is a certain bond of shared human experience.

To travel is to find oneself part of a larger commons, and it can serve the formation of a more spacious faith.[35] Mentoring communities on the road and back at home can create contexts in which young adults can tell their stories, surface their questions, debrief, and thus repattern their sense of meaning and faith on behalf of adequate knowing of self and world. If this happens well, young adults become more adequately prepared for leadership in an increasingly diverse and complex world.

Movements

Movements might be understood as another form of travel, into new ways of seeing, knowing, trusting, and faithing. One way young adults find a sense of meaning and purpose and develop critical, self-aware, and responsible faith is through participation in social movements. The reach for the ideal and a place of meaningful contribution in the adult world uniquely positions the energies of young adults to serve as vital fuel for transforming social movements (as it also makes the young adult vulnerable to exploitation by false mentors, who lead to death rather than to life). Not every generation has an opportunity to be part of a great social turning. But those who do tend to feel in later life a kind of privilege in having had one's adulthood forged in the fire of social conflict, in the service of high purpose.

If there is a groundswell of resistance to injustice and a stirring of the collective conscience that makes a claim for life-bearing patterns of institutional and communal practice, we can count on young adults to show up. The movement itself becomes a mentoring community, as critical dialogue, conscious conflict, powerful images, a host of mentors, a call to action, and a public stage upon which to test one's powers create a confluence of recognition, support, challenge, and inspiration—a crucible for the formation of young adult faith. It might be said that until we achieve a just and sustainable earth community, every generation of young adults deserves access to a worthy social movement. Movements are inevitably messy as well as meaningful, and they have their own kind of casualties. But it must be acknowledged that in the context of a great movement, many young adults discover purposeful participation in something larger than the self and gain access to worthy Dreams.

THE NATURAL ENVIRONMENT

Another context in which young adults travel and dwell and become is the natural world. Many young men and women know that "in human growth the road of development goes through nature, not around it," and they want to marry nature for vision, not possession.[36] The natural world may have particular power as a context for the reformation of young adult faith in our time because it is here that spirit and science may be at one rather than in conflict, and thus young adult integrity can find a home for faith in the largest dimensions we can imagine. Further, in the natural environment the attractions and bewilderments of a religiously pluralistic world may be transcended—at least temporarily. In 1994, Mark Jordahl, twenty-three, wrote a letter to his sister:

> This has been a busy month. It has sort of been a "pilgrimage month" or a month of Buddhism. It started on the 6th with the Dalai Lama's speech, then I went to Bodhgaya (where the Buddha gained enlightenment) and now I am up above Dharmsala where the Dalai resides.

It has been a very profitable month spiritually. I have come to what I think is a definite realization that I will never be a Buddhist. I still really like the ideas taught by the Buddha, and they will be a strong part of whatever beliefs I develop for myself, but the religion as it is practiced just ain't my thing. It has actually felt like a weight lifted off my shoulders. For quite some time I have thought I might want to become a Buddhist, and I expended a lot of energy trying to figure out how to start. I know I have a pretty solid academic understanding of it, but that's pretty meaningless by itself when you are talking about actually practicing religion. I am glad that so many people seem to benefit from the current practice of it, but . . . I tried. I tried meditating under a descendant of the same tree under which the Buddha gained enlightenment. It is in the same spot and it is, of course, one of the holiest places for a Buddhist. I felt nothing if not ridiculous. I looked at thousand year old *stupas* and felt nothing. I saw people bowing and touching the feet of images of the Buddha. I saw stone, bronze, gold statues. Nothing to bow to. I tried meditating in monasteries and I saw donation boxes. I was in a place that is supposed to be permeated with the presence of the Buddha, but I felt nothing.

Right now, however, I am sitting at about 10,000 feet in the Dhauladhor range in Himachal Pradesh, and I feel filled. I am surrounded with snow, but I feel warm, I feel power, awe, life, death, loneliness and home. I feel reverence and respect.

I have often wished that some sort of spiritual teacher would come and guide me to some higher knowing. But just today I have finally realized that I am sitting right on top of my spiritual teacher: The Earth generally but, more specifically, this mountain. I think that may be why I am so drawn to the mountains. They say that when you are ready for a guru, one will come to you. I have just needed to recognize my teacher. I have always had this feeling on the tops of mountains that I could never describe. My chest feels full, my body feels light, and I feel like I could cry. I can only guess that that's what a Catholic would feel like during a vision of Mary, or a Buddhist seeing the Buddha.

A mountain is the perfect teacher. It can teach you everything you need to know about living. It does not try to humble you or force you to bow down before it, but it absolutely demands respect. When you are on a mountain, you need to be there body and mind. You can't take the mountain carelessly or too lightly. It has the immediate law of karma, or responsibility for your actions. If you are careless and step in the wrong place the mountain may decide you would be happier in the valley and it will send you there.

The mountain teaches you how to live with other beings through the basic concept of ecological balance. There is enough for everybody but, once a person decides they need more, the whole balance gets thrown off. Also in relation to people, it teaches you how important it is to care about others. If you get into trouble, you need people or you will probably die. If you are alone and break your legs, what do you do if nobody cares enough to help, or if nobody knows you are out there? You need to be aware of your surroundings and act in relation to them. Is there water ahead? Is there a storm coming? Do I know where I am? Is my food safe from bears? Do I have enough food and warm clothes for the conditions I am likely to encounter?

The mountain also teaches not to acquire things you don't need because you will have to carry them. Pretty basic lessons. These ideas are still pretty fresh and unformed in my head. I am going to give them a lot more thought and try to develop them more clearly. But, more or less, I think I have found my religion! It's a great feeling. Want to join?

Young adults on the prowl for meaning and participation that is enlarging and trustworthy have a particular readiness to tune into the deep motion of life through communion with the more-than-human world. The natural world can be a source of revelation for those who have eyes to see, ears to hear, a heart that beats, and a soul that can be moved by the whisperings of the wind. As Thomas Berry articulates, wisdom about the complex unity of life is perhaps nowhere so eloquently expressed as in communion with creation itself: "[Though] no sense faculty can experience it directly and no equation can be written to express it, our immediate perception tells us that there is a unifying principle in the acorn that enables the complex components of the genetic coding of the oak tree to function as a unity—send down roots, raise the trunk, extend the branches and put forth leaves and fashion its seeds, then to nourish all this by drawing up tons of water and minerals from the Earth and distributing them throughout the entire life system."[37] Thus can the young adult's search for faith—a way of making meaning of the whole of life—lead them straight into the heart of creation.

If part of forming a worthy faith is initiation into big-enough questions, it may be essential to enable young adults to make the connections between whatever preoccupies them and the vast web of life in which they are emerging into adulthood. Some mentors know this. Linda Olds, a professor who works at the intersection of science, religion, and psychology, has written:

It is midnight. The stars are so bright they almost cast shadows on the black waters. Not too far away dark shapes toss in the warm wind, silhouettes of palm trees. It is an hour for wonder as the tropical night sky embraces the questions of the mind, somehow embodying them with a new density and significance. The sky always asks the largest questions.

They are old familiar questions from the evenings back home, when a quick glimpse up at the heavens seemed to give a breath of pause in a day too filled with human scale. Yet here, in the tropics, where vacation days roll back at night to uncover the great emptinesses, here is where the questions are imprinted in my mind. Perhaps when one need not bundle up against the cold, where you can sit on the damp sand and feel into the night, here there is time to get lost in the skies, the wonder, the infinite stretches away from this warm, green planet. There is no teacher of time and space as great as the evening sky, no greater prompter to the question why, no greater courier to the sense of majesty, of great and small, no greater dwarfer of one's own significance.[38]

FAMILIES

Rabbi Zalman Schacter-Shalomi has observed that although mentoring is an activity that is usually placed outside the family, "the model for mentoring clearly comes from the multi-generational family."[39] All families undergo significant stress in the context of today's society, especially as there is a crisis in the meaning of the family.[40] Families nevertheless play an important and underrecognized role in recomposing self and world and reforming faith in the young adult years.

As young adults seek to become at home in an enlarging world, there is an appropriate hunger to travel beyond the boundaries of family. But we never outgrow our need for connection and confirmation within that primary network of belonging. Indeed, if development is perceived less as a journey (leaving previously valued people and earlier ways of making meaning wholly behind) and more as a process of learning how to take more into account, families can meaningfully provide some of the gifts of a mentoring community. "Fruitful conversion [or transformation] . . . to a better path of life—. . . whether the conversion be sudden or gradual—is not so much an abandonment of what we have been as it is a transformation of what we have been, an inclusion of it into what we are becoming."[41]

I recently discovered this in a fresh way within the context of a family reunion. We are a close but scattered family of fifteen, presently living in two countries and ten cities. Seven of the fifteen of us are young adults. When we gathered several months ago to honor an occasion in mother's/grandmother's/step-grandmother's life, we managed to get all of us together for twenty-four hours and have one meal around the same table. I found myself wishing that we might have some way of sharing together what was happening in our varied lives.

After we concluded dinner with a yummy cake to celebrate both a fiftieth and a twenty-first birthday, with some trepidation (knowing the resistance of young adults to anything that seems contrived and inauthentic) I suggested that around the table we each take a turn, sharing something that had been particularly satisfying in the previous year, and something that we expected would be particularly challenging in the year to come. As each one did just that, we were able to catch a glimpse of each other's lives in fresh and shared ways. And then as mother/grandmother/step-grandmother affirmed the love and aspirations of the family circle, the kind of centering power that a family can provide was re-anchored for all of us.

In these and other ways, families can serve to confirm a worthy identity and continuity of self and integrity across time. In many families this requires healing—recomposing the family story in adequate terms to ground a deepening faith. In a good-enough family, however, the family primarily needs to discover the art of recognizing the young adult in new terms rather than simply drifting with the currents of prevailing patterns. Then visits home or other ways of touching base may add new layers of meaning to family belonging and play an important function as the young adult recomposes self, other, world, and God.

As we have recognized, the developmental journey includes both venturing forth and returning well. The awareness of the return has considerable power. For example, there are young adults who have limits imposed on their capacity for dreaming because the expectations within that primary network of belonging are perhaps subtly but strongly defined. In other families, by contrast, there is permission to dream good though perhaps unexpected Dreams, and there is support that honors them.

This is often hard work for parents who have made deep investments in the promise of the young adult life. A young woman who was headed off to the city to make her way in the arts had a thoughtful and loving father who was judiciously raising a long list of obvious questions. After patiently responding to most of them, she said, "Dad, I don't need your cold feet." He got the message, rented a truck, helped pack, and followed behind her small car, supporting her in her exploration of self and world, as she drove a thousand miles to Chicago. Later, I heard the same father remark that one of the challenges of parenthood is watching your children find "their own forms of faithfulness."[42]

Honoring the faithfulness of young adult children may take parents themselves into pathways that enlarge the soul and evoke new meaning. In her freshman year of college, Sara Kelly began to study the Holocaust. She had the opportunity to interview Samuel Bak, a Holocaust survivor and artist of enormous genius who is boldly addressing issues that are fundamental to the quality of life in our era. Later, when Doug Kelly went to visit his daughter at college, she took him to the gallery where Bak's work was being shown. After Doug's return home, he received a letter from the director of the gallery that began: "Many thanks to you for allowing your daughter to lead you to the gallery and the work of Samuel Bak."

When families serve well as part of a young adult's mentoring environment, their members become gracious and skilled in recognizing that we all participate in the ongoing motion of life. We all change over time. Their support, challenge, and inspiration carry great weight, if offered in ways that make sense in terms of the young adult's own experience. Families can steadfastly affirm the strength and promise of young adult lives. But as the young adult self is still appropriately fragile, families err if it is assumed that the young adult is now simply on her own.

Parents may begin to long for an empty nest, but though the path may feel at times like a maze, it is a gift to be able to find a new quality of conversation and relationship with young adult children who still return (often unexpectedly), hover, or in some cases actively resist moving out. Discovering that right mix of challenge and support is the mentoring two-step that is particularly complicated for parents. Sometimes an aunt, uncle, grandparent, or other family member or family friend may offer a "less weighted" but mentoring voice within the family.

Listen, for example, to excerpts of e-mail correspondence between an uncle and his nephew, who is a sophomore in college. In an English literature course, the nephew was given an assignment to write a sonnet, which received high commendation from his teacher. When the uncle heard about it, he asked his nephew to send him a copy. What follows is the nephew's sonnet and the uncle's response.[43] Hear the emerging inner authority of the young adult, the recognition from the uncle, the encouragement being offered to strengthen critical thought, and the exquisite process in which faith is held even as it is being recomposed.

"ON GROWING UP"

The womb is a lovely and welcome place.
Would that I had retained it as my home,
Instead of this Outside which now I roam.
Pilgrim that I am, I cannot retrace
My steps to find a youthful, blushing face.
My childish goods I've traded for a tome.
A colored coat appears from monochrome.
My playful trot has now become a race.
Yet amidst these uncertainties I feel
A branch of surety sprouting in my thoughts,
My doubts obscured by Illumination
From that Master Teacher bending to reveal
To me a Grace erasing all my spots
Of sin and conquering my trepidation.

Dear Josh—

Thanks for the sonnet. It's interesting seeing you working with this form nowadays. We have so thoroughly thrown out "tradition" that no one has the discipline any longer to work with so demanding a form. I, myself, had long since forgotten the distinction between a Spenserian and Petrarchan sonnet. Thanks for re-enlightening me.

You weave theology and introspection together in a way that is quite wonderful—and ought to be a good deal more common than it is. We have foolishly separated the two, relegating one to the church and the other to the couch, forgetting that the *psyche* of *psychology* meant "soul."

Anyway, I wanted to pass on a couple of reflections occasioned by your latest sonnet. I sensed a certain ambivalence in lines 6–8. That is, you seem to have mixed feelings about this growing up business. On the one hand, you have traded "goods" for a "tome." That sounds like a bad trade to me; a tome carries the sense of weight, complexity, and drudgery about it. Yet in the next line, you note that your world has become colored, somehow richer and more varied, clearly an emergence into something better. But then you see a shift from a "playful trot" to a "race." I like that image a lot, but it seems to struggle with the earlier one. Since I imagine the ambiguity is deliberate, I am intrigued by it.

I really liked the "branch of surety" sprouting in your thoughts. The image of your thought—indeed, your very *capacity* for a certain kind of newly complex thought—being like a growing tree is a lovely one. . . .

And then you do something really interesting in line 11. Your doubts are "obscured by Illumination." So we have a fascinating apparent paradox. How can Light (illumination with a capital I) *obscure* something? The root of "obscure" lies in darkness. Hmmmmm. So there is the sense of an overlay. In some way, Light provides darkness to put doubts to rest. But you did not use "remove" or "eradicate" or "utterly demolish." You used *obscure*. I like that. It suggests that there is something important, even valuable, about doubts. They provide a kind of salutary counter-balance to certainty. In some way, absolute certainty has a kind of suffocating too-much-ness about it that a healthy doubt or two can cut through as a touch of acidity gives character to a great wine. Doubts, of course, must be kept in line. . . . But to bounce around in a Disney world of saccharine certainties? Who needs that? The trick is to hold the tension. As a writer and critic, you know that it's at the border between conflicting platitudes where the creativity, the interest, resides.

So thanks! Since you have been kind enough to share your poetry, here's one I wrote (with much less discipline than you, I confess) some time ago.

Once
Somewhere in the Pacific,
Leaning out
Over the edge of a small boat,
I saw,
Down there,
Light.
It moved with us,
That light;
Glided beneath the boat
More silently than sharks.
And from its perfect center,
Shafts accompanied us,
Lancing the deep green,
Breathing certainty
With the faith of a blinded Saint.

Families as Healers

Some families serve as a mentoring community for other people's young adult children who are seeking confirmation and challenge, assessing possible templates of their future adulthood (especially the kind of family and community they do and do not want to create), and recomposing their own family story. Gina Higgins, in her book *Resilient Adults: Overcoming a Cruel Past,* recounts the experience of "Grady," who came from a family where his father was "severely alcoholic" and his mother was repeatedly hospitalized for depression: "It was really bad stuff, toxic stuff." His girl-friend's family became a surrogate family, and she later became his wife. Later in his thirties, he reflected: "She was a normal kid [from a] normal family. . . . *I threw the anchor out, and it hooked onto that island. . . .* What I really liked was that the parents respected each other, and they were nice to each other . . . but there was love; there was warmth. . . . I'd *never* seen that sort of respect that they had for each other. . . . *I wanted something stable.*"[44]

Diana, a young adult with a very painful family background, had the opportunity during her university years to spend time in the home of her aunt and uncle. "I used to go out to their house and then all their friends would come over, and they'd sit around usually and have dinner, and their kids, who were slightly younger than I was, would come and go . . . and their kids would tell a joke and everybody would laugh. . . . *I thought this was unbelievable. I'd never been listened to long enough to have a joke. . . . So I really got a lot from that family.*"[45]

Higgins observed that for many of the adults she studied (all of whom had suffered profoundly in childhood but were able to love well in adult-hood), the capacity for critical reflection and experiences in surrogate fam-ilies during their young adult years meant that they "gradually cast their previous family experience in high relief and then relativized them." In this process they were "aggrieved but relieved." The pain began to make sense. She concludes, "For those who are adept at sowing their seeds out-side the gardens into which they were born, recruited love certainly seems to have the capacity to flourish and thereby restore."[46]

Parent as a Keeper of the Promise

In a cultural era in which many young adults suffer from the absence of true mentors, from false mentoring, and from a variety of temptations to a lesser life in small and large ways, some parents experience considerable anguish as they sift and sort, trying to discern what powers they do and do not have as they watch their young adult children flounder and some-times head down paths that are dangerous and the absolute opposite of anything they have hoped for them. In Chapter Two, we spoke of parents and other caregivers in the life of the infant as "keepers of the promise."

In vastly different but vital ways, parents and families can be keepers of the promise for young adult lives as well.

One mother shared with me this account of her current relationship with her twenty-five-year-old son. A few months ago, she thought he was spending the holidays with his father. His father thought the son was spending the holidays with his mother. They discovered that neither of them knew where he was. When he did turn up, he had just returned from Europe with entirely too much unaccounted-for money. He would not tell his parents where he lived, though he gave them a number for his cell phone. Recently, he arranged to visit his mom for a couple of days.

"I struggled," she said, "with the question of how I would be with him. And after a long time, I had an image that helped me. I imagined that I had already totally lost him; he had died or simply disappeared forever. But he was going to be coming back for just two days. How would I want to be with him?" She continued, "Then I was able to be with him from a loving, not bitter, less fearful, un-accusing place. We had a remarkable visit. We could begin to at least walk around the things that matter. I could ask him, 'Can I rule out terrorism?' He said, 'Yes.' Can I rule out child prostitution? Again, 'Yes.'" This mother is dealing with deep anguish over her son. Tempted to just cut him off because the pain is so great, she is finding the strength of soul and imagination to remain connected, knowing her voice does matter, letting go to the degree she must, yet still conveying to her son that his life and his choices matter. On his behalf, she continues to hold the hope of a worthy Dream.

RELIGIOUS FAITH COMMUNITIES

When we wrestle with hope and fear, power and powerlessness, the known and the unknown, we are swept up in the Mystery. When a friend is dying too young, when the plan that everything hinges on is in disarray, when we are stressed out and someone surprises us with a bit of gentleness, we are awakened to wonder. We discover ourselves again on the edge of our knowing. Our imagination is activated, and our soul leans into another turn in the motion of our becoming. As the questions brew, we seek a language and a home in which to know and work them. We long for a religious faith.

A religion is a shared way of making meaning. In a time of profound cultural change, as science continues to make demands on religion and all religious traditions now share a single commons, every religious tradition is under review. In the words of physicist Arthur Zajonc, "The venerable and beautiful traditions in which we were educated are losing their hold on human belief, day by day; a restlessness and dissatisfaction in the religious world marks that we are in a moment of transition. . . . The old forms rattle, and the new delay to appear. We are born too late for the old and too early for the new faith."[47] This creates a complex set of challenges for both young adults and religious faith communities.

Since young adults are in the process of finding their place in a complex world and seek satisfying ways of ordering a sense of meaning and belonging, some religious communities primarily appeal to the undertow of longing for security and certainty, simply offering refuge in a conventional, unexamined faith. Usually well-intentioned, religious communities of this sort often convey zealous care for the integrity of conventional faith mediated by Authority; they reach out to those of young adult age in these terms, frequently with obvious success.

Other religious communities assume that, indeed, young adults are questioning Authority in the process of seeking adequate and owned faith, and that young people may push away from the dock and explore a "far country." These religious faith communities assume, therefore, that during the process of coming to critical, mature faith, young adults want to distance themselves from the religious community. It is also assumed that later, when they are older, they will come back. Neither is necessarily the case.

The spiritual quest is integral to the developmental process; it is a common work that generations young and old must share in today's world. Young adults are naturally renegotiating questions of their personal future, happiness, God, the ethical dimensions of their choices, suffering, and death. As Andres Nino writes, "These are 'big questions' in the sense that they carry the potential for meaning-making at a profound level, both personally and communally."[48] These are religious questions because they touch the whole of life. If they are seemingly set aside because there is no place for them, no language to give them public voice, the development of faith becomes disjointed. Some elements of meaning-making are being recast while others languish; there is little or no coherence.

A group of young adults, recently out of college, were speculating over coffee in Manhattan. They had attended colleges and universities where there was no particular encouragement to explore questions of spirituality and religious faith. They wondered together how it was that their consciousness of faith had been alive before they entered college but then seemingly gone underground. Now, in the harsh light of big-time needs for a faith that made sense, they were clearly in a new place and scrambling for a faith to live by. Collectively they came up with this analogy to describe their experience:

It's like high school was the period when you're trying to think up the paper topic, and you get a rough thesis, an idea of what you want to find out or prove, and the questions you need to ask in your research. Then you spend four years in the library researching, and you find out more than you ever knew you would, and maybe you lose sight of what you were supposed to be researching in the first place, and maybe think of a couple of new ideas while you're at it, or discover something that changes the entire idea you had coming in. And after four years, you step out of the library (where it's been very dark and quiet and safe) and it's noisy and you're blinking in the sun and you have a messy stack of note cards that you're supposed to organize into something cohesive to write the paper, and your original idea sort of comes back to you. But you know way too much to do that thesis, and you're disoriented and have no idea where to start, and the last thing you want to do, having been in the library for so long, is write the damn paper.

Even so, their shared intuition is that life is not likely to unfold well if that "damn paper" is never written.

Spiritual formation and religious faith development happen best in tandem with the whole flow of one's life. This means that young adults need access to religious faith communities the whole time they are "in the library." Their communities need to extend hospitality to big questions; recognize the claims of a plurality of religious traditions; create a meaningful network of belonging, comfort, and ethical challenge; give access to viable stories and myths, symbols, and songs; recognize the promise and contributions of young adult lives; evoke worthy Dreams; and hold mentors and young adults alike in a viable hope.[49]

Hospitality to Big Questions

Once when I was in conversation with Douglas Huneke, a Presbyterian minister whose congregation attracts a significant number of young adults, I asked, "Why do you think that so many young adults are present in your church?" He thoughtfully responded, "I think it is because we are willing to welcome a lot of questions." This means also, of course, not simply responding with traditional or easy answers, but rather engaging in serious and sustained dialogue. It means willingness to recognize the Mystery we all share.

Joining with young adults in recognizing the complex mystery of life has larger implications beyond creating a posture of tolerance for the questions posed by their inquiring minds. In the complex, diverse, and morally ambiguous frontiers on which we find ourselves, we have observed that those initiated into the Mystery by way of religious traditions are often better positioned for ethical leadership because they can tolerate ambiguity yet are committed to finding more adequate ways of perceiving and acting.[50]

Religious leaders and their communities have natural opportunities to gather with young adults around big questions and to honor the ultimate mystery of life, while affirming that we can learn to apprehend aspects of meaning and truth. For example, marriages and funerals (each in their own way) are woven into the lives of young adults and are occasions for walking again into those dimensions of experience that can only be understood in faith-sized terms. Campus clergy discover that funerals of young adults require a special kind of sensitivity and become a natural opening into questions of meaning, purpose, and significance.[51]

A freshman, Jennifer, reflected on the death of one of her classmates. She discovered that Rachel and her family knew that she had a condition that placed her in a precarious state of health. The physicians had told her, "You can either live the rest of your life between satin sheets, or you can simply live your life to the fullest for as long as it sustains you." So, Rachel went away to college and died midway through the first semester of her freshman year. Jennifer recalled how the professor of a course she shared with Rachel talked about this death with the class. She spoke about how meaningful—and inspiring—the funeral was. With a trace of tears in her eyes, she quietly said, "What could be more significant for us to learn than the importance of living our lives to the fullest?"

A Plurality of Religious Traditions

Later in the same conversation, Jennifer remarked: "I learned when I visited Northern Ireland that it is important not to insist on my own religious perspective as exclusive. I don't think that God thinks less of me, or that I am less a Christian because I respect those of other faiths, Buddhist, Jewish, Muslim, or others." She went on to reflect that although the professor wanted their freshman course to contend with the proof or disproof of God, "that isn't the question we are asking now—though maybe we will later. I am secure in my faith. What we are interested in now is, How do all of our differing religions relate to each other?"

Young adults now wander and wonder in a dramatically pluralistic landscape, exploring and sometimes discovering deep meaning in traditions other than those presumed to be their own. This means that religious faith communities that serve as mentoring communities have a distinctive opportunity to provide leadership in a world where we must learn to live together and often seem to be divided by religious passion.

As we have seen, development of critical thought and the growing strength of the inner authority of the young adult create readiness to transcend tribal norms and revise one's boundaries outward. A campus minister who worked to create a climate in which people could express their religious identities while honoring the experience and commitments of others described a poignant and precious moment in the regular flow of things. The Jewish students had celebrated the High Holy Days in the fall season, concluding with the building of the traditional Sukkos. After the service was over, a young Israeli woman was putting the Sukkos away when a Palestinian student happened by. He spontaneously offered to help carry one of the long beams. Then each of them paused a moment, recognizing that if they had been at home, this gesture would not have been possible. Such encounters can awaken a larger religious imagination, and faith can be recomposed profoundly and durably.

Often, it is feared, this means that students will no longer hold the faith of their inherited traditions. Sometimes this is the case. Very often it is not. When we encounter the other, there often arises not just greater appreciation for the integrity of the other but new appreciation as well for one's own heritage and its gifts. It is often through our encounter with the faith of others that we come to a deepened experience of our own.[52]

One young Jewish woman grew up in a very Protestant city with a small but strong Jewish community. In her college years, she participated in the E Pluribus Unum (EPU) program, which brought Catholic, Jewish, and Protestant students together for three weeks to practice and learn from interfaith dialogue and interreligious collaboration on issues of social justice.[53] Later, she reflected:

> After I went back home, I became friends with a Catholic. We had a big conversation one time after lunch about two big things, abortion and the death penalty. Before EPU, I was always afraid to bring up things like that. But now, as in EPU, we were able to talk with each other and to share with each other without being mad and without getting defensive. At the end, we agreed to disagree, but it was so good that I could come back home and still be able to talk in that way.
>
> The first time I went to services after I returned home was for Rosh Hashanah and Yom Kippur, which of course are the big, huge services every year where everyone comes. It was so good to be able to stand there and to not really feel the need to exactly follow along in the

prayer book because I knew from the EPU experience that I could find a prayer inside of me. I had my own spirituality, and it didn't need to be fed to me before like it was, from the prayer book and from the rabbi standing up there talking at me. And so as I stood near the back of the synagogue, I just looked at all the people and was totally in a world of complete prayer just standing there. On those holidays we're continually asking for forgiveness, and it was an amazing experience to stand there and genuinely be able to ask for forgiveness instead of just rambling off all the prayers as I had done in the years past. . . . I'm getting older and my thoughts are becoming more my own, just as my faith is.

This young woman is discovering a deeper experience of her own religious faith. What is also clear when we listen to those who have been engaged in genuine dialogue is that irrespective of what particular religious community one may claim as one's own, one does not remain untouched by the genuine faithfulness of others and the forms in which it is demonstrated. Increasingly, we all have opportunities to observe and in some measure participate in and understand the practices and beliefs of others. Religion is slowly but surely being reshaped in our time by this fact. As they do in every generation, young adults are leading the way.

Communities of Belonging, Comfort, and Challenge

Young adults look for places where they can be truly at home. If they are conscious of their own spiritual search and commitments, they seek places of belonging that can embrace the whole self as it is emerging in its new integrity. In the ongoing search for meaningful belonging, young adults, like the rest of us, value places and people where the spiritual dimensions of life are acknowledged and where it is possible to work that delicate mix of sustaining comfort and solace, along with a healthy dollop of stimulation and challenge. A young woman completing her senior year at a major university reflected, "One of my current unresolved questions is that I don't know where to tie my spirit into—there are the confines and dangers of different religions, yet religion provides a place of community and hope like no other."

Stories and Myths, Symbols, Songs, and Practices

Religion can offer a community "like no other" in part because of its capacity to give language to faith. Even in a time between stories, if the great traditions offer their stories, symbols, and songs—less as dogma and more as gifts to the faithful imagination—then with critical awareness they can be received as finite vessels to be treasured, reshaped, or cast aside according to their relative usefulness. This is not well done if it is merely a matter of personal selection from a religious smorgasbord. It is best done in the context of a community—and for young adults, a mentoring community. We all need a story to live by, symbols to anchor our meanings by, and songs and dances that confirm that we belong with each other. More, we need practices that discipline us into ways of life that make and keep us fully human.[54] Religious communities at their best provide this language of faith in profound measure. If its offering is or becomes resonant with the young adult soul, then the spiritual quest leads to a religious home.

In today's world, this increasingly means that religious communities explore and grapple with the new media. As Tom Beaudoin, in his thoughtful and articulate book *Virtual Faith,* has so boldly recognized, many young adults on the one hand tend to exhibit an experimental attitude toward orthodoxy, skepticism about religious institutions (partly because traditional hierarchies are being leveled by cyberspace), and a heightened ambiguity in their experience of faith.[55] At the same time, many young adults are creating new forms of searching for and articulating their faith, new images to convey their experience of Spirit, unprecedented modes of music—in short, new and often seemingly "irreverent" forms of credo. Great liturgy—the work of the people—is always an artful juxtaposition of the novel and the familiar. Communities of religious faith that respond to the hunger for mentoring environments are being stretched, sometimes almost to the breaking point, to maintain their embrace of these two poles. Embedded, however, in the irreverence, new sounds, and syncopations are gifts to the religious imagination.

Recognition of Young Adult Gifts

The religious community does not fulfill its role in the formation of young adult faith unless it can recognize the gifts of young adults, welcome their emerging competence, and give them power. This, again, is done in part through the power of recognition. A minister reflecting upon his own formation confirmed this:

> Attending a youth conference as a young minister to youth, I was in awe of some of the other ministers present. Men and women whom I respected, they were . . . inspirations to me in my ministry.
> One morning one of these men came up to me and said, "I would love the privilege of getting together with you. How about over a Coke this afternoon?"

I couldn't believe what I had heard. This successful, highly regarded man wanted to sit down with me? With me? Why? I felt both honored and scared. Why would he want to take his time and spend it with a young youth minister?

That afternoon we did get together . . . and had a great time getting to know each other. I can't recall all that this man shared with me, but I do remember one statement he made that has stayed with me as a real source of encouragement.

As our conversation came to a close he looked straight into my eyes and said, "Michael, I want to tell you something. This afternoon I'm buying stock in you as a person and as a minister. Right now, as you begin your ministry, the stock is not 'at a high.' But one day stock in you is going to pay big dividends, and I'm buying into it right now, because I believe in you. . . ."

There was a man with years of successful ministry, not yet knowing me closely, yet willing not only to sit down with me, but also willing to risk himself. He said, "I believe in you right now as you begin, even as you experiment and as you grow. . . ."

That afternoon as I walked alone among the pines, I prayed . . . "What is this all about? What can the words of this good man mean? Were they words from you? Were they the inspiration and encouragement you knew I needed to hear? Will the stock pay off and will there be dividends years down the road?"

. . . Now, years later, this incident, along with many others, brings to my mind the realization that God placed certain people in my life to be a source of encouragement and support both to my ministry and to me personally.[56]

I share this account here because of how frequently it is the case that when people in later life reflect on how religious faith communities have been part of their formation, they identify someone, lay or ordained, who singled them out in their young adult years and conferred a deepened sense of trust in their own potential and gave form to their Dream.

Recognition is ultimately, however, most powerful when it becomes a two-way street. Religious faith communities that serve as a home for the formation of faith in the young adult years are most effective if they are themselves open to possibilities for ongoing transformation at the hand of Spirit. Genuine dialogue affects us and alters the trajectory of our becoming. When young adults are present, we are opened into different questions that frequently make demands upon us and stretch us. This is particularly the case when the religious mentoring community invites young adults to active engagement in addressing issues that call for compassion and justice, and when it is willing to work side by side in the ongoing work of practical acts of faithfulness. In this kind of real work in the world, young adults discover their work as vocation. In mentoring communities where this takes place, the vocation not just of young adults but of all of us is deepened.

A Viable Hope

Recently, when I asked a group of civic leaders what they thought religion contributed to the new commons, the first reply was, "Hope." Perhaps religious faith communities serve their most profound function when they hold mentors and young adults alike in a viable hope. Hope is nourished in a host of ways, but one of the forms that is now needed is the opportunity for experiences of the commons—places where, finitely but profoundly, we can recognize our interdependence and have access to symbols that open us to the Mystery while at the same time inviting us to moral responsibility. At their best, religious faith communities can offer young adults a micro experience of the commons and nourish the imagination that seeks a worthy faith.

A campus minister, Mary Romer Cline, recently described a student panelist's response to a new Seattle University faculty member's question: "What do the students do on the weekend, anyway?" A student responded, "On Sunday evening we go to Mass." On this campus, the Mass is a place where a very large number of the campus community gather and the full spectrum of their lives is acknowledged. Sunday night at nine, students come pouring in from across the campus. They come to a place where they know they will see each other, they will have hearth and table, they will be "fed," and then they will be sent out with a sense of purpose. At the Mass, they are offered access to a living tradition: story and myth, symbol, song, and sacrament, by and through which they may discover and name their own spiritual experience and intuitions. They have the opportunity to know themselves as a community, not just as individuals. Here they have seen Bishop Tutu and Nelson Mandela. Here they have reflected on the protests around the meeting of the WTO, and they have been asked to consider Jubilee 2000 (a program for third-world debt reduction). Here they are connected not only with each other but also with the world. This is a place where they linger and talk (prompted also by the presence of cookies and cider). "It becomes," says Romer Cline, "a way that students mark the transition in the week to week rhythm of campus life."

Religious faith communities can serve as mentoring communities, initiating young adults into patterns of meaning-making and faith that assist young adults in discovering where and who they are in space and time, meeting them in their quest for both authenticity and hope.

CULTURE AS MENTOR

When the passionate, boundless energy of our youth is wasted
through the failure of our culture
to give meaningful direction and care,
we all court disaster.
Without elders, who grasp and protect
the mysterious core of culture,
inner purpose and spirit do not get valued and acknowledged
by an appropriate community
and people feel like victims and act like outcasts.

—Michael Meade

AS WE HAVE SEEN, the central task of young adulthood is to discover and compose a faith that can orient the soul to truth, and shape a fitting relationship between self and other, self and world, self and "God." It is not enough, therefore, to reconsider only the relationship between young adults and particular institutions such as higher education, religion, workplaces, and the family. We must enlarge our gaze and reflect upon the whole cultural milieu in which young adults and institutions dwell, the milieu that constitutes the full frame of the mentoring environment.

Every culture serves as a mentoring environment by mediating expectations of adulthood and the terms of faith. *Culture* as a word is closely linked with "cultivation." A culture is composed of the forms of life by which a people cultivate and maintain a sense of meaning, thus giving shape and significance to their experience. Culture unfolds in its politics—that is, the whole complex of relationships among people in their society—and the myriad forms both mundane and sublime (symbols, language, institutions, art, practices, customs, and habits) by which a people express their convictions of ultimate reality and thereby order their everyday life. Culture mediates a people's faith, ordering, teaching, creating "how things are" or "how life is." A culture coheres across time through the protection and maintenance of what Michael Meade describes as its "mysterious core": values or "worths" that nourish essential hungers and animate the ongoing imagination of life. Cultures die when there is a loss of correspondence between the forms and the values they hold and the felt conditions of human experience.

Since the purpose of the developmental perspective we have described is to ask, "What do we now mean to each other?" we must ask, "What do young adults and the present adult culture mean to each other? Does contemporary culture serve today's young adults as a worthy mentoring environment?"

A Single Place

In today's world, the cultural milieu functions on local, regional, national, and global scales. It has many dimensions; for example, we speak of ethnic culture, religious culture, political culture, and pop culture. Most of today's young adults dwell in a mix of cultures that sometimes complement each other but often collide in their efforts to capture the imagination and allegiance of the next generation. To some degree, this has been true in almost every age.

But certainly one primary fact of today's commons creates a significant change in the cultural milieu that defines the imagination of young adults. This is the development of globalization. If the function of a mentoring environment is to honor the potential and vulnerability of young adulthood by offering recognition, challenge, support, and inspiration—and thus initiation into a worthy Dream grounded in a viable faith—how are these functions manifest in this new cultural milieu?

Frederich Schweitzer has described globalization as "turning the world into a single place."[1] The term refers both to the compression of the world and to intensifying consciousness of the world as a whole.[2] Since the effect of globalization is both subjective and objective, it is a cultural process that entails psychological and educational consequences. In an increasingly interconnected world, it requires recomposing meaning at all levels.

Globalization is driven by developments in transportation, communication, and entertainment technologies, mediated primarily by commercial institutions that increasingly become international realities, transcending local, regional, and national boundaries and sweeping most of us along. Increasingly, hopes and anxieties are fueled by events taking place half a world away.[3]

Two primary features of globalization are its amplification of consciousness-shaping influences through new media technologies, and its creation of and affect upon youth culture. Schweitzer quotes Ronald Inglehart: "In a world that is highly interconnected, such influences do not stay in one place. The research on the change of values in the Western world, for example, has made this quite clear. Changing value orientations in youth are not limited to any one country anymore . . . such changes spread out like a 'silent revolution.' . . ."[4] This is particularly true in relation to the power of commercial and entertainment media—often intimately linked. Increasingly, young adults in diverse geographical locations long for the same athletic shoes, drink the same beverages, harbor similar ambitions. The voices that influence them and their networks of belonging may include others a continent or more away.

It follows that another significant consequence of globalization is that all cultural traditions are relativized. As the world becomes a single place, there is growing awareness of the radical diversity of people and lifestyles and endless ways of understanding self, other, world, and "God." This can foster a kind of precocious but conventional relativism. Within this relativism, faith tends to become regarded as a highly subjective and individual matter, leaving the individual little expectation of finding a home and community in the vast global sea. Some cope by making a reflexive grab for security, in either an exotic faith identity that "will do for me" or a fundamentalism that offers community and certainty but excludes big questions that may give rise to doubt. Similar dynamics spawn an ascendancy of subcultures of all sorts and a renewed tribalism that poses a major threat to the commons and to young adults seeking place and purpose.[5]

Interestingly, young adults themselves play a significant role in the globalization of culture and the birth of subcultures, since they are often among the first to experience the dissonance between established cultural forms and emerging global realities. On the other hand, critically aware young adults in search of the ideal may be acutely aware of some of the emerging opportunities and challenges revealed by a global perspective. Still uninitiated into traditional cultures, young adults are particularly vulnerable, however, to the images and apparent promise of any attracting future.

What globalization does and will mean cannot yet be very richly understood by any of us. Yet we can recognize that if global consciousness merely relativizes every culture or is defined exclusively by economic ideology alone, it does not offer an adequate ethical orientation for the formation of a worthy faith. But to the degree that globalization reveals and redefines the context of moral action in adequate terms and spurs the recomposing of meaning and purpose, it may awaken and stir new generations of meaningful commitment grounded in a vital faith.

Consumers

Within this emerging cultural milieu, there is growing awareness of a question that anyone concerned with mentoring the next generation must ask. Are we preparing the next generations to become consumers of stuff (including knowledge, credentials, success, opportunities, experiences, and so on) rather than stewards and creators of culture—that is, citizen-leaders committed to the common good? The dominant economic faith of our time, rooted in the belief that consumption based on individual choice creates a global marketplace that provides what we collectively need, invests billions of advertising dollars in the effort to ensure that all of us become individualized consumers.[6]

Embedded in this set of assumptions is a "dream" that is anchored in certain relatively narrow understandings of self, purpose, productivity, wealth, achievement, and success. As Lendol Calder has elegantly revealed in *Financing the American Dream: A Cultural History of Consumer Credit*, from the beginning the American dream has had a double nature. It is "both a set of 'free' ideals whose worth cannot be measured in market terms, and a wish list of goods with expensive price tags." In this two-sided dream there lies "a paradox inscribed so deeply in the everydayness of contemporary life it easily goes unremarked." By means of consumer credit, the American dream appears "both fabulously expensive *and* generally affordable. . . ." Calder is interested in the "core ministry of cultural traditions, the way they address the existential questions that confront all of us as we navigate our way through life: Who am I? What is worth doing? How am I to live, and what is the best way to cope with the hardships I must suffer? Cultures, including consumer culture, exist to answer such questions."[7]

Coupling the assumptions of consumer culture with technologies that speed up the pace at which commerce and every other form of communication and transportation occurs leaves all of us—old and young alike—vulnerable to being swept up in these assumptions and the supposed Dreams they offer. This is partly because there is limited time to critically examine the nature and effects of the emerging new cultural milieu and also because there is an ever "more alluring universe of distractions and greater social isolation. . . ."[8] These commercially mediated Dreams constitute powerful images of a future adulthood and, at the least implicitly, define a corresponding faith.

Yet such Dreams are essentially indifferent to those who are not viable players in the economic system. Moreover, the system's assumptions about production do not account for depleting the earth's resources or perceive any threat to the integrity of the planet upon which all generations depend. This economy has encouraged yawning gaps between the wealthy and the poor, the old and the young. On the other hand, this economy has a high level of need for the best and the brightest of the next generation. It needs them as consumers, and it needs to consume them—that is, to capture their imaginations and to harness and exhaust their talents, passions, and energy. To consume means to destroy utterly. Many bright and gifted young adults have been heard to say: "Well, I'll work eighty-plus-hour weeks for five to ten years and then I'll be free to live the way I want to live"—inadequately aware of how formative these years are for setting the trajectory and the habits of their entire adulthood.

Citizens

Although the word *consumer* is individually oriented and depends on a degree of passive compliance, the word *citizen* is relationally cast, suggesting rights, protection, and the capacity to act. Citizen is related to *civis*: city. A citizen is a person in responsible relationship to an identifiable sociality. The rights and responsibilities of citizenship may vary from one locale and culture to another, but being a citizen requires awareness and engagement.

Against this backdrop of globalization, the changing cultural milieu, and the images of consumers and citizens, how might we begin to reflect on the power of culture as a mentoring environment? What do we need to be alert to at this time in our cultural life if culture is to function meaningfully and accountably as a mentoring environment? How does the culture as a whole challenge, recognize, support, and inspire the next generations?

Challenge

In countless ways, the challenges and opportunities of citizenship are now heightened by the growing complexity, diversity, and moral ambiguity of the emerging cultural milieu. Unprecedented conditions set before the human community a significant array of adaptive challenges. Ronald

Heifetz, author of *Leadership Without Easy Answers,* has usefully distinguished "technical problems" from "adaptive challenges."[9] He suggests that even very difficult situations can sometimes yield to answers already in hand and thus may be understood as technical problems. In contrast, adaptive challenges exist whenever there is a gap between professed values and actual practice, or when there are conditions that require new learning. Here the word *adaptive* does not suggest mere accommodation. Rather, adaptive challenge signifies a recognition of dramatically new conditions and the learning required to make a creative and life-bearing response.

From this perspective, it is clear that today's prevailing culture can be a context of significant and meaningful challenge. For example, it is increasingly evident to growing numbers that a central challenge of our time is posed by threats to the integrity of creation. No longer can ecological concerns merely be a favorite issue in a long list of possible choices. Rather, this set of concerns is so fundamental to human existence that serious engagement with them touches every other domain of interest: health, education, economics, politics, religion, commerce, and the claims of justice for all.

At the core of this challenge is a cluster of big questions: How will we all dwell together on the small planet home we share? How will we reimagine what we mean by quality of life? Will we have the psychic energy, the soul energy, the spiritual energy to do what must be done? What do we now need to learn, through science, the arts, the humanities, and through relationships with the vast others (human and the more-than-human) who constitute our world?

These are some of the great questions of our time, arising from our present circumstances. Avoiding them puts all of us at risk. Young adults can hear and respond to these questions. But as we have seen, they are appropriately dependent upon a mentoring milieu that presents challenges they can rise to, be engaged by, and wrestle with in ways that are enlivening rather than simply defeating.

Intensifying social diversity is a challenge to us all. But if young adults are hobbled by ethnic prejudices or gendered assumptions (whether they are the prejudices of others or their own) such that recognition of their potential is precluded, then yes, they are being challenged, but not in a manner that encourages fulfillment of the promise of their lives. The growing economic divide ensures that many young people are defined as "marginal" and merely allowed to cope as best they may. They are vulnerable to "feeling like victims and acting like outcasts." Indeed, young adults in the most marginalized domains of our global culture are vulnerable to the exploitation and numbing (if not death-bearing) effects of prostitution, prisons, and warfare.

Those privileged on the other side of the divide may be encouraged, even required, to achieve, sometimes in narrow terms. In this they may, in fact, be cheated—trapped in golden handcuffs before anyone has invited them into great questions and meaningful Dreams. At a later point in life, they too may feel like victims, and some will break and act like outcasts.

Many young adults on both sides of the economic divide are under-challenged; arrested in conventional thought; and rendered distracted, numb, and essentially passive by some of the pervasive realities of the emerging culture: glamorization and normalization of alcohol and other drug abuse, affirmation of casual sex, the distractions and preoccupations of media entertainment (print, video, audio) and the subjects it exploits (exhibition sports, superficial celebrity, cynical politics, and violence of all sorts), and habits of technology that often prepare people to be technicians rather than enliveners of thought, word, and gesture.

The story of the development of faith offered here tells us that the central challenge a mentoring culture can offer those of young adult age is initiation into critical and connected thought and inner-dependence, by means of awakening into the realities of our time. The adaptive challenges our times present, the great questions to which they give rise, and the Dreams that they suggest are the birthright challenges of young adults. A mentoring culture must mediate these challenges by offering young adults opportunities to work alongside mentoring presences, skillfully engaging those adaptive challenges in meaningful and faithful ways.

Recognition and Support

Within a healthy cultural milieu, mentoring presences may take many forms, but as we have seen they are in essence people, communities, places, and contexts that *recognize* young adults in their distinctive expressions of potential and vulnerability. By including young adults *as young adults,* these presences help to pave the way into a flourishing adulthood. The question we want to pose here is, Does our emerging culture afford access to genuinely mentoring presences and environments that are worthy of the promise of young adult lives?

The response is, of course, both yes and no. For those who go to college after graduating from secondary school, there may be access to a mentoring community, particularly in those colleges where there is clear commitment to undergraduate teaching and to community. Yet even in these environments, severe and growing pressures erode these commitments. For example, in one relatively small yet "successful" liberal arts college, it was deemed economically strategic to sell off part of the campus. This put such pressure on the remaining facilities that there was no time in the day or week when a majority of the faculty or of the students could be available for a common meeting, meal, program, or other event. There was no longer a commons of *time*. The sense of common purpose, shared learning, and communal inspiration has been, it is reported, inevitably weakened. Moreover, the pressures on faculty everywhere, as mentioned earlier, to do research, publish, and secure grants for themselves and those who become dependent upon them mitigate against time for that lingering cup of coffee; or seminar; or presence at the game, concert, or art exhibit.

Very similar pressures are at work in other organizations and throughout the professions. For example, a notably fine twenty-six-year-old attorney with significant commitments to the common good chose to work in a state attorney general's office. He admired the attorney general and hoped he could learn from her aspects of the art of the legislative process and the administration of the law. In the course of the work, however, their paths rarely crossed, and there was essentially no time in the hurly-burly of a legislative session for occasions of conversation and reflection. The young attorney had many responsibilities, but there was limited opportunity to work at the matters that represented his central commitments and ideals.

Still seeking a place where he could work on issues that have long-term importance for the region, he moved into a large private law firm, having been assured that he would work with someone who shared his commitments and interests. The promise of shared work proved illusory; when he looked elsewhere in the firm for mentoring presences, they did not seem to exist. He asked others in the firm just slightly older, "Where did you get feedback when you were first working here?" The response was, "We didn't get it either."

There was a time when informal mentoring did occur within the professions and notably within law, but we are now at least two generations deep in the erosion of that kind of natural mentoring. As one attorney put it, "It isn't profitable for two lawyers to talk with each other; when they do, they aren't billable hours."

Stepping Stones

James Keen has observed that we dramatically underestimate the significance of the loss of community that young people experience the day they graduate, whether it be from secondary school or from college. If young adults are still making their way into full adulthood and do not move directly into an educational program or a permanent work position, they face a significant unknown; often for the first time, the future is not structured for them.

During her senior year of college, Kate Daloz became aware that she was not the only person undergoing this kind of transition. She began to ask her young adult friends for metaphors that captured its quality. One young adult, recently graduated from college and about to look for a job but without much sense of direction, decided, "It's like a trapeze artist, when it comes to that moment where you're at the end of one swing and you gotta let go and grab onto the other trapeze but you *really just don't want to let go* and you're not sure if there's a safety net or not and you know you can't just swing backward either or you'll hit the wall (and the whole time there are thousands of people watching you)."

With a similar awareness of needing to leave the nest, another recent university graduate who was about to look for a job in his home city said: "I feel like I got a new set of beautiful angel wings and I'm admiring them and preening them and everyone's giving me compliments, but then I try to fly and jump off a cliff and realize I don't know how to use them. I'm scared to death and flapping and falling, and even though I know I'll never hit the bottom because every once in a while I hit the wind right and bounce up a little, I have that constant tension in my stomach."

Another echoed this sense of inner-dependence coupled with uncertainty and varying degrees of anxiety: "I feel like I'm about to get on a train, and I know exactly what the train looks like, how long I'm going to be on it, what baggage I'm taking, what the other passengers are like, and everything else about the train. I just don't have a clue where the train is going."

Two graduates, sorting through possible career and location options, yearned for the orientation of a broader perspective:

> I picture heat lightning—it's all dark and then all of a sudden it lights up and you see everything branching out and it's amazing. But then it's dark again, and then it lights up and branches out in a different part of the sky, and you completely forget what the first one was like.

> I feel like I'm a pioneer, trying to make my way west on no trail and I'm kind of lost in the bushes and tumbleweeds and don't know which way to go and what I really want is some sort of guide to stand up on a cliff above me, where they can see the place I'm trying to get to, and call down directions to me about which way to head.

Each of these young adults reflects a mix of strength and vulnerability, and the legitimate need for recognition and mentoring company in the transitions of young adulthood. Though it has been said that the world is always ready to receive talent with open arms, this is not the experience of many young adults. To be sure, there are some enterprises that actively seek the best and the brightest and offer certain kinds of opportunities. But this is different from providing time, presence, meaningful respect, and support for young adults as they must discern and test the pathways available to them. It is another matter altogether to recognize the potential of young adult lives and ask how the firm, business, organization, department, work crew, training program, or research lab can call forth the best unfolding of young adults at this time in our cultural life.

There often seems to be a trade-off for young adults between "doing work I value" and "doing work where I will make a lot of money—a *lot* of money." Where might support for the former come from? The stakes seem high, and in a deeply divided economy mentoring presences are loath to counsel what they cannot themselves model or what they fear may quite literally cost the young adult too much. This feature of economic life, coupled with the fact that there is ever less expectation that one will remain with a given firm (a form of community), means that neither potential mentors nor protégés can see much point in making an investment in the relationship. Individual tracks to success become the norm, utilitarian relationships abound, and the kind of support that makes it possible to flourish in place or else entertain a different horizon of possibility shrivels.

Comfort and Healing

For many young adults, inadequate access to even minimal emotional sustenance creates dramatic barriers to flourishing adulthood. Young adults are very vulnerable to the attitude that "you're old enough now to be on your own." For too many, this translates into simply being alone. Most foster care systems set eighteen as the age beyond which family presence and care is no longer provided; yet a social worker administering the system recognized that her own child was not yet ready at eighteen to simply be on her own.

Even young adults who are not entirely alone may be hampered by significant wounds that need healing before an inner-dependent self can confidently move into the future with full energy and strength. As the social fabric has become strained and weakened, the responses to a recent study of young adults were not surprising (they also broke on ethnic lines). Asked what they thought had shaped their generation the most, African Americans gave as the key response "crack cocaine." From Caucasians, the response was simply "divorce."[10]

These wounds, along with others that could be similarly named, cannot be well addressed apart from the support of mentoring communities that recognize that young adulthood can be a time of healing. The young adult self has begun to individuate sufficiently from powerful but painful relationships and can reflect critically upon both the world of others who have inflicted pain and the life of the self. The young adult's whole framework for understanding suffering can be enlarged and recomposed, given time and wise dialogue within a mentoring culture. Young adults are appropriately dependent upon a culture, its institutions, and mentoring presences who offer life-bearing support by recognizing their promise, creating contexts that serve as stepping stones into a meaningful future, and offering comfort and healing where there has been wounding and pain.[11]

Inspiration

It is not enough, however, for a mentoring culture to engender only challenge, recognition, and support. There must also be inspiration. By this we mean images of a promising and viable future for self and world that evoke engagement and commitment. Thus the question becomes, In this culture, what do young adults "breathe in," what is made accessible to in-spirit them? Specifically, what images and ideologies are offered to shape the imagination of the young adult soul?

Earlier we noted that the emerging cultural milieu within which young adults are formed is significantly shaped by modern media technologies and their enormous power to amplify any prevailing image and pour it into the heart and hearts of the new global commons. The media can attract and distract, form and deform with rapid-fire power. These media determine in significant measure what it is that young adults are breathing in. As international markets create an appetite for violent images (because they do not have to be translated), and as these images must be constantly heightened in order to yield the same effect, it becomes increasingly important to raise our awareness of the makeup of the human brain in at least two respects.

The first is that the limbic part of our brain plays a vital though primitive function. It alerts us to danger. Anything that may be dangerous can command our attention—anything with shock value, anything that might terrorize. But as soon as we discover that there is, in fact, no immediate danger, the limbic mind is immediately bored.[12] Market-driven media most easily succeed if an appeal is made to anxiety or terror. To sustain our attention, the messages must change and the charge must escalate. The subtlety here is that even much of what appears not violent but instead beautiful, glamorous, or entertaining is designed to raise the fear that without it we are not attractive and do not belong (a not-so-subtle form of terror). We are awash in images of seemingly infinite possibilities of what presumably we may have, and be, or lose. In large measure, these media messages—directly and indirectly—dominate what young adults, seeking a faith to live by, breathe in.

The second vital aspect of mind to recognize is that what we breathe in remains imprinted within. It may fade from the conscious mind, but it nevertheless takes up residence somewhere within us. We become what we breathe in. But as one person, reflecting upon having grown up with many images but none that were deemed more important or valuable than any other, remarked, "If you grow up in a world where every image is of equal value, you don't have any." The consequence is that there is no satisfying home place. The young adult lives in a "hotel culture,"[13] where essential needs appear to be met but there has been none of the sorting out of the superficial from the truly worthy, the toxic from the life-bearing, that makes it possible for the young adult to become meaningfully at home in the world.

Young adulthood is an ideological time, when whatever ways of seeing that appear worthy and potent may be fiercely grasped and incorporated into the young adult Dream. Thus the ideologies—systems of images and their effects—that a culture makes available are a central ingredient in the formation of young adult faith. The ideology may be political, economic, religious, or of some other type. It may be held cynically or reverently, but it is what the young adult breathes in and becomes in the quest for a faith to live by.

In a culture of sound bites and multitasking, it has been said that we are becoming "masters of fragmentation, and we hunger for wholeness."[14] A mentoring culture inspires young adults by offering worthy images that, as suggested in Chapter Seven, have the power to shape into one the whole force field of our experience, thereby evoking moral vision and a sense of vocation that inspires the finest aspirations. In his book *The Real American Dream: A Meditation on Hope*, Andrew Delbanco contends that "today hope has narrowed to the vanishing point of the self alone," and that "the most striking feature of contemporary culture is the unslaked craving for transcendence." Arguing that the symbols that might link us with this transcendence have been terribly weakened, he suggests that something new is being born: a new and more adequate faith.[15] In such a context, a mentoring culture will initiate young adults into big questions and encourage the search for right images by which to name one's sorrows and joys—right images to breathe in for the composing of self, others, world, and "God."

Recalling how the process of imagination forms us, the quest for right images will include recognizing dissonance and conflict. It will also make provision for pause and contemplation, countering the temptations to infinite distraction and yielding images of power and value.

Accountability

Finally, it is inappropriate to speak of mentoring in any extensive way without acknowledging that mentors must do more than offer challenge, recognition, support, and inspiration. They must also be accountable (a function implied in the other four). They must be responsible for the power they exercise as individuals. As a culture inevitably mentors its young, likewise it must be accountable. A primary form of cultural accountability is the offering of a positive and worthy future to the next generations. Every culture has a stake in its image of the future, for the future shapes the present. A culture's imagination of the future must be mediated through the faithfulness of the generations. Each generation receives, recreates, and nurtures that mysterious core of culture. In our time, the generations are asked to respond to the invitation of an increasingly global society to create a mentoring culture for an emerging world.

It is difficult, however, for adults in any society to serve as citizens of a mentoring culture if they themselves are cynical, burned out, sold out, or otherwise bereft of worthy meaning and faith. Yet wherever adults are located in the fabric of culture, each affects the viability of that culture to mentor young adults well. Thus it is of enormous importance that a culture support ongoing development of meaning and faith throughout adulthood. Again and again, faith must be reconsidered and renewed if it is to continue to viably nourish the life of the self and the wider community. Because we are individually and as a people standing on a new threshold in history, we especially need people in the adult culture who are willing to reconnect with its essential, vitalizing spirit so as to mentor the future. How is this to be done?

Particularly in times of potential transformation—those developmental openings termed midlife crisis, or other transitions—it is important for adults to remember, reclaim, and renew their own young adult Dream. Having in some measure gone underground in the tested adult years, the Dream resurfaces in later adulthood, at forty-five, fifty-five, sixty, or beyond. If the young adult Dream is to have mature power and serve the full potential of self and world, then it must be *critically* reexamined from time to time throughout adulthood. The still unrealized potential depends on the person's willingness to wrestle yet again with what it asks. Though the Dream often resurfaces forcefully, it can be welcomed or it can be muzzled—and either one usually exacts a cost. If dreams are welcomed, they must then be reknown, and the formative power they held, for better or for worse, must be recognized.

The young adult Dream that dwells in the older adult was formed in interaction with a particular historical era that is no more; it was formed in a particular place and circumstance in a person's journey that has now passed. If the adult is to continue to become at home in the world, big questions must be asked again and again, and there must be an ongoing realignment of the Dream with the evolving fabric of life. What was worthy and full of promise must be reclaimed, and what was limited and limiting—even destructive to the self and others—must be grieved and relinquished. Wounds in which the Dream was embedded, and any wounds the Dream created, may now be laid open for healing.

This is not easy work.[16] One man discovered that he had not had a Dream—a sense of aspiration and purpose—other than to stay out of the Vietnam War. He accomplished that through educational deferments, which landed him in an admired profession, but his own spirit never had the opportunity for the kind of exploration and imagination that he could claim as his own. At the age of fifty, he recognized that the formation of his Dream had been constrained by historical circumstance, and he began to interrogate it and recompose a more faithful adulthood for all the good years still ahead.

A woman recognized that in her young adult years she wanted to be a social worker, work that her father feared was too difficult, too dangerous, or beneath her. Across the years of her adulthood, however, she steadily found ways of reaching out beyond her safe professional role and social location, eventually finding pathways into working in the local prison. She created a meeting ground between prisoners and community volunteers, transforming the experience of both.[17] At the age of fifty-five, she now stands on another new threshold, plumbing again that young adult impulse, seeking the next steps of faithfulness to her Dream.

Once, listening to the story of a man who emigrated to New Zealand as a young adult, I hastily surmised that he had a powerful young adult

Dream. He quietly responded, "It was my father's dream." Now in midlife and realizing that he simply inherited a "Dream," he hungered to assess whether and how he might refashion it as his own.

If adults are willing to undergo this critical reexamination of young adult Dreams, there is the possibility that a deepened, more mature and wiser passion becomes available. The self is renewed so as to beckon the promise of the next generation of young adults.

Worthy Dreams

Similarly, if a culture's Dream has exhausted its initial energy, or is unworthy, the culture too must reexamine its prevailing ideology and reawaken passion and imagination. This requires a recovery of spirit, reconnection with the master currents of the soul—the mysterious core that is worthy of being protected, sustained, and renewed across the generations. It requires reassembling the community—networks of belonging, trust, and commitment—in which a positive vision can thrive. It requires a new search for right images, an imagination more fitting to our ongoing collective experience and our deepest hungers.

Such images have the capacity to give form to excellence (now more richly and compassionately understood), to the ideal (now understood in its complexity), and to the necessity within the motion of life for both holding on and letting go (now more trusted). Thus can a mature adult culture hold and embody the wisdom of interdependence (now more self-consciously experienced) and a consciousness upon which a viable imagination of a positive future depends.

Self-conscious practices of interdependence and a renewed consciousness of the commons are perhaps the most significant strengths that a mature culture has to offer to a young adult world. Consciousness of the wholeness—the holiness—of life confirms the lives of young adults while inviting participation in commitments beyond mere self-interest, narrowly defined. In our political life, the press toward profound recognition of the interdependent reality in which we dwell is evident in issues of inclusion and entitlement, and growing ecological awareness. Though these issues ebb and flow, their persistence manifests the deep current of democracy that seeks to rejoin an ethic of rights, competition, and detached justice with an ethic of responsibility, connection, and love. This motion is toward wisdom; toward maturity as a culture; and toward a faith that knows that the one who is other is the one to whom, inextricably, the self is related in the mutual interdependence we are.

This kind of faithful alignment with the motion of life invites young adults to imagine not only a job, a career, or a lifestyle. It invites them to claim Dreams that are the fruit of a deep sense of vocation, that place, as we saw earlier, where the heart's deep gladness meets the world's deep hunger. It invites them to participate in what some have spoken of as the Great Work of our time.[18] The strength of that invitation is dependent upon those who will practice a faithful, generous, and mentoring adulthood.

NOTES

CHAPTER ONE: YOUNG ADULTHOOD IN A CHANGING WORLD

1. John Kotre, and Elizabeth Hall. *Seasons of Life: The Dramatic Journey from Birth to Death.* Ann Arbor: University of Michigan Press, 1990, p. 219.

2. Brigid McMenamin. "The Tyranny of the Diploma." *Forbes,* Dec. 28, 1998, pp. 104–109.

3. Conversation at Barton-Glover Friends Meeting with Sarah Waring, student at Haverford College, Jan. 3, 1999.

4. Meaning is, broadly speaking, the awareness of connectedness, importance, and felt significance among perceived objects both external and internal; narrowly speaking, it is the attribution of positive value to a particular configuration of attitudes, ideals, and connections that stand close to the center of one's identity and are the key to judging importance in relation to time, persons, events, and the natural world. Adapted from William R. Rogers. "Defense and Loss of Meaning." Paper delivered to the Society for Scientific Study of Religion, Philadelphia, 1976, p. 8. See also Michael Lerner. *The Politics of Meaning: Restoring Hope and Possibility in an Age of Cynicism.* Reading, Mass.: Perseus, 1996, p. 21.

5. See Sharon Parks. *The Critical Years: Young Adults and the Search for Meaning, Faith, and Commitment.* San Francisco: Harper San Francisco, 1986; Daniel Levinson. *Seasons of a Man's Life.* New York: Knopf, 1978; Daniel J. Levinson, with Judy D. Levinson. *Seasons of a Woman's Life.* New York: Knopf, 1996; and Kotre and Hall (1990), chapters ten through twelve.

6. Kotre and Hall (1990), p. 221.

7. Wade Clark Roof. *A Generation of Seekers: The Spiritual Journeys of the Baby Boom Generation.* San Francisco: HarperCollins, 1993, p. 3.

8. Personal conversation with Valerie Russell, April 1996.

9. Laurent A. Parks Daloz, Cheryl H. Keen, James P. Keen, and Sharon Daloz Parks. *Common Fire: Leading Lives of Commitment in a Complex World.* Boston: Beacon Press, 1996.

10. "New England's First Fruits," quoted in S. E. Morrison. *The Founding of Harvard College.* Cambridge, Mass.: 1935, p. 168. See also Perry Miller. *The New England Mind: The Seventeenth Century.* Cambridge, Mass.: Harvard University Press, 1939, pp. 75–76; and Steve Moore (ed.). *The University Through the Eyes of Faith.* Indianapolis: Light and Life Communications, 1998, pp. 19–21.

11. See Derek Bok. *The Cost of Talent: How Executives and Professionals Are Paid and How It Affects America.* New York: Free Press, 1993.

12. Zalman Schachter-Shalomi. *From Age-ing to Sage-ing.* New York: Time-Warner, 1995, p. 192.

13. Levinson (1978), p. 73.

CHAPTER TWO: MEANING AND FAITH

1. Parker Palmer. *The Courage to Teach: Exploring the Inner Landscape of a Teacher's Life.* San Francisco: Jossey-Bass, 1998.

2. Wilfred Cantwell Smith. *Belief and History.* Charlottesville: University Press of Virginia, 1977, pp. 41–45.

3. Smith (1977), pp. 13–61.

4. Smith (1977), p. 78.

5. William F. Lynch, S.J. *Images of Faith: An Exploration of the Ironic Imagination.* Notre Dame, Ind.: University of Notre Dame Press, 1973, p. 9.

6. Lynch (1973), p. 125.

7. Charles Spezzano. "Prenatal Psychology: Pregnant with Questions." *Psychology Today,* May 1981, pp. 49–57.

8. Erik Erikson. *Childhood and Society.* (2nd ed.) New York: Norton, 1963, pp. 247–251.

9. James W. Fowler. *Stages of Faith: The Psychology of Human Development and the Quest for Meaning.* San Francisco: Harper San Francisco, 1981, pp. 16–23; and *Faithful Change: The Personal and Public Challenges of Postmodern Life.* Nashville: Abingdon Press, 1996, pp. 20–22.

10. H. Richard Niebuhr. *Radical Monotheism.* London: Faber and Faber, 1943, p. 25.

11. Wilfred Cantwell Smith. *Faith and Belief.* Princeton, N.J.: Princeton University Press, 1979, p. 20.

12. Sharon Lea Parks. "Faith Development and Imagination in the Context of Higher Education." Th.D. dissertation, Harvard University, 1980, p. 42.

13. Smith (1979), p. 13.

14. Niebuhr (1943), pp. 24–39.

15. John Tarrant. *The Light Inside the Dark: Zen, Soul, and the Spiritual Life.* New York: HarperCollins, 1998, p. 114.

16. Anthony Lawlor. *A Home for the Soul: A Guide for Dwelling with Spirit and Imagination.* New York: Clarkson Potter, 1997, p. 26.

17. Smith (1979), pp. 61–62.

18. Smith (1979), pp. 65–66.

19. For an extended discussion of education for faith as act, see Thomas H. Groome. *Sharing Faith: The Way of Shared Praxis.* Part II. San Francisco: Harper San Francisco, 1991.

20. Lynch (1973), pp. 39–40.

21. Richard R. Niebuhr. *Experiential Religion.* New York: HarperCollins, 1972, pp. 42–43. See also Tom Beaudoin. *Virtual Faith: The Irreverent Spiritual Quest of Generation X.* San Francisco: Jossey-Bass, 1998, especially chapter six.

22. R. R. Niebuhr (1972), pp. 91–104.

23. Karen Thorkilsen has helpfully recognized that though the structure of an earlier faith may undergo collapse, often it is some element of the wreckage that saves our lives until the new shore comes up to meet our feet.

24. Viktor Frankl. *Man's Search for Meaning: An Introduction to Logotherapy.* New York: Washington Square Press, 1963, p. 106. See also the writing of Elie Wiesel. *An Interrupted Life: The Diaries of Etty Hillesum.* (Arno Pomerans, trans.) New York: Pantheon Books, 1983.

25. R. R. Niebuhr (1972), p. 97.

26. James Carroll. *A Terrible Beauty.* New York: Newman Press, 1973, p. 102.

27. Lynch (1973), p. 25.

28. Tarrant (1998), p. 106.

29. James Fowler and Sam Keen. *Life Maps: Conversations on the Journey of Faith.* (J. Berryman, ed.) Waco, Tex.: Word Books, 1978, p. 37.

30. See Robert Kegan. *The Evolving Self: Problems and Process in Human Development.* Cambridge, Mass.: Harvard University Press, 1982, pp. 121–132.

CHAPTER THREE: BECOMING AT HOME IN THE UNIVERSE

1. Jedediah Purdy. *For Common Things: Irony, Trust, and Commitment in America Today.* New York: Knopf, 1999, p. 25.

2. Parker Palmer. *Let Your Life Speak: Listening for the Voice of Vocation.* San Francisco: Jossey-Bass, 2000, p. 70.

3. Smith (1979), p. 12. For a history of the idea of a hospitable universe in American religion, see William A. Clebsch. *American Religious Thought: A History*. Chicago: University of Chicago Press, 1973.

4. Here, I am again indebted in part to conversation with Karen Thorkilsen.

5. See chapter two of Daloz, Keen, Keen, and Parks (1996).

6. Robert Fulghum. *All I Really Need To Know I Learned in Kindergarten: Uncommon Thought on Common Things*. New York: Villard Books, 1988, pp. 6–7.

7. Emily Souvaine, Lisa Laslow Lahey, and Robert Kegan. "Life After Formal Operations: Implications for a Psychology of the Self." In E. Langer and C. Alexander (eds.), *Beyond Formal Operations*. New York: Oxford University Press, 1990, p. 8.

8. Reflecting in *Women, Art, and Power and Other Essays* (New York: HarperCollins, 1988, pp. 157–158), Linda Nochlin has put it nicely:

> When the right questions are asked about the conditions for producing art, of which the production of great art is a subtopic, there will no doubt have to be some discussion of the situational concomitants of intelligence and talent generally, not merely of artistic genius. Piaget and others have stressed in their genetic epistemology that in the development of reason and in the unfolding of imagination in young children, intelligence—or, by implication, what we choose to call genius—is a dynamic activity rather than a static essence, and an activity of a subject *in a situation*. As further investigations in the field of child development imply, these abilities, or this intelligence, are built up minutely, step by step, from infancy onward, and the patterns of adaptation-accommodation may be established so early within the subject-in-an-environment that they may indeed *appear* to be innate to the unsophisticated observer. Such investigations imply that, even aside from metahistorical reasons, scholars will have to abandon the notion, consciously articulated or not, of individual genius as innate, and as primary to the creation of art.

9. See "Reconstructing Larry: Assessing the Legacy of Lawrence Kohlberg." *Harvard Education Bulletin*, 1999, 43(1), 6–13.

10. Robert Kegan. "There the Dance Is: Religious Dimensions of a Developmental Framework." In *Toward Moral and Religious Maturity*. Morristown, N.J.: Silver Burdett, 1980, p. 407.

11. Robert Kegan. *In Over Our Heads: The Mental Demands of Modern Life*. Cambridge, Mass.: Harvard University Press, 1994.

12. Carol Gilligan. *In a Different Voice: Psychological Theory and Women's Development.* Cambridge, Mass.: Harvard University Press, 1982.

13. Carol Gilligan. "Remapping the Moral Domain: New Images of Self in Relationship." Paper presented at Reconstruction Individualism, Stanford University Humanities Center, Feb. 1984.

14. Kegan (1980), p. 409.

15. Kegan (1980), p. 410. See also Robert Kegan. *The Sweeter Welcome— Voices for a Vision of Affirmation: Bellow, Malamud, and Martin Buber.* Needham Heights, Mass.: Wexford Press, 1977.

16. Fowler (1981).

17. See especially Fowler (1996); and James W. Fowler. *Becoming Adult, Becoming Christian.* San Francisco: Jossey-Bass, 1999.

18. See William G. Perry Jr. *Forms of Ethical and Intellectual Development in the College Years: A Scheme.* San Francisco: Jossey-Bass, 1998; and Sharon D. Parks. "Led to Places We Did Not Plan to Go . . ." *The Cresset* (Valparaiso University), Summer 1996, pp. 6–7.

19. Kenneth Keniston. *Youth and Dissent: The Rise of a New Opposition.* Orlando: Harcourt Brace, 1960, p. 7.

20. Keniston (1960), p. 5.

21. Keniston (1960), p. 6.

22. See Parks (1986).

23. See John Broughton. "The Political Psychology of Faith Development Theory." In Craig Dykstra and Sharon Parks (eds.), *Faith Development and Fowler.* Birmingham, Ala.: Religious Education Press, 1986.

24. See Laurent A. Daloz. *Mentor: Guiding the Journey of Adult Learners.* San Francisco: Jossey-Bass, 1999. (First edition published 1986)

25. Joseph Campbell. *The Hero with a Thousand Faces.* Princeton, N.J.: Princeton University Press, 1949, p. 30.

26. Nancy Chodorow. *The Reproduction of Mothering: Psychoanalysis and the Sociology of Gender.* Berkeley: University of California Press, 1978.

27. Kegan (1982), pp. 107–108.

28. Mary Belenky, Blythe Clinchy, Nancy Goldberger, and Jill Tarule. *Women's Ways of Knowing: The Development of Self, Voice, and Mind.* New York: Basic Books, 1986.

29. Sharon D. Parks. "Home and Pilgrimage: Companion Metaphors for Personal and Social Transformation." *Soundings,* 1989, 52(2–3), 297–315.

30. Richard R. Niebuhr. "Pilgrims and Pioneers." *Parabola,* 1984, 9(3), 6–13.

31. Martin Heidegger. *Poetry, Language, Thought.* New York: HarperCollins, 1975, p. 147.

32. Thomas W. Ogletree. *Hospitality to the Stranger: Dimensions of Moral Understanding.* Philadelphia: Fortress Press, 1985; Linda J. Vogel. *Teaching and Learning in Communities of Faith: Empowering Adults Through Religious Education.* San Francisco: Jossey-Bass, 1991, pp. 84–88; Carol Lakey Hess. *Caretakers of Our Common House: Women's Development in Communities of Faith.* Nashville: Abingdon Press, 1997.

33. Robert Bellah and colleagues have captured some of the implications of a linear, individualized, decontextualized understanding of human development. One of these is the decoupling of individual opportunity understood as accumulation in monetary terms from other social goods. They quote Lewis Mumford: "When the pioneer had skinned the soil, he moved on; when the miner had exhausted his mine, he moved on; when the timber cutter had gutted out the forests of the Appalachians, he moved on. All those social types left rack and ruin behind them. . . . [N]o civilization can exist on this unstable and nomadic basis; it requires a settled life, based on the possibility of continuously cultivating the environment, replacing in one form what one takes away with another." *The Good Society.* New York: Knopf, 1991, p. 265.

34. Tarrant (1998), pp. 37–38.

CHAPTER FOUR: IT MATTERS HOW WE THINK

1. Perry uses initial capitals for the terms *authority* and *truth* to indicate the particular way that these are constructed in early developmental positions. The same pattern is employed here.

2. Perry (1998), p. 33.

3. Belenky, Clinchy, Goldberger, and Tarule (1986), chapter two. See also M. F. Belenky. "Public Homeplaces: Nurturing the Development of People, Families, and Communities." In Goldberger, Tarule, Clinchy, and Belenky, *Knowledge, Difference, and Power.* New York: Basic Books, 1996, pp. 393–394.

4. Perry (1998), pp. 121–148.

5. For the term *unqualified relativism,* I am indebted to George Rupp's work *Beyond Existentialism and Zen.* New York: Oxford University Press, 1979, chapter one.

6. Perry (1998), pp. 36–37.

7. Quoted in Robert Rankin. "Beginning." In Robert Rankin (ed.), *The Recovery of Spirit in Higher Education: Christian and Jewish Ministries in Campus Life*. New York: Seabury Press, 1980, p. 10.

8. Erik H. Erikson. *Identity: Youth and Crisis*. New York: Norton, 1963, pp. 261–263.

9. Erikson (1963), p. 211.

10. Fowler and Keen (1978), p. 70.

11. Keniston (1960), p. 8. (The language in the citation has been modified to be inclusive in terms of gender.) This is resonant with "subjective knowing," as described by Belenky, Clinchy, Goldberger, and Tarule (1986) and discussed in Chapter Five of this book.

12. Keniston (1960), p. 6.

13. Ernest L. Boyer Jr. *A Sailor's Journal.* Volant, Pa.: Napier Press, 1974, pp. 19–20.

14. Keniston (1960), p. 8.

15. Perry (1998), pp. 149ff.

16. Boyer (1974), pp. 27–28.

17. Keniston (1960), pp. 8–9.

18. Howard Brinton. *Quaker Journals.* Wallingford, Pa.: Pendle Hill, 1972, pp. 6–68. In the study described in *Common Fire* (Daloz, Keen, Keen, and Parks, 1996), it was similarly observed that a coalescence of vocation typically occurred by the ages of twenty-six to twenty-eight.

19. Keniston (1960), pp. 17–18.

CHAPTER FIVE: IT ALL DEPENDS . . .

1. Kegan (1980), p. 408.

2. Note that this volume addresses the mind-heart dualism but often assumes, and only modestly addresses, the body/embodied dimension of human personality. This undoubtedly reflects in part the body-spirit dualism that prevails in much of Western culture. Beverly Harrison, a mentoring voice for many, has traced the fallacies and dangers of the traditional body-spirit or heart-mind dualisms that fail to recognize persons as fully embodied, psychosexual, spiritual unities: "We are not split, 'compounds' of mind and emotion or body and spirit. Our emotions mediate our basic interactions with the world. Our minds are an integrated aspect of our body-systems, shaped by the matrix of our sensuous being in the world" (p. 147). Pervasive sex-negativity in the Christian tradition has left us with a great deal of

bodily repression: "With bodily repression comes a *loss of a sense of our connectedness* to the rest of nature, the cosmos, and to each other" (p. 148). See Beverly Wildung Harrison. "Human Sexuality and Mutuality." In Judith L. Weidman (ed.), *Christian Feminism*. San Francisco: Harper San Francisco, 1984. See also Tu Wei-Ming. "The Confucian Perception of Adulthood." *Daedalus,* Spring 1976, p. 115.

3. See Robert Jay Lifton and Richard Falk. *Indefensible Weapons: The Political and Psychological Case Against Nuclearism.* New York: Basic Books, 1982, especially chapter ten.

4. My awareness of dependence as a key dimension of development was initially informed by the work of William Weyerhaeuser; see "One Person's View of Conscience with Special Reference to His Therapy." Ph.D. dissertation, Fuller Graduate School of Psychology, 1975.

5. Patricia O'Connell Killen and John de Beer. *The Art of Theological Reflection.* New York: Crossroad, 1994, pp. 27–28.

6. Mirra Komarovsky. *Women in College: Shaping New Feminine Identities.* New York: Basic Books, 1985, p. 10.

7. See George C. Lodge. *The American Disease.* New York: Knopf, 1984.

8. W. R. Rogers. "Dependence and Counterdependency in Psychoanalysis and Religious Faith." *Zygon,* Sept. 1974, *9,* 191.

9. See Robert A. Ludwig. *Reconstructing Catholicism for a New Generation.* New York: Crossroad, 1996, p. 60.

10. Gilligan (1982).

11. See Beaudoin (1998), chapter seven.

12. Belenky, Clinchy, Goldberger, and Tarule (1986), pp. 52–62.

13. Belenky, Clinchy, Goldberger, and Tarule (1986), chapter three.

14. Robert E. Quinn. *Deep Change: Discovering the Leader Within.* San Francisco: Jossey-Bass, 1996, pp. 73–78.

15. Fowler (1981), pp. 197–198.

CHAPTER SIX: . . . ON BELONGING

1. See Sharon Lea Parks. "Communities as Ministry: An Exploration of the Role of Community in Undergraduate Faith Development." *NICM Journal,* Winter 1977. In the face of this dynamic, the school created forums by means of which students who had traveled were invited to convey their experience and learning to the wider community, which did, in turn, serve as a positive contribution to the consciousness of the college as a whole.

2. See Parker Palmer. *The Company of Strangers: Christianity and the Renewal of America's Public Life.* New York: Crossroad, 1980.

3. In his recent writing, Fowler (1996) has suggested that he uses the word *stage* in a double sense: first to signify the phases or recognizably different levels of activity and understanding in psychosocial growth, and second, to refer to the theaters of interplay and interaction shared with the significant people in one's life.

4. James W. Fowler. "Stages in Faith." In T. Hennessey, S.J. (ed.), *Values and Moral Development.* New York: Paulist Press, 1976, p. 184.

5. See Daloz, Keen, Keen, and Parks (1996), chapter three.

6. Daloz, Keen, Keen, and Parks (1996), pp. 206–209.

7. Kegan (1982), p. 90.

8. Seminar conversation with Dwayne Huebner, Auburn Theological Seminary, March 1982.

9. See Kegan (1980), pp. 411–413.

10. Fowler and Keen (1978), p. 63.

11. John Henry Newman. *The Idea of a University.* Notre Dame, Ind.: University of Notre Dame Press, 1982, p. 110.

12. Keniston (1960), pp. 18–21.

13. Early on, Fowler observed that individuating faith sometimes had to collapse the dichotomies one way or another; elsewhere he suggested that the tensions could be tolerated. I believe that this contradiction in Fowler's early work is another instance of the discrepant data that, under reexamination, distinguish the young adult from the tested adult.

14. Ronald Marstin. *Beyond Our Tribal Gods: The Maturing of Faith.* Maryknoll, N.Y.: Orbis, 1979.

15. Marstin (1979), p. 34.

16. Marstin (1979), p. 34.

17. Marstin (1979), p. 44.

18. Marstin (1979), p. 37.

CHAPTER SEVEN: IMAGINATION

1. Phillip Wheelwright. *The Burning Fountain.* Bloomington: Indiana University Press, 1954, p. 82.

2. See Richard R. Niebuhr. "Symbols in Reflection on God and Ourselves." *Princeton Seminary Bulletin,* new series 1999, 20(2), 131–137.

3. In the era of the Enlightenment (1675–1830), it was as though Western philosophical-theological thought came to the same point in the epistemological pilgrimage as does the emerging young adult. Philosophical reflection articulated renewed awareness of the powers and limits of the human mind. In Germany, Kant made distinctions between forms of knowing (theoretical, speculative, practical), particularly distinguishing knowing of the sensible world from that of the supersensible. In his view, only what could be apprehended through the five senses could be "known." Apprehension of moral and religious claims was perceived as inaccessible to knowing, but he affirmed the postulation of religious categories as essential to practical or moral life, life in the lived world where human actions have consequences. Philosophical and theological reflection became more fully aware of and responsible for its own composing activity, particularly in relationship to spiritual, theological, and moral questions. (Similarly, in our postmodern period, we are learning to recognize not only the relative character of our knowing of the supersensible but also the relative character of every discrete point of view, that is, the culturally conditioned nature of every claim to truth and the exercise of power justified by such claims.)

As part of his critique of the powers of the human mind, and central to our concerns here, Kant identified imagination as the active, creative, constructive power of the knowing mind. To Kant, imagination is the free composing activity of the mind, essential to all perception and to the power of the mind to hypothesize. But as critical a role as he gave to imagination in knowing the sensible world, he did not allow it a central role in practical reason. Thus he did not give imagination a role in faith and moral choice. See his *Critique of Practical Reason*. (L. Beck, trans.) Indianapolis: Bobbs-Merrill, 1956 (originally published 1788), especially pages 3–19 and 92–93. See also A. D. Lindsay. *Kant*. London: Ernest Benn, 1934, in particular pages 95 and 275.

In Kant's view, as imagination strains to its utmost to know the sublime, it has a sense of being unbounded. It thereby activates practical reason, which then deduces the nature of the sublime. Lindsay suggests that Kant did not extend the role of imagination because he never saw that freedom and necessity somehow had to be reconciled within reason itself.

4. See Suzanne Langer. *Philosophy in a New Key: A Study of Symbolism of Reason, Rite, and Art*. Cambridge, Mass.: Harvard University Press, 1942, p. 42.

5. Coleridge remarked in a notebook entry: "How excellently the German *Einbildungskraft* expresses this prime and loftiest faculty, the power of coadunation, the faculty that forms the many into one—*in-eins-bildung!*" Quoted in Ray L. Hart. *Unfinished Man and the Imagination: Toward an*

Ontology of Rules and Rhetoric. New York: Herder and Herder, 1968, p. 338.

6. Lynch (1973), p. 119. See also Charlene Spretnak. "Don't Call It Romanticism!" In *The Resurgence of the Real: Body, Nature, and Place in a Hypermodern World.* Reading, Mass.: Addison-Wesley, 1997, chapter four.

7. Samuel Taylor Coleridge. *Biographia Literaria; Vol. 1.* (Two volumes; J. Shawcross, ed.) Oxford: Oxford University Press, 1907, p. 202. (Originally published in 1817)

8. Lynch (1973), p. 63.

9. Lynch (1973), p. 69.

10. Samuel Taylor Coleridge. "The Statesman's Manual." In R. White (ed.), *Lay Sermons.* Vol. 6 of K. Coburn (gen. ed.). *The Collected Works of Samuel Taylor Coleridge.* Princeton: Princeton University Press, 1972, pp. 59–61.

11. See Stephen Talbot's presentation of Owen Barfield in reference to the implications of computer technology for the ongoing evolution of consciousness: *The Future Does Not Compute: Transcending the Machines in Our Midst.* Sebastopol, Calif.: O'Reilly and Associates, 1995; and David Abram's *The Spell of the Sensuous: Perception and Language in a More-Than-Human World.* New York: Pantheon Books, 1996.

12. Coleridge (1907), vol. 1, p. 202.

13. D. W. Winnicott has addressed this paradox by observing that the child composes that which the child finds (*The Maturational Processes and the Facilitating Environment.* New York: International University Press, 1965). See also Ana-Maria Rizzuto, *The Birth of the Living God: A Psychoanalytic Study.* Chicago: University of Chicago Press, 1979.

14. James E. Loder. *The Logic of the Spirit: Human Development in Theological Perspective.* San Francisco: Jossey-Bass, 1998, p. 113.

15. Wheelwright (1954), p. 79.

16. Gaston Bachelard. *The Poetics of Space.* (M. Jolas, trans.) Boston: Beacon Press, 1969, p. 39. See also R. R. Niebuhr (1972), pp. xi–xiv.

17. Barbara E. Rooke (ed.). *The Collected Works of Samuel Taylor Coleridge.* (K. Coburn, gen. ed.) Vol. 4: *The Friend* (vol. 1 of vol. 4), p. cii.

18. James E. Loder. *The Transforming Moment: Understanding Convictional Experiences.* San Francisco: Harper San Francisco, 1981, p. 53.

19. Scott R. Sanders. *Hunting for Hope: A Father's Journeys.* Boston: Beacon Press, 1998, pp. 8–9.

20. Loder (1981), p. 32. Loder draws on Harold Rugg, who described this moment as allowing the "transliminal mind to be at work. The true locus

of the creative imagination is the border state that marks off the conscious from the nonconscious. This is the stage between conscious alert awareness, . . . and the deep nonconscious in which Freud was intensely absorbed. James was aware of it, calling it 'the fringe,' 'the waking trance'. . . . This is the Taoists' state of 'letting things happen,' where day dreaming and reveries go on, where Whitehead's prehension and Wild's intuition as primal awareness function; where we know before we know we know . . . the true creative center. . . . I think of it as 'off-conscious,' not unconscious, for the organism is awake, alert, and in control." Harold Rugg. *Imagination.* Orlando: Harcourt Brace, 1963, pp. 39–40.

21. Bachelard (1969), p. xviii.

22. Coleridge (1907), vol. 1, pp. 85–86.

23. Coleridge (1907), vol. 1, p. 167.

24. Evelyn Fox Keller. *A Feeling for the Organism: The Life and Work of Barbara McClintock.* New York: Freeman, 1983, pp. 115, 117.

25. The Krista Foundation's gift to the first Krista Colleagues was Wayne Mueller's *Sabbath: Restoring the Sacred Rhythm of Rest.* New York: Bantam, 1999.

26. See also Andres Nino. "Spirit Quest Among Young Adults." In Victor H. Kazanjian Jr. and Peter Laurence (eds.), *Education as Transformation: Religious Pluralism, Spirituality, and a New Vision for Higher Education in America.* Baltimore: Lang, 2000, p. 52.

27. Loder (1981), p. 36.

28. Horace Bushnell. "Dissertation on Language." In *God in Christ.* Hartford, Conn.: Brown and Parsons, 1886, pp. 20–21.

29. Bushnell (1886), pp. 24–25.

30. Bushnell (1886), p. 23.

31. Bushnell (1886), p. 52.

32. See Gordon Kaufman. *The Theological Imagination: Constructing the Concept of God.* Philadelphia: Westminster Press, 1981; and Sallie McFague. *Metaphorical Theology: Models of God in Religious Language.* Philadelphia: Fortress Press, 1982.

33. Langer (1942), pp. 40–41.

34. R. R. Niebuhr (1999), p. 130.

35. Sara Eileen Kelly, college application essay, 1998.

36. Beaudoin (1998), pp. 74–77.

37. H. R. Niebuhr. *The Meaning of Revelation.* New York: Macmillan, 1952, p. 93.

38. H. R. Niebuhr (1952), p. 109.

39. H. R. Niebuhr (1952), p. 93.

40. H. R. Niebuhr (1952), p. 154.

41. Alfred North Whitehead. *The Aims of Education and Other Essays*. New York: Free Press, 1929, p. 25.

42. Bushnell (1886), pp. 81–82.

43. Loder (1981), p. 55.

44. From a lecture by Richard R. Niebuhr, a paraphrase from Coleridge: "with feelings as fresh as if all had then sprang forth at the first creative fiat" (1907, vol. 1, p. 59).

45. Lynch (1973), p. 63.

46. Arthur Zajonc. "Molding the Self and the Common Cognitive Sources of Science and Religion." In Kazanjian and Laurence (2000), pp. 61–63.

47. Northrop Frye. "The Expanding World of Metaphor." *Journal of the American Academy of Religion*, 1985, 53(4), 591.

48. Loder, unpublished paper.

49. H. R. Niebuhr (1952), pp. 95–109.

50. Patricia M. Sparks. *The Female Imagination*. New York: Avon, 1976, p. 4.

51. Owen Barfield. *What Coleridge Thought*. Middletown, Conn.: Wesleyan University Press, 1971, p. 155.

52. H. R. Niebuhr (1952), p. 96.

53. H. R. Niebuhr (1952), p. 80.

54. See Kegan (1994), chapter ten.

55. H. R. Niebuhr (1952), pp. 108 and 96.

56. See Sharon D. Parks. "Reimagining the Role of the Human in the Earth Community." In Fritz Hull (ed.), *Earth and Spirit*. New York: Continuum, 1993.

57. Mary Moschella, baccalaureate address, Harvard Divinity School, June 8, 1983. See also her "Back Doors and Other Openings." In Allison Stokes (ed.), *Women Pastors*. New York: Crossroad, 1995.

58. R. J. Lifton, *The Broken Connection: On Death and the Continuity of Life*. New York: Simon & Schuster, 1979, p. 39.

CHAPTER EIGHT: THE GIFTS OF A MENTORING ENVIRONMENT

1. Richard J. Light. *The Harvard Assessment Seminars: Explorations with Students and Faculty About Teaching, Learning, and Student Life*. Harvard University Graduate School of Education and Kennedy School of Government, 1992.

2. For an excellent portrayal of the mentor in relationship to older adults, see Laurent A. Daloz. *Mentor: Guiding the Journey of Adult Learners.* (2nd ed.) San Francisco: Jossey-Bass, 1999.

3. Agnes K. Missirian. *The Corporate Connection: Why Executive Women Need Mentors to Reach the Top.* Upper Saddle River, N.J.: Prentice-Hall, 1982, p. 47.

4. Martin Buber. *I and Thou.* (R. G. Smith, trans.) New York: Scribner, 1958.

5. Gary Whited. Essay in Edward F. Mooney (ed.), *Wilderness and the Heart: Henry Bugbee's Philosophy of Place, Presence, and Memory.* Athens: University of Georgia Press, 1999. See also Daloz, Keen, Keen, and Parks (1996), pp. 80–101.

6. See the twenty-two-minute teaching video of Daloz, Keen, Keen, and Parks's *Common Fire: Leading Lives of Commitment in a Complex World.* (Terry Strauss, producer.) Clinton, Wash.: Whidbey Institute, 1997.

7. Coleridge (1907), vol. 1, p. 98.

8. A. Storr. *Feet of Clay. Saints, Sinners & Madmen: A Study of Gurus.* New York: Free Press, 1996.

9. Mary Jo Bona, Jane Rinehart, and Rose Mary Volbrecht. "Show Me How to Do Like You: Co-Mentoring as Feminist Pedagogy." *Feminist Teacher,* 9(3), 116–124.

10. See Daloz, Keen, Keen, and Parks (1996), pp. 45–46, 206–207.

11. Steve Garber has observed that people who have formed a viable adult faith have in their young adult years "(1) formed a worldview that could account for truth amidst the challenge of relativism, (2) found a mentor whose life 'pictured' that possibility of living with and in that worldview, and (3) forged friendships with folk whose common life offered a context for those convictions to be embodied." *The Fabric of Faithfulness: Weaving Together Belief & Behavior During the University Years.* Downers Grove, Ill.: InterVarsity Press, 1996, p. 160.

12. For an account of this program see J. P. Keen. "Appreciative Engagement of Diversity: E Pluribus Unum and the Education as Transformation Project." In Kazanjian and Laurence (2000).

13. See Sharon D. Parks. "Is It Too Late?" In T. Piper, M. Gentile, and S. D. Parks (eds.), *Can Ethics Be Taught? Approaches, Perspectives, and Challenges at Harvard Business School.* Boston: Harvard Business School, 1993.

14. See Daloz, Keen, Keen, and Parks (1996), chapter three.

15. Douglas Steere. *Dimensions of Prayer.* General Board of Global Ministries, United Methodist Church, 1982.

16. See Jon C. Dalton and Anne Marie Petrie. "The Power of Peer Culture." *Educational Record: The Magazine of Higher Education,* Summer/Fall 1997, pp. 19–24.

17. See Beverly Daniel Tatum. "Changing Lives, Changing Communities: Building a Capacity for Connection in a Pluralistic Context." In Kazanjian and Laurence (2000), p. 88.

18. See Daloz, Keen, Keen, and Parks (1996), chapter four.

19. Diana Eck. *Encountering God: A Spiritual Journey from Bozeman to Banaras.* Boston: Beacon Press, 1993, p. 37.

20. Renee Lertzman. "Living on the Rim: Notes from the Ontologically Insecure." *The Symposium,* 1999, *1*(6), 1–2, 5.

21. Levinson (1978), pp. 91–93; and Levinson with Levinson (1996), pp. 238–239.

22. Levinson (1978), p. 91.

23. Carol Gilligan. "Moral Development." In Arthur W. Chickering and Associates (eds.), *The Modern American College.* San Francisco: Jossey-Bass, 1981, pp. 139–57. Note that for Kohlberg, "principled moral judgment *solved* the problem of moral relativism; for Perry, relativism *found* the problem in principled moral judgment" (p. 153).

24. Gilligan (1981).

25. Gilligan (1981), p. 149.

26. Gilligan (1981), p. 148.

27. Gilligan (1981), p. 148.

28. Gilligan (1981), p. 150.

29. Gilligan (1981), p. 151.

30. Gilligan (1981), pp. 145–146.

31. Gilligan (1981), p. 155.

32. See Frederick Bueckner. *Wishful Thinking: A Theological ABC.* New York: HarperCollins, 1973. See also Daloz, Keen, Keen, and Parks (1996), chapters five and seven; Tarrant (1998); Gregg Levoy. *Callings: Finding and Following an Authentic Life.* New York: Harmony Books, 1997; and Palmer (2000).

33. See Daloz, Keen, Keen, and Parks (1996), p. 148.

34. See the chapter "Suffering Has a Religious Dimension" in Beaudoin (1998).

35. Rosemary Radford Ruether. "Beginnings: An Intellectual Autobiography." In Gregory Baum (ed.), *Journeys.* New York: Paulist Press, 1975, pp. 40–41.

36. See chapter four of Alexander W. Astin. *What Matters in College: Four Critical Years Revisited.* San Francisco: Jossey-Bass, 1993.

37. R. R. Niebuhr (1999), p. 135.

38. See Linda E. Olds. *Metaphors of Interrelatedness: Toward a Systems Theory of Psychology.* Albany: State University of New York Press, 1992.

39. See Dorothy Bass (ed.). *Practicing Our Faith: A Way of Life for a Searching People.* San Francisco: Jossey-Bass, 1996; and C. Dykstra. *Growing in the Life of Faith: Education and Christian Practices.* San Francisco: Jossey-Bass, 1999.

40. Bachelard (1969), p. 6.

CHAPTER NINE: MENTORING COMMUNITIES

1. See Daloz (1999).

2. See Richard A. Morrill. *Teaching Values in College.* San Francisco: Jossey-Bass, 1980, pp. 59–62.

3. See Smith's review of "The University: The Anatomy of Academe" by Murray G. Ross. *Dalhousie Review,* 1977, *57,* 546; and Douglas Sloan. *Faith and Knowledge: Mainline Protestantism and American Higher Education.* Louisville, Ky.: Westminster John Knox Press, 1994.

4. George Rupp. *Beyond Existentialism and Zen.* New York: Oxford University Press, 1979, pp. 8–9.

5. For example, see Kazanjian and Laurence (2000); William H. Willimon and Thomas H. Naylor. *The Abandoned Generation: Rethinking Higher Education.* Grand Rapids: Erdmands, 1995; George M. Marsden. *The Soul of the American University: From Protestant Establishment to Establishment of Nonbelief.* Oxford: Oxford University Press, 1994; and Mark R. Schwehn. *Exiles from Eden: Religion and the Academic Vocation in America.* New York: Oxford University Press, 1993.

6. See Sharon D. Parks. "The University as a Mentoring Environment," Indiana Office for Campus Ministries, Indianapolis, 1992.

7. Harvey Cox. *Seduction of the Spirit.* New York: Simon & Schuster, 1973, pp. 100–101, 103–104. The language has been modified to be inclusive, as is now the practice of the author.

8. Nancy Malone. "On Being Passionate: Reflections on Roman Catholic Approaches to Spirituality." In R. Rankin (ed.), *The Recovery of Spirit in Higher Education.* New York: Seabury, 1980, pp. 58–67.

9. See "Preventing Cultural Clashes in Academe: Reports from 3 Countries." *The Chronicle of Higher Education,* Feb. 25, 2000, pp. A56-A59.

10. See Thomas Berry. *The Great Work: Our Way into the Future.* New York: Bell Tower, 1999, chapter seven; and David Orr. *Earth in Mind: On Educa-*

tion, Environment, and the Human Prospect. Washington D.C.: Island Press, 1994, and Abram (1996).

11. Cheryl H. Keen. "Spiritual Assumptions Undergird Educational Priorities: A Personal Narrative." In Kazanjian and Laurence (2000).

12. Coleridge (1907), vol. 2, pp. 5, 16. "The imagination of the poet remains under . . . control of will and understanding," but its vocation above all is to make manifest "the original gift of spreading . . . the depth and height of the ideal world around forms, incidents, and situations, of which for the common view, custom had bedimmed the luster, had dried up all the sparkle and the dew drops." Vol. 2, p. 11, and vol. 1, p. 59.

13. Coleridge (1907), vol. 1, p. 59.

14. Jacques Barzun. *Teacher in America.* Indianapolis: Liberty Press, 1981, pp. 42–43. (Originally published 1945)

15. See, for example, bell hooks. *Teaching to Transgress: Education as the Practice of Freedom.* New York: Routledge, 1994; Stephen Brookfield. *The Skillful Teacher.* San Francisco: Jossey-Bass, 1990; Palmer (1998); Daloz (1999); and Kazanjian and Laurence (2000).

16. Kenneth Keniston. *The Uncommitted: Alienated Youth in American Society.* New York: Dell, 1960, pp. 338–339.

17. Patricia Killen. "Gaps and Gifts." *Prism,* Spring 1999, *12,* 8.

18. Erik Erikson. *Insight and Responsibility.* New York: Norton, 1964, p. 133.

19. See T. Piper, M. Gentile, and S. D. Parks. *Can Ethics Be Taught? Perspectives, Approaches, and Challenges at Harvard Business School.* Boston: Harvard Business School Press, 1993.

20. Purdy (1999).

21. "The Future of Callings—An Interdisciplinary Summit on the Public Obligations of Professionals into the Next Millennium." *William Mitchell Law Review,* 1999, *25*(1), 43–192.

22. "The Future of Callings" (1999), p. 186.

23. Parks (1993).

24. See "A Contemplative Approach to Law." Mirabai Bush (ed.). A program of The Center for the Contemplative Mind in Society, Williamsburg, Ma., 1999.

25. See Herminia Barra. "Provisional Selves: Experimenting with Image and Identity in Professional Adaptation." *Administrative Science Quarterly,* Dec. 1999, pp. 764–791; and "Making Partner: A Mentor's Guide to the Psychological Journey." *Harvard Business Review,* Mar.–Apr. 2000, pp. 146–147.

26. "Start Making Sense! Meet the Irresistible Search Engine." *Wired*, Feb. 2000, p. 177.

27. Susan Bratton is a professor of biology at Whitworth College.

28. Brian T. Johnson. "An Essay on Lost Arts and Common Callings." *Mitchell Law Review*, p. 184. See also Douglas Sloan. *Faith and Knowledge: Mainline Protestantism and American Higher Education*. Louisville, Ky.: John Knox Press, 1994.

29. Adelaide Winstead, with Catherine Kapikian. In *The Awful Rowing Toward God*. Washington, D.C.: Potter's House Press, 1988, pp. 16–18.

30. See also Roberto Mangaberira Unger. "The Critical Legal Studies Movement." *Harvard Law Review*, Jan. 1983.

31. Eric Wallen. "The Mindless Carpenter." *The Symposium*, 1999, *1*(6), 1, 4–5.

32. Personal conversation with Charlie Murphy, Whidbey Institute, Jan. 2000.

33. Conversation with Sarah Waring, student at Haverford College.

34. Todd Daloz is a student in history and political science at Oberlin College. Bridges is directed by Carter Via, and is based in Chappaqua, N.Y. See also Ronald Frase. *Discovering the Stranger Next Door* (unpublished manuscript).

35. In our study of people who can sustain commitment to the common good, more than 70 percent had significant travel experiences by their mid-twenties (Daloz, Keen, Keen, and Parks, 1996), p. 3B.

36. Robert Bly (ed., with critical commentary). *The Winged Life: The Poetic Voice of Henry David Thoreau*. New York: Harper Perennial, 1992, p. 5.

37. Berry (1999), p. 79.

38. Olds (1992), p. 53.

39. Schachter-Shalomi (1995), p. 204. See especially "Mentoring in the Family," in the same book, pp. 203–207.

40. See Mary Pipher. *The Shelter of Each Other: Rebuilding Our Families*. New York: Ballantine Books, 1996, especially pp. 10–26.

41. R. R. Niebuhr (1999), p. 148.

42. This story is shared with the gracious permission of the father, James W. Fowler. In the study for *Common Fire*, we learned that when people chose a vocation that sets them on a road less traveled, parental and other family confirmation can play a particularly valued and meaningful role. See Daloz, Keen, Keen, and Parks (1996), p. 207.

43. Josh Avery, poet and nephew; Larry Daloz, uncle and poet, Aug. 1999.

44. Gina O'Connell Higgins. *Resilient Adults: Overcoming a Cruel Past*. San Francisco: Jossey-Bass, 1994, pp. 166–167.

45. Higgins (1994), pp. 156–158.

46. Higgins (1994), pp. 158, 169.

47. Zajonc (2000), p. 68.

48. Nino (2000), p. 48.

49. See Keith R. Anderson and Randy D. Reese. *Spiritual Mentoring: A Guide for Seeking and Giving Direction.* Downers Grove, Ill.: Inter-Varsity Press, 1999; V. James Mannoia Jr. *Christian Liberal Arts: An Education That Goes Beyond.* Lantham, Md: University Press of America, 2000. Rev. Scotty McLennan. *Finding Your Religion: When the Faith You Grew Up with Has Lost Its Meaning.* San Francisco: Harper San Francisco, 1999; Sam Portaro and Gary Peluso. *Inquiring and Discerning Hearts: Vocation and Ministry with Young Adults on Campus.* Atlanta: Scholars Press, 1993.

50. See Daloz, Keen, Keen, and Parks (1996), chapters four and seven.

51. See Sarah Birmingham. "A Terrible Tragedy, a Tenuous Time: Bereavement and the Search for Meaning in the Campus Community." Unpublished thesis, Harvard Divinity School, 1997.

52. See Eck (1993).

53. Interview by James Keen in the E Pluribus Unum program. See also Keen (2000).

54. See Craig Dykstra. *Growing in the Life of Faith: Education and Christian Practices.* San Francisco: Jossey-Bass, 1999.

55. Beaudoin (1998), chapter seven and pages 56–57.

56. Michael Slater. *Stretcher Bearers: Giving and Receiving the Gift of Encouragement and Support.* Ventura, Calif.: Regal Books, 1985, pp. 16–18. The mentoring pastor in this story was my father, Emmett F. Parks. Though it is characteristic of his life, I did not know about his encounter with Slater until this book was given to me after my father's death.

CHAPTER TEN: CULTURE AS MENTOR

1. Friedrich Schweitzer. "Global Issues Facing Youth in the Postmodern Church." *1998 Princeton Lectures on Youth, Church, and Culture.* Princeton, N.J.: Princeton Theological Seminary, 1999, p. 73.

2. Schweitzer (1999), p. 73.

3. See Richard J. Barnet and John Cavanagh. *Global Dreams: Imperial Corporations and the New World Order.* New York: Simon & Schuster, 1994.

4. Ronal Inglehart quoted in Schweitzer (1999), p. 74.

5. See Arthur Levine and Jeanette S. Cureton. *When Hope and Fear Collide: A Portrait of Today's College Student.* San Francisco: Jossey-Bass, 1998, chapter two.

6. Sharon D. Parks. "The University as a Mentoring Environment." Indianapolis: Indiana Office of Campus Ministry, 1992.

7. Lendol Calder. *Financing the American Dream: A Cultural History of Consumer Credit.* Princeton: Princeton University Press, 1999, pp. 4–6.

8. Andrew L. Shapiro. *The Nation,* June 21, 1999, p. 14.

9. Ronald Heifetz. *Leadership Without Easy Answers.* Cambridge, Mass.: Harvard University Press, 1994, chapter four.

10. Peter D. Hart Associates. "Key Findings from a Study on Youth, Leadership, and Community Service." Aug. 28, 1998. [www.publicallies.org]

11. For rich insight into the power of "public home places," see M. F. Belenky, L. A. Bond, and J. S. Weinstock. *The Tradition That Has No Name.* New York: Basic Books, 1997.

12. D. Goleman. *Emotional Intelligence.* New York: Bantam, 1995.

13. Cornell West. "The Moral Obligations of Living in a Democratic Society." In D. Batstone and E. Mendieta (eds.), *The Good Citizen.* New York: Routledge, 1999, p. 6.

14. Purdy (1999), p. 25.

15. Andrew Delbanco. *The Real American Dream: A Meditation on Hope.* Cambridge, Mass.: Harvard University Press, 1999, pp. 103, 114–115.

16. See Palmer (2000), especially chapter four.

17. See Daloz, Keen, Keen, and Parks (1996), chapter three.

18. See Berry (1999).

THE AUTHOR

Sharon Daloz Parks has spent much of her career teaching and reflecting upon the formation of meaning and faith, particularly in the experience of young adults. She began as a residence hall director at the University of Redlands, became associate in ministry at University Presbyterian Church in Seattle, and then associate chaplain at Whitworth College. Subsequently, she took her deepening questions to Harvard University, where she earned her doctorate in theology and human development. She remained there for more than sixteen years, becoming an associate professor at the Harvard Divinity School and later a visiting professor and senior research fellow in leadership and ethics at the Harvard Business School and the Kennedy School of Government. She has also taught at the Weston Jesuit School of Theology. Her publications include *The Critical Years: Young Adults and the Search for Meaning, Faith, and Commitment,* and she is coauthor of *Can Ethics Be Taught? Approaches, Perspectives, and Challenges at Harvard Business School.*

In 1988, she joined Larry Daloz in both marriage and professional colleagueship; along with Cheryl and James Keen, they conducted a study of people committed to the common good. The result was *Common Fire: Leading Lives of Commitment in a Complex World.* Currently she is associate director and faculty member of the Whidbey Institute near Seattle, Washington, a center dedicated to encouragement of creative and committed leadership for earth, spirit, and the human future. She also teaches in the Executive Leadership Program at Seattle University and lectures and consults nationally for professional and other organizations. She is a member of the Religious Society of Friends (Quaker). She is a stepmother, an aunt, and a godmother. She and her husband live on Whidbey Island and in Glover, Vermont.

NAME INDEX

Page numbers in square brackets refer to textual references to endnotes.

A

Abram, David, 107, [166], 238n10
Anderson, Keith, [199], 241n49
Aristotle, 27
Astin, Alexander W., [151], 237n36
Avery, Josh, [193–195], 240n43

B

Bachelard, Gaston, [110], [113], [153], 157, 233n16, 234n21, 238n38
Baez, Joan, 149
Bak, Samuel, 193
Baldwin, James Mark, 38
Barfield, Owen, 107, [122], 235n51
Barnet, Richard, [208], 241n3
Barra, Herminia, [176], 239n25
Barzun, Jacques, 169–170, 239n14
Bass, Dorothy, [157], 238n40
Beaudoin, Tom, [80], 118, [149], 203, 230n11, 234n36, 237n34, 241n55
Beer, John de, 73, 230n5
Belenky, Mary, 12, 50, 54, [57], 82, [216], 227n28, 228n3, 230(nn12, 13), 242n11
Bellah, Robert, [50], 228n33
Berry, Thomas, [166], 190, [221], 238n10, 240n37, 242n18
Birmingham, Sarah, [200], 241n51
Bly, Robert, [188], 240n36
Bok, Derek, [11], 224n11(ch1)
Bona, Mary Jo, 134, 236n9
Bond, L. A., [216], 242n11

Boyer, Ernest L., Jr., 65–66, 67, 229(nn13, 16)
Bratton, Susan, 177, 239n27
Brinton, Howard, 70, 229n18
Brookfield, Stephen, [170], 239n15
Broughton, John, [48], 227n23
Buber, Martin, 44, 131, 236n4
Bueckner, Frederick, [148], 237n32
Bugbee, Henry, 131, 132
Bushnell, Horace, [115], 116, 119–120, 234(nn28, 29, 30, 31), 235n42

C

Calder, Lendol, 209, 242n7
Campbell, Joseph, [49], 227n25
Carroll, James, [31], 225n26
Cavanagh, John, [208], 241n3
Cedrick, Ron, 85
Chodorow, Nancy, 49, 227n26
Clinchy, Blythe, 50, 54, [57], 82, 227n28, 228n3, 230(nn12, 13)
Cline, Mary Romer, 205
Coleridge, Samuel Taylor, 106–109, 111, 113, 121, 133, 162, 167–169, 232–233n5, 233(nn7, 10, 12), 234(nn22, 23), 236n7, 239(nn12, 13)
Cox, Harvey, 164, 238n7
Cureton, Jeanette S., [208]

D

Daloz, Kate, 214
Daloz, Laurent A., 48, [90], [128], [159], [170], [193–195], 223n9, 226n5, 227n24, 231(nn5, 6),

236(nn2, 6, 10, 14), 237(nn18,
  33), 238n1, 239n15, 240n43,
  240(nn35, 42), 241n50, 242n17
Daloz, Todd, 186–187, 240n34
Dalton, Jon C., [140], 237n16
de Beer, John. *See* Beer, John de
Delbanco, Andrew, 217–218, 242n15
Dewey, John, 38
Dykstra, Craig, [203], 241n54

E

Eck, Diana, 142, [201], 237n19,
  241n52
Erikson, Erik, 12, 21, 36, 40, 62–63,
  64, [172], 224n8, 229n8, 239n18
Erikson, Joan, 37

F

Falk, Richard, [72], 230n3
Fowler, James, 12, 21, 32, 41, 44–45,
  61, [64], 66, [86], [89], 93, [100],
  224n9, 225n29, 227(nn16, 17),
  229n9, 230n15, 231(nn3, 4, 10,
  13), 240n42
Frankl, Victor, 30, 225n24
Frase, Ronald, 240n34
Freud, Sigmund, 77
Frost, Robert, 35
Frye, Northrup, 122, 235n47
Fulghum, Robert, 38–39, 226n6

G

Garber, Steve, [135], 236n11
Gentile, M., [174], 239n19
Gilligan, Carol, 12, 41, 43–44, 49, 78,
  147–148, 227(nn12, 13), 230n10,
  237(nn23, 24, 25, 26, 27, 28, 29,
  30, 31)
Goethe, Johann Wolfgang von, 168
Goldberger, Nancy, 50, 54, [57], 82,
  227n28, 228n3, 230(nn12, 13)

Goleman, D., [217], 242n12
Groome, Thomas H., [26], 225n19

H

Hall, Elizabeth, [4], 8–9, 223(nn1, 5, 6)
Harrison, Beverly, 229–230n2
Hart, Peter D., 242n10
Hart, Ray L., 232–233n5
Heidegger, Martin, 50, 228n31
Heifetz, Ronald, 211–212, 242n9
Higgins, Gina O'Connell, 196,
  240(nn44, 45), 241n46
Holmes, Oliver Wendell, 60
Huebner, Dwayne, [90], 231n8
Hull, Timothy, 35
Huneke, Douglas, 199

I

Inglehart, Ronal, [208], 241n4

J

Johnson, Brian T., 178, 240n28
Jordhal, Mark, 188–190

K

Kant, Immanuel, 38, 106, 160, 232n3
Kapikian, Catherine, [179], 240n29
Kaufman, Gordon, [116], 234n32
Kazanjian, Victor, [163], [170],
  238n5, 239n15
Keen, Cheryl, [90], 167–168, 223n9,
  225n29, 226n5, 231(nn5, 6),
  236(nn6, 10, 14), 237(nn18, 33),
  239n11, 240(nn35, 42), 241n50,
  242n17
Keen, James P., [90], [136],
  [201–202], 213, 223n9, 226n5,
  231(nn5, 6), 236n12, 236(nn6, 10,
  14), 237(nn18, 33), 240(nn35, 42),
  241(nn50, 53), 242n17

Keen, Sam, [32], [64], [201–202], 229n10, 231n10

Kegan, Robert, 12, 13, [33], [40], 41–43, [42], 44, 49, 61, 66, 72, 74, [90], [91], [124], 225n30, 226(nn7, 10, 11), 227(nn14, 15, 27), 229n1, 231(nn7, 9), 235n54

Keillor, Garrison, 37

Keller, Evelyn Fox, 114–115, 234n24

Kelly, Doug, 193

Kelly, Sara Eileen, [118], 193, 234n35

Keniston, Kenneth, 8, 46–47, 64–65, 66, 67–68, 70, 96, 170, 227(nn19, 20, 21), 229(nn11, 12, 14, 17, 19), 231n12, 239n16

Killen, Patricia O'Connell, 75, 171–172, 230n5, 239n17

Kohlberg, Lawrence, 41, 43–44, 147–148, 226n9

Komarovsky, Mirra, [76], 230n6

Kotre, John, [4], 8–9, 223(nn1, 5, 6)

L

Lahey, Lisa Laslow, [40], 226n7

Langer, Suzanne, 106, 116, 232n4, 234n33

Laurence, Peter, [163], [170], 238n5, 239n15

Lawlor, Anthony, [23], 225n16

Lerner, Michael, [7], 223n4

Lertzman, Renee, 143–144, 237n20

Levine, Arthur, [208], 241n5

Levinson, Daniel, [8], 12, 13, 146, 223n5, 224n13(ch1), 237n21, 22

Levinson, Judith, [8], 146, 223n5, 237n21

Lifton, Robert Jay, [72], 126, 230n3, 235n58

Light, Richard J., [127], 235n1

Lindsay, A. D., 232n3

Loder, James, 108–109, 111–113, [113], [115], [120], [122],

233(nn14, 18), 233–234n20, 234n27, 235(nn43, 48)

Lodge, George, [77], 230n7

Lucas, George, 127

Ludwig, Robert A., [77], 230n9

Lynch, Michael, 177

Lynch, William F., 13, 20, 26, 27, [31], [106], [107], [121], 224(nn5, 6), 225(nn20, 27), 233(nn6, 8, 9), 235n45

M

Macy, Joanna, 184

Malone, Nancy, 165, 238n8

Marsden, George M., [163], 238n5

Marstin, Ronald, 100–102, 231(nn14, 15, 16, 17, 18)

McClintock, Barbara, 114, 120

McLennan, Scotty, [199], 241n49

McMenamin, Brigid, [5], 223n2

Mead, George Herbert, 38

Meade, Michael, 206, 207

Medea, 26

Miller, Perry, [11], 224n10(ch1)

Missirian, Agnes K., [129], 236n3

Moore, Steve, [11], 224n10(ch1)

Morrill, Richard, [159], 238n2

Morrison, S. E., [11], 224n10

Moschella, Mary, 124–125, 235n57

Mueller, Wayne, 234n25

Murphy, Charlie, 184, 240n32

N

Naylor, Thomas H., [163], 238n5

Newman, John Henry, 94–95, 231n11

Niebuhr, H. Richard, 21, 22, 23, 118–119, 122, [123], [124], 234n37, 235(nn38, 39, 40, 49, 52, 53, 55)

Niebuhr, Richard R., 27–28, 31, [50], [106], [117], [121], 152, [191], 224n10(ch2), 225(nn14, 21, 22,

25), 228n30, 231n2(ch6), 234n34, 235n44, 238n37, 240n41
Nino, Andres, [115], 198, 234n26, 241n48
Nochlin, Linda, [41], 226n8
Norena, Carlos, 143

O

Ogletree, Thomas W., 50, [50], 228n32
Olds, Linda E., 190–191, [238], 238n39, 240n38
Orr, David, 238n10

P

Palmer, Parker, 16, 34, [89], [170], [219], 224n1(ch6), 225n2, 231n2, 239n15, 242n16
Palmer, Robert, 150
Parks, Emmett F., [204]
Parks, Sharon Daloz, [8], [47], [88], [90], []092, [124], [139], [164], [174], [175], 223(nn5, 9), 224n12, 226n5, 227(nn18, 29), 230n1 (ch2), 231(nn5, 6), 235n56, 236(nn6, 10, 13, 14), 237(nn18, 33), 238n6, 239(nn19, 23), 240(nn35, 42), 241n50, 242(nn6, 17)
Peluso, Gary, [199], 241n49
Perry, William G., Jr., 12, 45–46, 55, 58, 66, 71, 227n18, 228(nn1, 2, 4, 6), 229n15
Peter D. Hart Associates, [216], 242n10
Petrie, Anne Marie, [140], 237n16
Piaget, Jean, 12, 38–41, 41–43, 89, 162, 226n8
Piper, T., [174], 239n19
Pipher, Mary, [191], 240n40
Portaro, Sam, [199], 241n49

Purdy, Jedediah, 34, [174], [217], [218], 225n1, 239n20, 242n14

Q

Quinn, Robert E., 85, 230n14

R

Rankin, Robert, [60], 229n7
Reese, Randy D., [199], 241n49
Rinehart, Jane, 134, 236n9
Rogers, William R., [7], 77, 223n4, 230n8
Roof, Wade Clark, 9, 223n7
Rooke, Barbara E., [111], 233n17
Ross, Murray G., 238n3
Ruether, Rosemary Radford, 150, 237n35
Rugg, Harold, [113], 233–234n20
Rupp, George, [57], 162, 228n5, 238n4
Russell, Valerie, 9, 223n8

S

Sanders, Scott Russell, 112–113, 233n19
Schacter-Shalomi, Zalman, [12], 191, 224n12, 240n39
Schwehn, Mark R., [163], 238n5
Schweitzer, Freidrich, 207, 241(nn1, 2)
Shakyamui, 51
Shapiro, Andrew, [210], 242n8
Slater, Michael, [204], 241n56
Smith, Wilfred Cantwell, 16, 18, [22], 24, 34, 160–161, 224(nn2, 3, 4, 11, 139[ch2]), 225nn17, 18, 226n3
Souvaine, Emily, [40], 226n7
Sparks, Patricia, [122], 235n50
Spezzano, Charles, [20], 224n7
Spretnak, Charlene, [106]

Steere, Douglas, [139], 236n15
Storr, A., [133], 236n8

T

Talbot, Stephen, [107], 233n11
Tarrant, John, [23], [31], 51,
 225(nn15, 28, 34), 230n13
Tarule, Jill, 50, 54, [57], 82, 227n28,
 228n3, 230n12
Tatum, Beverly Daniel, [141], 237n17
Thompson, Steve, 85
Thorkilsen, Karen, [28], [36], 225n23,
 226n4

U

Unger, Roberto Mangaberira, 179,
 240n30

V

Volbrecht, Rose Mary, 134, 236n9

W

Wallen, Eric, 180–181, 240n31
Waring, Sarah, [6], [185], 223n3,
 240n33
Wei-Ming, Tu, 229–230n2
Weinstock, J. S., [216], 242n11
West, Cornell, [217], 242n13
Weyerhauser, William, [73], 230n4
Wheelwright, Phillip, [105], [110],
 233n15
Whited, Gary, 131–132, 236n5
Whitehead, Alfred North, 44, 119,
 235n41
Wiesel, Elie, 225n24
Willimon, William H., [163], 238n5
Winnicott, D. W., 233n13
Winstead, Adelaide, [179], 240n29
Wired magazine, 177

Z

Zajonc, Arthur, 122, 197–198,
 235n46, 241n47

SUBJECT INDEX

A

Academy as place for faith formation, 159–160, 163

Accountability in cultural milieu, 218–220

Act as form of faith, 25–26

Adaptive challenges, 211

Adolescence stage, 62–63

Adolescents, 60–61

Adult, connotation of word, 70

Adult faith: composing of, 144; emerging, 61; eras of development of, 70; formation of, 60–61, 135, 143, 236n11; journey toward, 102–103; limitations of, 100; making meaning, composition of, 33

Adult knowing, 151

Adult workers, 182–184

Adulthood: capacity for responsible, 85; formation of, 6–7; life stage of full, 47; making meaning in, 69; mark of psychological, 91; steps toward, 43

Adults, young. *See* Young adults

Ages of human unfolding, 36–38

Amazement as faith metaphor, 27–31

Ambivalence, 65–66

American culture: contemporary myths, 50; journey metaphor in, 46, 49; passion in, 170

American dream, 209

Analogy for consciousness of faith, 198–199

Apprenticeship, 179–180

Asraddha, 24

Atheism, 22

Authority: forms of, 46; new kind of, 80; questions about, 53; recomposing, 76; responsiveness to, 78; use of term, 228n1

Authority-bound faith, 71

Authority-bound form of knowing, 54–57, 60

B

Belief, 17–18

Belonging: communities of, 202; conventional, 140; forms of community and, 91–102; freedom/boundaries in, 90; importance of, 88–89, 93; power of tribe in, 89–90; yearning for, 91, 101

Belonging, networks of: community as, 88–89; forms of, 90; freedom and boundaries, 90; mentoring environments, 127

Betrayal of faith, 26–27

Beyond Our Tribal Gods (Marstin), 100–102

Bible, 165

Big-enough questions, 165–166

Biographia Literaria (Coleridge), 107–108

Books as mentors, 133

Boundaries and freedom, 90

Buddhism, 23, 113, 149

C

Callings: future of, 239n21; Future of Callings symposium, 174–175; vocations as, 148

Canopy as form of faith, 24–25
Certainty, loss of, 71–72
Challenge, 130, 202
Challenges, 198, 210–212
Child development investigations,
    226n8
Childhood and Society (Erikson),
    36–38
Christian tradition, 229–230n2
Citizens in cultural milieu, 210
Civitas, 156
Co-mentoring, 134
Cognition, 41–43
Cognitive development, 69, 101
Coherence, formation of, 59
Comfort, communities of, 202
Comfort and healing in cultural
    milieu, 215–216
Commitment: to the common good,
    140, 240n35; formation of, 59;
    probing, 66–69; in relativism form
    of knowing, 59
*Common Fire: Leading Lives of Com-
    mitment in a Complex World*
    (Daloz, Keen, Keen, Parks), 10,
    [37], [90], [100], [132], 135, [139],
    [141], [148], [187], [193], [219]
Common goals, 154
Common good, 140, 240n35
Common sense, 166
Commons: concept of, 9–10; and cul-
    tural milieu, 207; making meaning
    in today's, 11; practice of the,
    156–157, 176–177; of time, 213
Communion with creation, 190
Communities: of belonging/comfort/
    challenge, 202; of confirmation/
    contradiction, 123; dependence on,
    121; mentoring, 134–135; of prac-
    tice, 154–157; purposes of, 123;
    religious faith, 197–199
Community: making meaning in, 90;
    network of belonging, 88; role of,
    91

Community, forms of: complexity and
    inclusion, 100–101; conventional,
    92; in development of life, 91; dif-
    fuse, 92–93; ideological, 95–99;
    mentoring, 93–95; openness to
    other, 101–102; self-selected group,
    99–100
Compassion, 140
Competing points of view, 99
Complexity and inclusion as form of
    community, 100–101
Composing, making meaning as, 19
Composing the real, 106
Concrete operations, 40
Confident inner-dependent form of
    dependence, 84
Confirmation, community as, 123. *See
    also* Recognition; Support
Conflict, 109–115, 111–112, 113
Connected thought, 185–187
Connections, 120
Connective-systemic-holistic thought,
    144–145
Conscience, power of, 85
Conscious conflict, 109–115
Consciousness, 13, 113
Consciousness shaping influences,
    208
Constructive-developmental theories,
    56, 61
Consumers in cultural milieu, 209–210
Contemplation, 113–114. *See also*
    Pause, importance of
"Contemplative Approach to Law,
    A," [176], 239n24
Contemplative mind, 145–146
Contemplative Mind in Society, 145
Contemplative silence, 114
Contradiction, community as, 123
Conventional form of community, 92
Conversation, 142–143. *See also*
    Dialogues
Convictional commitment form of
    knowing, 60

Cosmology, functional, 166
Counterdependent form of depen-
    dence, 75–76
Courage and intellectual life, 171–173
Creation, acts of, 121
Creation of life, 105
Creative imagination, 233–234n20.
    See Imagination
Critical awareness, 101
Critical-systemic faith, 13
Critical thought, 65, 143–144,
    164–165, 185–187
Cultural assumptions, 78
Cultural ethos, 77
Cultural milieu: accountability in,
    218–220; challenges of, 210–212;
    citizens in, 210; comfort and heal-
    ing in, 215–216; consumers in,
    209–210; globalization and, 207–
    209; inspiration from, 216–218;
    origins of, 206–207; recognition/
    support in, 212–213; stepping
    stones from, 213–215; worthy
    dreams from within, 220–221
Culture: definition, 206; globalization
    of, 208; "hotel," 217; vocation of
    a, 126
Culture clashes, 238n9
Cynicism, 19, 154

D

*Deep Change: Discovery of the Leader
    Within* (Quinn), 85
Deep purpose, 182
Deep self, 86
Definitions: belief, 17–18; community
    groupings, 92; compassion, 140;
    consciousness, 113; culture, 206;
    dependence, forms of, 73, 77; edu-
    cator, 167; ethics, 174; fanciful,
    106; globalization, 207; home, 34;
    humanness, 7; ideology, 95; images,
    105; imagination, 106, 107–108;

making meaning, 223n4; mentor-
    ing, 127; professor, 167; reason/
    knowledge, 160; revelation, 119;
    sincerity, 116; vocation, 148
Dependence: appropriate, 81–82;
    attention to development of, 87; as
    dimension of development, 230n4
Dependence, forms of: Authority,
    new kind of, 80; confident inner-
    dependence, 84; counterdependence,
    75–76; definitions, 73, 77; depen-
    dent, 74; fragile inner-dependence,
    82–84; inner-dependence versus
    independence, 77–80; interdepen-
    dence, 86–87; interiority and ethi-
    cal life, 84–85
Development: of adult faith, 70; child,
    226n8; of cognition, 69; cognitive,
    69, 101; cognitive-affective-social-
    moral, 160; cognitive-intellectual,
    71, 101; of community life, 91;
    constructive-developmental theo-
    ries, 56, 61; of dependence, 87;
    dimensions of, 102, 230n4; eras of,
    70, 74; of faith, 100; faith journeys
    as, 61; human, theories of, 41–45,
    46–47; journey of (Gilligan), 43;
    metaphors of, 48; as motion of
    faith, 44–45; understanding human,
    38; understanding of human, 51;
    during young adulthood, 51–52
Developmental moral decision-making,
    50
Developmental openings of transitions,
    218–219
Dialogues: affect of genuine, 204–205;
    as habit of mind, 142–143; inner,
    84; interfaith, 201–202; between
    self and society-world-other, 96;
    "talking through," 155; young
    adult's inner, 131–133
Differentiation, 49
Diffuse form of community, 92–93
Dimensions of experience, 200

Dimensions of human development, 41–42

Disability, 111–112

Disequilibrium, 109

Divided self, 67

Doubt, 109

Dreams: formation of worthy, 146–148, 151, 176; reexamination of, 219; worthy in cultural milieu, 220–221

Dualism, mind-heart, 229–230n2

Dualistic thinking, 57

E

"E-motion," 72

E Pluribus Unum (EPU) program, 201–202

Economic life of young adults, 215

Einbildungskraft, 232–233n5

Embeddual meaning, 43

Emerging self, 80. *See* Self

Emptiness, 23

Encounters with otherness, 141

Enlightenment era, 77, 107, 232n3

Epistemological assumptions, 159–164

Equilibrium, 109

Eras of development, 70, 74

Eternal truth, 106

Ethical life, 84–85

Ethical orientation, 50

Ethical questions, 173

Ethical reasoning, 77

Ethics: definition, 174; faith as ground of, 26; interpersonal versus systemic, 175–176; making meaning as ground for, 15

Etymology. *See* Definitions; Word origins

Evolving Self: Method and Process in Human Development, The (Kegan), 42

F

Faith: activity of, 21; and belief, 17–18, 18; betrayal of, 26–27; critical-systemic, 13; cross-cultural, 24; development as motion of, 44–45; emancipation from narrow, 123; formation of, 8; giving language to, 202–203; as human universal, 16–17, 24; and importance of meaning, 19–20; individuating, 231n13; life of, 139; limitations of adult, 100; maturing of, 45; metaphors of, 27–31; as motion of life, 31–32; origin of word, 17, 24; as quality of living, 34; rational and passional, 32; re-formation of, 12, 172; reconsideration of, 218; relativism of, 208; and religion, 15–16; responsibility for one's, 64; and skepticism, 18–19; and spirituality, 16; stages of, 61; and truth, 18; understanding of word, 16, 18–19, 23; as verb and noun, 32–33; young adult, 109–110

Faith, forms of: as an act, 25–26; as a canopy, 24–25; as center of power/value/affection, 21–22; monotheism, 22; polytheism, 22; as primal force of promise, 20–21; setting one's heart, 24; as suffering, 26–27; truth and trust, 23–24

Faith journey, 70

Faithfulness, 16

"Faithing," 24

False mentors, 133–134

Families, 191–197. *See also* Parents

Fanciful, usage of word, 106

Fantasy versus imagination, 106

"Far country," 198

Fiddler on the Roof, 25

Financing the American Dream: A Cultural History of Consumer Credit (Calder), 209

Focus, shifting, 41–43
Formal operations, 40
Formation of faith, 8
Forms of dependence. *See* Dependence, forms of
Forms of Ethical and Intellectual Development in the College Years: A Scheme (Perry), 45
Forms of faith. *See* Faith, forms of
Forms of knowing. *See* Knowing, forms of
Fragile inner-dependent form of dependence, 82–84
Free association of fantasy, 106
Freedom and boundaries, 90
Friends. *See* Quakers
Fusion, 81
Future of Callings symposium, 174–175

G

Gender differences, 49
Gifts, 203–205
Gladness as faith metaphor, 27–31
Global commons, 157
Globalization and cultural milieu, 207–209
Goals, 154, 174
God, 21–22, 23, 72–73
Good-enough families, 192
Growth, personal, 42–43

H

Habits of mind, 142–146
Harvard College, 11
Healers, families as, 195–196
Hearth, practice of, 154, 156, 176–177. *See also* Home
Henotheism, 22, 23
Heroes versus mentors, 170
Heroic separation, 49

Higher education, 10–11, 169
Higher education as mentoring community: about, 158–159; big-enough questions about, 165–166; epistemological assumptions about, 159–164; intellectual life in, 171–173; passion in, 168–171; professor as spiritual guide, 166–168; syllabus (confession of faith), 164–165
Holiness of life, 220
Holistic thought, 144–145
Holocaust, 30
Home: becoming at, 50–51; function of the house, 157; meaning of word, 34; seeking a place in society, 64–65. *See also* Hearth, practice of; Families
Hope, 150, 184, 205
"Hotel culture," 217
Human becoming, 89, 91
Human behavior, 14
Human development, understanding of, 38
Human growth and development theories, 41–45
Human universal, faith as, 16–17, 24
Humanizing practices, 154–157
Humanness, 7
Hunting for Hope: A Father's Journeys (Sanders), 112–113
Hypocrisy, 148

I

Ideal, the, 65, 105, 146–148
Idealism, young adults' capacity for, 174
Identity, 62, 63
Ideological form of community, 95–99
Ideologies, 147–148, 216
Idolatry, 119
Image (insight), 115–120

Imagery, religious-spiritual, 49

Images: access to, 148–154; associations carried by, 119; definition, 105; false, 124; finiteness of, 123; as fitting forms, 169; of leadership, 180–181; of other, 152–153; as revelation, 118–119; of self, 151–152; for shaping imagination, 216; strength/limitations of, 119; as symbols, 116–117, 118

Imagination: activity of, 106; Coleridge on, 106, 107–108, 239n12; faithful, 103; versus fantasy, 106; highest power of knowing mind, 107; isolated, 122; moments in act of, 109; and moral life, 123–124; as part of Reason, 162; power of, 104–105; practice of right, 167; process of, 107, 108–109, 218; repatterning reality through, 121; strength and precariousness of, 122; in Western culture, 106

In Over Our Heads (Kegan), 42

Individuating faith, 231n13

Infants, 21, 39

Information overload, 164–165

Inner-dependence versus independence, 77–80, 93, 214

Inner dialogue, 84

Inner life, 145–146

Inner Light, 85

Inner/outer realities, 78

Insight (image), 115–120

Inspiration, 130–131, 216–218

Intellectual affection, 31

Intellectual awareness, 72

Intellectual communities, 168

Intellectual life, 171–173

Interdependent form of dependence, 86–87

Interfaith dialogue, 201–202

Interiority form of dependence, 84–85

"Interlive," 89

Internet as mentor, 133

Interpersonal ethic, 175–176

Interpretation, 121–122

Interrelatedness, 153–154

Interreligious dialogue, 201–202

Irreverence, 203

J

Journey, origin of word, 50

Journeys: of development, 43; faith, 70; of faith development, 61; human, in pre-Civil War America, 46; *Hunting for Hope: A Father's Journeys* (Sanders), 112–113; of intellect/soul, 46; *Life Maps: Conversations on the Journey of Faith* (Fowler, Keen), [92]; toward mature adult faith, 102–103

K

Keepers of the promise, parents as, 196–197

Knowing: as composing activity, 106; structure of, 101; subjective, 229n11

Knowing, forms of: authority-bound, 54–57; commitment in relativism, 59; convictional commitment, 60; revisions of, 69–70; unqualified relativism, 57–59

Knowing mind, 107

Knowledge: as an event, 122; domain of, 160; "irrational," 17; relationship between what we know/how we know, 13; relativity of, 57, 60

Krista Foundation, [115], 234n25

L

Language, 43, 202–203

Leadership, 180

Leadership Without Easy Answers (Heifetz), 211

Life Maps: Conversations on the Journey of Faith (Fowler, Keen), [92]

Life span, 46

Life stages: adolescence, 62–63; emergence of new, 8–9; Erikson's, 36–38; full adulthood, 47; of full adulthood, 47; making meaning in different, 6; transitions in, 6–7, 62

Life tasks, 37

Lifetime, sense of, 86

Limbic brain, 216

Listening, art of, 45–46

Liturgy, 203

Loss: of assumed certainty, 71–72; of community, 213–214; of sense of home, 83

M

Making meaning: activity of, 23; broadening scope of, 175; in community context, 90; as composing, 19; critical reflection of one's way of, 143; cultural milieu effects on, 69; definition, 223n4; in different life stages, 6; dynamics of adult, 7; faith as, 20, 23; human need for, 14; as motion of faith, 31; movement into interdependent form of, 86–87; ongoing, 101–102; religion as shared way of, 197–198; seeking patterns for, 7; stresses of, 12

Manifestations of faith, 26

Marriage, 87

Master/apprentice relationships, 179–180

Mature wisdom, 60

Maturing of faith, 45

Maturity, 107

Meaning: evolution of, 72; importance of and faith, 19–20; re-forming of, 172; of self, transformation of, 90; threats to, 30; will to find, 20

Meaning-making. *See* Making meaning

Media, influence of, 216–217

Men, storytelling by, 49–50

Mentoring: art of, 130; co-, 134; deep purpose of in work environment, 182; as form of community, 93–95; good environment of, 115; informal, 213; multi-generational families and, 191; nature of relationship, 81; presences of, 212; recognition and support in, 182–183; restoring practice of, 12; two-step, 193

Mentoring communities: encounters with otherness in, 141; engagement of work in, 183–184; families, 191–197; higher education, 158–172; natural environment, 188–191; professional education/professions, 173–179; purpose of, 134–135; religious faith communities, 197–205, 201; travel, 184–188; workplace, 180–184. *See also* Cultural milieu; Higher education as mentoring community; Natural environment as mentoring community; Travel

Mentoring ecology, 173

Mentoring environments: access to images in, 148–154; big-enough questions of, 137–139; characteristics of good, 149; communities of practice in, 154–157; creating, 13; encounters with otherness in, 139–142; habits of mind in, 142–146; higher education as, 172; as networks of belonging, 135–136; purpose of, 107, 157; worthy dreams fostered by, 146–148

Mentors: appropriate time for, 80–81; becoming, 177; characteristics of good, 98, 128, 130, 131, 133, 181; with clay feet, 133; Coleridge's, 133; having many, 176–177; parents as, 193; as peers, 84; power of, 132; professors as, 168; public

relations, 170–171; roles of, 11–12, 129–134; use of term, 128
Metaphors: computer, grasp of reality, 41; of development, 48; for faith, 27–31; home, 50–51; journey, 48–50; journey, in American culture, 46; searching for, 214
Midlife, 86
Mind, evolving capacities of the, 38–41
"Mirror test," 85
"Mission, the," 181
Mistrust, 32
Monotheism, 22, 23
Moral conscience, 10
Moral judgment, 237n23
Moral life, 123–124
Morality, 147
Motion of faith, 44–45
Motion of life, faith as, 31–32, 221
Motion of self-other differentiation, 42
Movements, 187–188
Multi-generational families, 191
Mystery, 149, 197, 199–200
Myths: contemporary, 50; importance of, 202–203; Medea, 26; spiritual significance of, 35

N

Naming, 103, 105
Natural environment as mentoring community, 188–191
Needs, 116–117, 140
Neglects, 41–42, 47–48
Networks of belonging. See Belonging, networks of

O

Operations, concrete/formal, 40
Opposites, 152
Order of consciousness, 13
Orthodoxy, 203

Other, images of, 152–153
Otherness, 101, 139–142, 152
Overdistancing, 110

P

Paradigms, 108–109
Paradoxes, 149
Parents, 129, 193, 196–197. See also Families
Passion, 168–171
Passional faith, 32
Patterns, 56, 75–76, 95
Pause, importance of, 113–115, 145–146. See also Reflection
Peer groups, 91
Peer mentors, 84
Perception, relative character of, 71
Pervasive ambivalence, 65–66
Place in society, seeking a, 64
Pluralism Project, 142
Plurality of religious traditions, 200–202
Points of view, competing, 99
Polytheism, 22, 23
Post-midlife, 86, 102
Postadolescence, 67
Power, 21–22, 31–33, 107
Power of Hope program, 184
Practical reason, 107
Practice communities: the commons, 156–157, 176–177; hearth, 176–177; of hearth, 154–155; the table, 156
Practices, religious, 202–203
"Preventing Cultural Clashes in Academe," 238n9
Primal force of promise, 20–21
Probing of self and world, 67–68
Process of imagination, 104–105, 108–109
Professional education/professions as mentoring community, 173–179

Professions, 173–174, 175
Professors: as mentors, 168; responsible, 170; as spiritual guides, 166–168; testimony of, 165
Protestant religious faith, 77
Puberty, 62
Purpose, deep, 182. *See* Vocation

Q

Quakers, 70, 85, 114
Questions: about home, 34; alchemy of powerful, 103; asked by young adults, 137–139; big-enough, 165–166; at core of challenge, 211; ethical, 173; of faith, 30, 110; hospitality to big, 199–200; life's, 53; outside realm of knowledge, 160; posed by mentoring environment, 139; when one becomes adult, 5–7; of young adult faith, 109–110; of young adulthood, 184

R

Rapport, 111–113
Rational faith, 32
Re-formation of faith, 12, 172
Re-formation of meaning, 172
Reality: domain of objective, 160; handling, 119; inner/outer, 78; repatterning, 120–121
Reason, 107, 160, 162
Received knowing, 54
Recognition: as adult worker, 182–184; in cultural milieu, 212–213; as role of mentor, 128–129; of young adults' gifts, 203–205. *See also* Support
Reflection, 85. *See also* Pause, importance of; Contemplation
Relation, phenomenon of, 42, 43
Relational perspectives, 43–44

Relationships: face-to-face, 92; faculty/student, 166; human understanding/whole of reality, 162; master/apprentice, 179–180; mentor/protégé, 130, 132, 133, 170; of objects/self, 43; questions about self/world, 138; self-other, 42
Relative character of perception, 71
Relativism: faith within, 208; unqualified, 59, 92–93, 162
Religion and faith, 15–16, 118–119
Religious faith, 199
Religious faith communities as mentoring community, 197–205, 201
Religious traditions, 200–202
Repatterning reality, 120–121
Resilient Adults: Overcoming a Cruel Past (Higgins), 196
Respect for young adults, 5–6
Responsibility: capacity for adult, 85; conscious, 78; for one's faith, 64; for self, 63
Revelation, 118, 119
Right imagination, 167
Roles of professors, 167–168

S

Sacramentals, 118. *See also* Religion and faith
Self: divided, 67; essence of, 110; relationship of to world, 138; self-aware, 63, 64–65
Self-authoring pattern of relationship, 75–76
Self-identity, formation of, 64
Self-other differentiation, 42
Self-selected group as form of community, 99–100
Self-superintending, 106
Sense of lifetime, 86
Sense of the world, 74
Separation, heroic, 49

Setting one's heart as form of faith, 24, 64
Shifting focus, 41–43
Shipwreck as faith metaphor, 27–31, 147, 155
Sincerity, 116
Skepticism and faith, 18–19
Social awareness, 93
Social diversity, 211
Social environment, power of, 94–95
Social movements, 187–188
Social reality, 11
Society of Friends. *See* Quakers
Songs, 202–203
Soul, 16, 78–79, 140
Spirit: apprehension of, 16; origin of word, 31, 116; recovery of, 220; separating from, 110
Spiritual formation, 199
Spiritual quest, 198
Spirituality and faith, 16
Sraddha, 24
Stages of faith, 61
Stages of Faith: The Psychology of Human Development and the Quest for Meaning (Fowler), 45
Stages of life. *See* Life stages
"Start Making Sense!", 239n26
Stepping stones from cultural milieu, 213–215
Structure of knowing, 101
Subcultures, 208
Subjective knowing, 229n11
Suffering: in cognitive-intellectual development, 71; as feature of enlightenment, 149; as form of faith, 26–27; framework for understanding, 216; meaning of, 28
Sunyata, 23
Support, 129–130, 212–213
"Surround, the," 90
Syllabus, 164–165
Symbolization as basic need, 116–117

Symbols: images as, 116–117, 118; importance of, 202–203; linking to transcendence, 217–218; meaning expressed by, 116–117
Systemic ethic, 175–176
Systemic thought, 144–145

T

Table, practice of the, 156
Tasks: in becoming a self, 49; of faith, 116; of imagination, 106; of infants, 21; of life, 37, 65; of mentors, 131; of young adulthood, 9
Tensions, 96, 111
Tested commitment, 69
Testimony, 121–122, 123, 165
Theism, 22
Theories: cognition (Piaget's), 42; constructive-developmental, 44, 56, 61; faith development, 61; human development, 41–45, 46–47; limitations of, 47–48
Thinking: adolescent, 62–63; connective-systemic-holistic, 144–145; critical, 65; patterns of, 56. *See also* Knowing, forms of
Thought, critical and connected, 185–187
Three-step model of knowing, 60–69
Threshold existence, 105–106
Traditions, plurality of religious, 200–202
Transformations: from Authority-bound faith, 71; in community, 91–102; and conversions, 191; images of, 150–151; in meaning of self, 90; travel as experience of, 185; in ways of dependence, 73
Transitions: developmental openings of, 218–219; dynamic of, 66; life stages, 6–7; mentor to peer, 84; to reliance on inner authority, 79;

stages in, 62; to young adulthood, 80–81

Transliminal mind, 233–234n20

Travel, 184–188, 230n1

Tribe: as form of community, 100; having one's own, 141; power of, 89

Trust, 23–24, 32, 53–54

Truth: eternal, 106; exploring forms of, 67; and faith, 18; as form of faith, 23–24; images as conveyors of, 119, 148–149; insulation from, 149; mediators of, 74; as relational phenomenon, 43; search for, 163; ultimate, 169; understanding of personal, 58–59; use of term, 228n1; ways students compose, 45

U

Ultimate reality, 106

Uncertainty, 79. *See also* Doubt

Unqualified relativism form of knowing, 57–59, 60–61

V

Value as form of faith, 21–22

Values, competing, 96

Virtual Faith (Beaudoin), 203

Vocation: calling as, 148; coalescence of, 229n18; deepening of, 205; of higher education, 169

Voice: of developmental moral decision-making, 50; different languages of development, 43–44; of journey of development, 43

Vulnerability, 79, 83, 140

W

"We," sense of, 135

Western culture, 77, 91, 106

Western philosophical-theological thought, 232n3

Wheelwright, Phillip, 231n1

Wholeness, 153–154, 220

Wisdom, 60, 190

Women, storytelling by, 50

Wonder, 149

Word origins: faith, 17, 24; journey, 50; mentor, 127; sincerity, 116; spirit, 31, 116. *See also* Definitions

Workplace as mentoring community, 180–184

World coherence, 59

Worthy dreams: in cultural milieu, 220–221; formation of, 146–148, 151, 176

Y

Yearnings, 49, 101

Young adult faith, 109–110

Young adulthood: ambiguity of, 4–5; coming to in faith, 7–8; development during, 51–52; exploratory quality of, 68; identity at threshold of, 62–63; ideology of, 217; issues of, 1–4; network of belonging in, 96; nurturance of, 93; postadolescent period of, 70; questions about home, 34–35; stresses of, 12–13; tasks of, 9; threshold of, 146; value of recognizing era of, 102–103

Young adults: attitudes toward orthodoxy of, 203; critical thought of, 65–66; in faith, 143; initiation of into adult knowing, 150; making meaning of, listening to, 45–46; recognition of by family, 192; recognition of gifts of, 203–205; search for faith of, 190

Young people, "marginal," 211–212

"Youth," 70